YOU SHALL NOT STEAL

Robert Gnuse

YOU SHALL NOT STEAL

Community and Property
in the Biblical Tradition

ORBIS BOOKS

Maryknoll, New York 10545

The Catholic Foreign Mission Society of America (Maryknoll) recruits and trains people for overseas missionary service. Through Orbis Books Maryknoll aims to foster the international dialogue that is essential to mission. The books published, however, reflect the opinions of their authors and are not meant to represent the official position of the society.

Bible quotations are from the *Revised Standard Version*.

Manuscript Editor: William E. Jerman

Indexes prepared by James Sullivan

Library of Congress Cataloging in Publication Data

Gnuse, Robert Karl, 1947-
    You shall not steal.

    Bibliography: p.
    Includes index.
    1. Stealing—Biblical teaching.   2. Property—Biblical teaching.   3. Bible—Criticism, interpretation, etc.
4. Ten commandments—Theft.   I. Title.
BS680.S76G59   1985   241′.62   85-4810
ISBN 0-88344-799-1 (pbk.)

Contents

Preface

If all who are thieves, though they are unwilling to admit it, were hanged on the gallows, the world would soon be empty, and there would be a shortage of both hangmen and gallows. . . . A person steals not only when he robs a man's strongbox or his pocket, but also when he takes advantage of his neighbor at the market, in a grocery shop, butcher stall, wine- and beer-cellar, work shop, and in short, wherever business is transacted and money is exchanged for goods or labor. . . . These men are called gentlemen swindlers or big operators. Far from being pickpockets and sneak-thieves who loot a cash box, they sit in office chairs and are called great lords and honorable, good citizens, and yet with great show of legality they rob and steal. . . . Those who can steal and rob openly are safe and free, unmolested by anyone, even claiming honor from men. Meanwhile the little sneak-thieves who have committed one offense must bear disgrace and punishment so as to make the others look respectable and honorable [Martin Luther on the Seventh Commandment, "Large Catechism," 395–96].

The prohibition against stealing has commonly been viewed as the sanction that undergirds the right to private property—the protection of the diligent and prudent against the idle and improvident. Christians have dutifully included it among the commandments to be memorized in religious instruction. By some (Catholics, Lutherans, Episcopalians) it is numbered the Seventh Commandment, and by others (Protestants in general) it is the Eighth Commandment. All denominations impress upon their members that the command prohibits an individual from taking away the property of a reasonably unwilling owner. More sensitive religious instruction has insisted upon a positive emphasis as well: to be of service to one's neighbor by helping to "protect his property and business" (Martin Luther, "Small Catechism").

Use of this command as a pedagogical tool is good for the purpose of teaching children (and adults) to respect the possessions of others. However, there can be a dark side in the moral application of this command, which has left its impact upon Western civilization. Emphasizing respect for someone else's property may lead individuals to hold on firmly to their own property to the selfish exclusion of those around them. The command was designed to combat the selfish urge to appropriate the goods of others, but it may foster the selfish hoarding of one's own property.

In addition, a new rationale alien to the spirit of the commandment may develop. When individuals are able to bring more possessions into their personal domain, the command may be used to protect this new accumulation against all outsiders, including those who may have need of those goods. To be sure, the Christian tradition has encouraged the generous sharing of goods with those in need, and the imperative to open one's abundance to the community is sometimes stated in strong terms (James 5:1-5). But these moral encouragements may be downplayed or ignored by hoarders who steadfastly quote the commandment in literal fashion to ward off encroachment upon their accumulated wealth.

Ironically the commandment, which was designed to protect individuals by protecting their possessions, has been built into the cornerstone for the inviolability of private property in Western civilization. It serves as the theological rationale for those who maintain, "This is mine, that is yours; be content with what you have!" With the rise of a more complex society and its attendant economic structures in recent centuries, the prohibition against theft has become the justification for private property, the limitless accumulation of wealth, and the entrenched disparity between rich and poor. The command has been misused in Western history by those who accumulate wealth in order to be able to do whatever they wish. They gather wealth and defend its accumulation not because an affluent lifestyle is a necessity, but because they crave the power that such wealth brings (see Harrelson, *Commandments,* 136). For with power comes the ability to manipulate persons, the highest form of selfish gratification. But an appeal to the commandment on theft to justify such activity perverts the intent of the commandment. As I hope to demonstrate in this book, the purpose of the commandment was to protect individuals by assu:ing them of the right to access to those goods and possessions necessary for a productive existence.

Reflective individuals have realized how this commandment has been misused over the years, and a few solitary voices of protest have been raised. Luther's biting explication left no segment of society unscathed. The passages quoted at the beginning of this preface reflect his awareness of the inequity in the application of the commandment in his day. Later, in the Enlightenment, Rousseau would make more critical observations of society. He believed the golden age ended when individuals staked a plot of land and said, "This is mine." The institution of private property consolidated the unfair accumulation of wealth, led to human depravity, and provoked cruel injustice. More recently Proudhon, the nineteenth-century French socialist, went so far as to declare private property to be theft in general (Poggioli, 21).

Only on rare occasion have such solitary voices been raised in protest on behalf of the poor and dispossessed whose exclusion from property may be counted as theft committed by those who have legally monopolized wealth. Protection afforded the common individual to safeguard cherished possessions is unfortunately extended to those who amass large amounts of wealth under questionable circumstances. Appalled by this inequity the sensitive individual may be perplexed at how to resolve the problems created by modern misinterpretations of the commandment not to steal. To this end a consideration of the social milieu from which the prohibition arose may clarify the issues and give insight to possible resolutions.

The scope of this work includes a consideration of many affiliated laws that came from the same milieu as did the commandment against theft. This more specific legislation will serve to clarify the true and deeper meaning of the commandment by providing the particulars behind the general rule. The command not to steal might seem to justify accumulation, but it was balanced by laws designed to protect the poor and by theological rhetoric promoting a humanitarian concern for the poor. In the wider context this command actually condemns those who steal from society at large by amassing great wealth, for such theft breaks down society by destroying the economic and political equality of all its members. Laws in the biblical tradition indicate that the transfer of property that comes into a person's possession without the owner's consent, even if acquired legally, is still theft!

The biblical laws, therefore, do not limit the application of the commandment against theft to instances of a poor person's stealing an object from a rich person. Rather they call into question whether the superiority of riches is real or imagined, and whether the rich are permitted to withhold from members of society at large a quality of life that is rightfully theirs.[1]

Walter Harrelson reflects on the deeper meaning of the commandment:

Rather than its being used (as often it has in fact been used) to assure wealthy individuals that they may proceed unchecked in the amassing of wealth, confident that the laws will protect their property at whatever cost to the poor or the weak or the desperate, this commandment can be applied precisely against those who amass wealth and accumulate goods by any and all means. When equally applied, the eighth commandment has much more to say to the giver of bribes for political favors, to the manipulator of the economic system for unjust and unearned assets, to the destroyer of businesses for the sake of a favorable tax advantage, to the issuer of stocks who having made his millions then sells out as the vast new enterprise is about to collapse, or to the governmental figure who sets out to make a fortune by compelling the offering of bribes. The stealing with which our society is more and more familiar lies in such areas as these [*Commandments,* 138–39].

We may also discover implications of the command that extend to other aspects of our life and society. The command seeks to protect possessions not only because they sustain the life of individuals, but because they give meaning to life. Possessions of a sentimental nature that enhance our identity must be respected. In addition, there is a natural tendency to share them with others. And to share something priceless, whether it be in the private or public sphere, is to share meaning and value with others, and this fosters community (see Harrelson, *Commandments,* 140–42).

PART ONE

The Commandment

Chapter 1

Context of the Commandment

Setting of the Ten Commandments

The origin of the Ten Commandments lies in the early history of ancient Israel. Tradition attributes their origin to Moses in the wilderness of Sinai. Though scholars disagree on the exact origin, their precise original wording, and their actual application in that ancient society, all agree that the commandments reflect the ethos of early Israelites.

The Israelites were typical pastoralists—shepherds and cattle herders of the wilderness. They have been called nomads, seminomads, and more recently pastoralists by historians and sociologists. All agree that Israelite society was one of rustic simplicity with basic equality of all adult male members in economic and legal matters. They were inclined to disdain the values of settled farmers and city dwellers with their class structures, fertility religions, political and economic oppression, decadent morals, and polytheism. Thus Israelite traditions recall that Sodom and Gomorrah were models of evil urban existence and how Cain the farmer (settled society) killed Abel the shepherd (pastoral society). Later prophets attacked the abuses of polytheism and social oppression stemming from cities such as Jerusalem and Samaria. Bards, prophets, and reform-oriented lawmakers such as the Deuteronomists idealized the pastoral ethos as the norm for Yahwistic society, and they sought to recapture the golden age of Moses with its monotheism and egalitarianism.

The history of Israel suggests that the settlement process caused it to move from an early pastoral economic and political model for society based on tribal or kinship structures to a model based on mercantile economics and state-oriented political structures in the era of kingship. The prophets saw the abuses in their society created by this process and called for a return to the pure Mosaic covenant, which entailed the earlier social, political, and economic structures.

The roots of the Ten Commandments tap this pastoral ethos. The commandments originate somewhere in the early period and are attached to old

3

traditions of the community. As such they are a reaction against social abuses of the early monarchical period and the attendant social change. They reflect the early values of society.[2]

In their earliest form the commandments were remembered in oral form (the tradition describes the tablets of stone being stored in the Ark of the Covenant), inasmuch as few of the early Israelites could read or write. The original form of the commands may have arisen anytime between the age of Moses (late thirteenth century B.C.) and the united monarchy (tenth century B.C.). Scholars have tried to reconstruct the original wording as a series of simple prohibitions composed of one or two words after the negative particle.[3] Early parallels to the commandments may be found in the ritual decalogue or dodecalogue of Exodus 34:14–26, the curse rituals in Deuteronomy 27:15–26, or prohibition lists in Leviticus 18:6–18, 20:2–16, and Ezekiel 18:5–9 (Harrelson, *Commandments*, 26–40).

The commandments may have functioned as a civil law code in this early period, and the penalty for breaking them might have been death or expulsion from the community. If so, the meaning of several of the commandments might be different from the interpretation given by later Israelites and Christian tradition.[4]

The later development saw the commands lengthened, two commands restated in positive rather than negative fashion (holy day and parents), and the scope broadened to render the commands as a moral code rather than a civil code. The written form we possess in the biblical text (Exod. 20, Deut. 5) reflects the reinterpretation of the later reform-oriented era (seventh and sixth centuries B.C.). When oral tradition precipitated into written form, usually in an era of crisis or social change, the exact articulation of the commands reflects the theology of the editors. Deuteronomy 5 may reflect the concerns of the Deuteronomic reform movement, for the Sabbath observance is connected with social humanitarian rationales, and coveting of a neighbor's wife is placed before property. Exodus 20 may reflect the cultic concerns of priestly reform in the exilic and postexilic era, for Sabbath observance is connected to cultic concerns and the creation of the universe.[5]

The type of legal formulation we observe in the commandments is called apodictic or absolute law. It is characterized by the absolute statement, "You shall" or "You shall not" do something. The imperative is addressed to universal or abstract situations in a general fashion. The scope is broad and the application absolute. The rationale behind the command appears to be the divine will. As such the law contrasts with casuistic or case laws, which address specific situations. Their formulation is in the "if . . . then . . ." structure, so that various laws would read: "If this be the situation or offense, then this should be the result or punishment." The book of the covenant in Exodus 21–23 is replete with such laws. Casuistic law is conditional in that it sets guidelines for specific situations and does not seek universal application. Furthermore, casuistic conditions are not absolutely binding, for local elders or courts could adjust penalties under mitigating circumstances.

The Ten Commandments are classic examples of apodictic laws and they contrast with the bulk of Old Testament—casuistic—legislation. The commandments contrast vividly with other laws of the ancient Near East, which are almost exclusively casuistic. This observation has led some scholars to declare apodictic law to be the unique contribution of Israel, for it is legislation uniquely rooted in the divine will of a righteous God who sought the transformation of persons into a religiously motivated community of brothers and sisters. This intent would contrast vividly with the secular motivation of lawmakers in the rest of the ancient world.[6]

This classic understanding, first articulated in its fullest form by Albrecht Alt, has been criticized by more recent scholars. Some have noted that apodictic laws are found more frequently in the ancient Near East than we had earlier suspected.[7] Other scholars point out the existence of biblical laws that appear to be a combination of apodictic and casuistic. The implication is that we are making too great a distinction between them; perhaps apodictic is merely a variation of casuistic—apodictic laws deal with the general scope of legal situations and casuistic laws deal with concrete cases.[8]

Despite the criticisms leveled at Alt's theory, his description of the unique nature of the Ten Commandments may not be without foundation. Even though there are parallels with apodictic law in the ancient world, no example of an extended collection of such laws as we have in the Ten Commandments has been found. They are unique in terms of their extent and their scope for society as a whole (Boecker, 201; Harrelson, *Commandments*, 25–26).

This implies that Israel had a vision of itself and its destiny that made Israelites distinct from their surrounding neighbors. The appeal to obey the commandments was rooted in the will of Yahweh, the God of Israel. Yahweh was the God who liberated slaves from Egypt and sought to create a fellowship of equals by means of such laws as the Ten Commandments. Though the form may not be unique, the depth of the vision and the appeal for such a radical change in society was a new experience on the horizon of the ancient near eastern social world.

Stealing

The prohibition against stealing reflects the pastoral bias and theological imperative of early Israel. The community created by the exodus experience and molded in the wilderness was a society that emphasized the value of persons. The Ten Commandments as a whole reflect the importance of persons and their relationship to Yahweh. The commandments of the first table of the law outline divine-human relationships; the second table outlines the social obligations among persons. The laws seek to protect human life, family, possessions, and reputation. Taken together they seek to protect the total integrity of individuals within the community. The command against stealing must be understood within the matrix of this imperative to protect human integrity.

The primitive economy of Israel was communal in orientation. As is typical among pastoralists, the flocks and land were often owned by the community or tribe as a whole. When a pastoralist tribe settles, land may be divided up by families, but often large segments of land remain as common property for grazing. Even the land that is distributed is subject to periodic redistribution by lot or assigned rotation. In this system individuals do not view the land as exclusively their own property. At a later stage of development individual families may come into permanent possession of some land, but it remains the property of the family, and an individual may not dispose of that familial inheritance. It must stay within the possession of the extended family. Thus, if an individual dies with no heir, the next of kin must purchase the land, lest it fall into the hands of someone else (Lev. 25:23–34). The commandment against stealing does not serve to protect private property; important possessions belong to the entire community/family. Some have called this a primitive democracy or primitive socialism; both terms are naive generalizations with respect to pastoral society and economics. But it is important to realize that there was no notion of the inviolability of property owned by individuals; this is a later, Western notion.

As Israel reflected on this economic situation theologically, it viewed Yahweh as the true owner and imparter of the land. The conquest under Joshua and the judges was accomplished when Yahweh led them as a divine warrior. Their receipt of the land was a gift of divine grace, and all persons stood as equals before Yahweh when the land was distributed. According to the later Deuteronomic historian (622–550 B.C.) in the books of Joshua, Judges, Samuel, and Kings, the land was an ever renewed gift from Yahweh. If the Israelites obeyed the commands of God, they would be blessed; they would keep their land and it would bring forth abundant harvest. If they disobeyed the laws, followed other gods, and oppressed their fellow Israelites, the land would become infertile or be taken away by foreign powers. Such a theological understanding cut away at any idea of the individual's inviolable right to land. The affirmation that Yahweh gives the land is sounded throughout biblical tradition (Gen. 12:7; Exod. 3:8, 32:13; Lev. 20:24, 25:2, 38; Deut. 7:13; 1 Kings 8:34–40; 2 Chron. 20:7–11). The whole world belongs to Yahweh (Deut. 10:14; Ps. 24:1; Isa. 42:5; 1 Cor. 10:26). Land is given to human beings only to manage in the name of Yahweh (Gen. 2:8–15).

Property and land were given to be used for the glory of Yahweh and the good of all. The command not to steal spoke against those who sought to appropriate communal possessions for their own private use. Such hoarding could result in the lowering of the quality of life or even in death for others in the community. Persons had right of access to those things upon which their life depended. Goods were viewed as an extension of the self, and families, tribes, and communities had a right to maintain and use them. This imperative is vital for continued existence in any unfavorable environment, and the land of Palestine was such that the continued existence of the community depended upon the cooperation of all its members. The enfeeblement or death of members in the community would adversely affect even those who hoarded. (Though the analogy is not perfect, the sin of Achan in Josh. 7:1–26 in taking for himself those goods placed under the religious ban of destruction may typify such a sin of individual appropriation of goods to the detriment of the community.) Thus, the command may have slowed the growth of individual ownership rather than protected it. The command may have meant, "Do not take communal property for your own individual ownership." How ironic that modern society uses the commandment to defend the opposite course of action!

The purpose of the command was to curb those who steal from society at large by amassing great wealth, for such theft will ultimately break down that society. This explains the ire of the prophets who inveighed against the wealthy classes of Samaria and Jerusalem.

The biblical legislation in Exodus 20 and Deuteronomy 5 reflects the attempts by later generations of Israel to restore the equality of the early pastoral period. Much of the legislation may be an idealistic projection that was never attained; nevertheless, the religious ethos sought to restore the essential equality of all Israelites before God in all human endeavors. The Israelite preacher would declare, "You shall take care of the poor, the widow, the orphan, the stranger in your land; for once you were slaves in Egypt, and I the Lord your God brought you out with an outstretched arm and a mighty hand!"

In its original oral formulation the command read, "You shall not steal." The Hebrew word *gnb* implies secrecy—taking something by stealth. Other Hebrew words for stealing, such as *lqh* or *gzl*, imply more force. The verb may have a person or a thing as its object: persons as well as property may be stolen (Childs, 423).

In the early period theft may have been punished by death, especially if the Ten Commandments were used as a code of civil law. But later the punishment was reduced to severalfold restitution. Ancient Babylon went through a similar process: first theft was punished by death, then only the theft of sacred objects was punishable by death, and finally all theft was punished by restitution. With the economic development that brought the establishment of private property to Israel, the infliction of a fourfold repayment for stolen sheep and fivefold repayment for stolen oxen became the standard (Exod. 21:37, 22:2). This would have been effective in a society where individuals were economically equal. But as a gap developed between rich and poor, the rich could more easily pay the penalty, but the poor person who could not repay might be sold into debt-slavery (Meek, 66–67; Hyatt, *Exodus*, 132–33). The law continued in force, for society needed a deterrent. It is important to realize that as this gap between rich and poor developed, later reform legislation was designed to mitigate the unfairness it caused in society. Theft was to be prevented, but laws were created to preclude situations in which the poor had to steal in order to survive. To appeal to Israelite restitution laws in order to justify the concept of inviolable private property ignores the legislation that sought to alleviate the plight of the poor by redistributing wealth.

Some modern scholars, most notably, Albrecht Alt, have hypothesized that the original command referred to stealing an adult free Israelite male to sell him into slavery. The following arguments are offered: (1) Such an interpretation fits the model and needs of early pastoral Israel. It is difficult to understand why a command against property theft would be placed in the commandments by a pastoral society that owned little property (unless it referred to communal property). (2) The commandments are oriented toward the protection of persons. This command would fit its context better if it referred to kidnapping. (3) There is a clear parallel with Exodus 21:16 and Deuteronomy 24:7, which command the death penalty for selling an Israelite into slavery. (4) The command against coveting property overlaps with the prohibition of theft in its common interpretation. If stealing originally meant kidnapping, there is no duplication. (5) If one posits that the Ten Commandments were once a code of civil law with the death penalty as punishment, the kidnapping interpretation of the commandment is more appropriate. Theft was only a tort, whereas kidnapping was a capital offense in other legal codes. (6) The sequence of our commandments would then make better sense. The second table of the law would protect life, family, *freedom*, honor, and possession in that order. (7) Inasmuch as the list of things to be coveted does not include an adult male, this particular instance must have been covered in the earlier command on theft.[9] Scholars posit that with the rise of commercialism in Israel the law was altered by omitting reference to the man. The command referred to property by inference. But the command still protected persons, for it was designed to guard the property of the poor from the rich. The early meaning was, "do not reduce a man to slavery by kidnapping," and the later meaning was, "do not reduce a person to slavery by monopolizing the wealth" (Hamel, 86).

This theory also posits a parallel development in the meaning of the commandment on coveting. Coveting originally referred to stealing, and the Hebrew verb *ḥmd*, which we translate as "covet," really meant "seize." Other texts in the Old Testament pair this verb with other verbs of stealing (Deut. 7:25; Josh. 7:21; Mic. 2:2), and the verb may occur by itself and mean "steal" (Exod. 34:24; Ps. 68:16). The meaning may include intrigues that lead to possession. Furthermore, an ancient inscription from Karatepe uses a similar verb (*nḥmd*) with the meaning of seize. The version of the commandments found in Deuteronomy 5:21 replaced the *ḥmd* of Exodus 20:17 with a new verb, *hit'awwe*. The Deuteronomic movement of the seventh century B.C. thus redefined *ḥmd* as an interior mental disposition by the use of the verb *hit'awwe*, "desire." Thus the meaning of Exodus 20:17 was originally "take pains to get" or "seize," but the Deuteronomy 5:21 version, "desire," softened the meaning of the older Exodus text. This process of "softening" continued when the Greek Septuagint (200 B.C.) translated the verb in Exodus 20:17 as *epithumeseis*, "desire." With the modification of the concept of coveting to become an internal mental disposition, the command against stealing could refer to theft in general rather than kidnapping. [10]

Recent scholarship, however, has cast doubt on this theory by questioning whether we have tried to read too much into the text and stretch the meaning of *ḥmd* too far. There is no real textual evidence that the commandment on theft referred to persons. Kidnapping would have been rare in early Israel, and inasmuch as a law in Exodus 21:6 treated it, why should the same law be included in the decalogue? The use of *ḥmd* with other verbs of stealing may not imply that it means the same thing. Rather, it may be used to indicate the mental disposition that is prior to the act of theft in passages such as Joshua 7:21, Deuteronomy 7:25, and Micah 2:2. The individual had it in mind to steal (*ḥmd*) and then stole something. Finally, because Deuteronomy 5:21 and the Septuagint translation of Exodus 20:17 imply that coveting is an interior disposition, we should respect their interpretation of the earlier verb until we have more convincing information to the effect that they were trying to alter the original meaning. If "coveting" is a mental act, then "stealing" can refer to any act of theft. [11]

This debate is important whether Alt and his followers are correct or not, for it confirms that if the commandment underwent any development at all, it remained throughout a command designed to protect persons. This is all the stronger if the position of Alt is correct. Modern scholars are sensitive to this insight, for both sides recognize the command to be an attempt to protect persons, especially the poor.

The insight that the commandment against stealing was designed to protect persons and not property may challenge our ideologies. We have for too long used this command as the safeguard for the institution of private property against the human needs of the poor and dispossessed. A return to the biblical roots is necessary for a correct understanding of the commandment.

Up to this point the argument may not appear convincing. To place the meaning of the commandment in its proper context we must consider the further legislation of Israel. Specific laws of Israel demonstrate that the prohibition of theft was designed to protect the property of the poor and preserve the economic equality of all for the maintenance of a healthy society.

Chapter 2

The Laws of Israel: Mandate for the Poor

A proper understanding of the Israelite prohibition against theft must be obtained by consideration of the laws and legal decisions that cover the various acts of theft. The command not to steal is the generic prohibition and the various related laws are specific applications of this general principle. A closer evaluation of those laws will clarify what Israel meant by "theft" of property.

Israel believed that human need was more important than property. The commandment not to steal was designed to protect persons and their access to those things necessary for an adequate life. Though the commandment itself does not spell this out, references to other civil laws in Israel verify this thesis. The laws of Israel called for the release and redistribution of property for the sake of human need. The commandment not to steal meant that no individual had the right to deprive another person of possessions necessary for meaningful existence. Consideration of legal directives that pertain to simple theft, land, slaves, and debts, will demonstrate this concern. The laws also indicate that Israel had no concept of an inalienable right to private property; rather, personal needs took priority over private property.

Law in the Ancient Near East and in Israel

The word "Torah" or "law" means "guidance" or "instruction," for this is the purpose of law in society. Direction is given to administrators of law, whether they be judges in courtrooms or local elders in small villages, so that justice might be administered properly. Law promotes uniform decisions in all parts of the land by providing standards, and this means there will be stability in the social fabric of society. Not all legal decisions are made strictly in accord with the law, but the law provides a guideline for the dispensation of legal decisions. Punishment may not exceed that exacted by the specific law, but the judges or elders may moderate the punishment according to the circumstances of individual cases. Common sense is to prevail over the legalistic application of a specific law.

The accumulated legal lore and precedents of a society were usually remembered in oral form throughout the ancient Near East. However, the occasion to fix them in a written form, usually by carving them in stone tablets (steles) or upon large monuments, was brought about by several factors. The creation of a unified nation-state under one ruler often necessitated legal reform to unify local customs in the dispensation of justice. Promulgation of law codes then unified disparate practices. Such may have been the case with Hammurabi's law code. Movement of new ethnic groups into an area may have led to the reform of legal practices in order to deal with the new situations that arose as a result of different social and economic customs. Dislocation of large segments of the population in a given area may have precipitated the recording of laws in written form lest they be forgotten in the turmoil of social upheaval. Such may have been the case with Israel during the sixth-century B.C. exile in Babylon. Finally, some law codes were carved in stone and placed in shrines of deities as acts of piety by kings to demonstrate that justice and order had been brought to the land. (Whether those laws were then actually enforced or whether the inscriptions were merely royal braggadocio cannot be ascertained.)

We know of several law codes of kings in a period preceding by a thousand years the existence of Israel as a people. These codes were found in Mesopotamia and attest to a long-established legal tradition there. The reforms of the Sumerian King Urukagina of Lagash (ca. 2350 B.C.), though they do not constitute a law code, are our earliest reference to legal reform, an activity often associated with law codes. The neo-Sumerian law code of Ur-Nammu of the third dynasty at Ur (ca. 2050 B.C.) is the earliest formal law code of which we know. The entrance of the Amorites into Mesopotamia brought about the creation of three other law codes. Lipit-Ishtar, king of Isin, produced his code around 1850 B.C. A law code from the city of Eshnunna dates to 1750 B.C. It was formerly attributed to King Bilalama, but now there is uncertainty as to its royal promulgator. The best known code is that of Hammurabi of Babylon (ca. 1700 B.C.), who presented his law code after the unification of a large part of Mesopotamia. The laws of Eshnunna coincide closely with Hammurabi's laws, which implies a common legal tradition. It also suggests that a king does not really create law codes, but he inherits a tradition to which he may add his own reforms and particular modifications. We also have laws and courtroom decisions from Hittite and Assyrian sources in the second millennium B.C. In addition to these law codes there are records of courtroom decisions discovered at archeological sites such as Nuzi and Mari in northern Mesopotamia.[12]

Consideration of these ancient law codes and courtroom decisions brings several insights. First, none of the law codes seems to be a complete attempt at covering all possible legal situations. Oral tradition apparently still functioned in most cases for legal administrators. The law codes perhaps functioned in situations where uniform law was necessary to bring divergent practices into standard procedure or new socio-economic conditions required the modification of existing practices.

Secondly, throughout the codes we sense a fairly high morality and a strong sense of consideration for the weaker elements of society. Judges are to provide for the poor, widows, and orphans, and the king sees it his duty to protect them. The king would mention his protection of the poor in supplications before his deity, because defending them brought justice and order to the land. In return the deity would grant stability in the cosmos, fertility to the land, and permanence to the royal dynasty.

Thirdly, we see that decisions rendered by judges in various courts were based on common sense rather than on quoted passages from a law code (Loewenstamm, "Law," 232–33). This indicates reliance on oral legal tradition. But it makes us wonder about how extensively the law codes were actually used in day-to-day legal practice. The royal law codes may have been propaganda or expressions of religious piety rather than normative law.

Fourthly, a significant degree of correspondence exists between Old Testament and Mesopotamian laws and legal decisions. In most areas there is overlap between the two; the formulation and penalties often are similar (Greengus, 533–34). This is no surprise: Israel arose in the same cultural milieu and was ethically related to the Mesopotamian. Inasmuch as this legal tradition was well established by the time of the emergence of Israel, it is logical to assume that the Israelites adopted much of it when they settled in the land of Canaan. They may have received much of this legal tradition through the Canaanites. (There are, however, some significant points of divergence, which we shall consider later.)

The laws of Israel are attributed to Moses, for he was seen as the first lawgiver and instrument by which Yahweh created the community of Israel. Hence, all later legal reform was attributed to him as the founder of the legal process. The same was true in later Greece: the laws in the Solonic code of the sixth century B.C. really date from later periods, but they were attributed to Solon, because he created the original law code.

Attribution of the laws to Moses clearly identifies these laws as revelation from Yahweh. Placed in the context of the Sinai experience, all the laws became a mandate not only for the proper functioning of society but as a religious obligation to Yahweh. Israel infused religion into its law, whereas other surrounding cultures restricted religion to ritual cult and sacrifice. One might be tempted to think that Mesopotamian culture, separating cult and juridical practice, was more sophisticated than that of Israel, for it reminds us of the separation of church and state enshrined in American practice. But closer inspection reveals that Israel grounded its law in its religion and thereby elevated the quality of religious practice above that of its neighbors. Religious obligation was measured by more than simply cult and sacrifice, though these elements were important. Emphasis upon the law as religious obligation placed the worshiper in the realm of social interaction, ethics, and interpersonal relationships in the community, so that the rights of individuals in society received religious undergirding. This became the basis for Western political as well as religious values. As Micah declared:

> With what shall I come before the Lord, and bow myself before God on high? Shall I come before him with burnt offerings, with calves a year old? Will the Lord be pleased with thousands of rams, with ten thousands of rivers of oil? Shall I give my first-born for my transgression, the fruit of my body for the sin of my soul? He has showed you, O man, what is good; and what does the Lord require of you but to do justice, and to love kindness, and to walk humbly with your God? [6:6–8].

The legal corpora in the Old Testament arose over the centuries. The codes originate from the period between the settlement in Canaan and the Babylonian exile.

The oldest law code appears to be the book of the covenant or the covenant code in Exodus 20:22–23:33. The laws come from the era of early settlement in the land (thirteenth to tenth centuries B.C.), for the instances in the law code often refer to a simple agrarian economy with small farms and livestock in the possession of families.[13] It has been suggested that the laws are Canaanite, and their adoption by Israel in this early settlement period reflects partial accommodation to the ways of the land.[14] The code contains a combination of civil laws, cultic laws, and theologizing tendencies. Laws are stated in casuistic fashion: the condition or crime is stated and is followed by the penalty to be imposed. A typical law would read, "If so and so does thus, then you shall do thus."

Throughout the text the principle of *lex talionis* is evident. This principle of retribution demands the imposition of punishment equal to the crime. This does not reflect primitive morality or mentality but rather a concern for equality and justice. The Code of Hammurabi introduced the principle of *lex talionis* for the same reason. When the punishment is the same as the crime, the rich person is reduced to equal status with the poor person, for the payment of money for the penalty is not an option. Nor is there any class distinction in the laws of Israel. Elsewhere a crime by a lower-class person against a higher-class person warrants greater punishment than does the reverse situation. *Lex talionis* protects the poor from abuse by the rich.[15]

The ritual decalogue or dodecalogue is an interesting collection of cultic regulations found in Exodus 34. Its present position in the text implies that it was written on the two tablets of stone to replace those broken by Moses. Whether this means that the ritual decalogue is older and is the more original version of the Ten Commandments cannot be ascertained. Its directives are concerned with feasts and other cultic matters.

The Deuteronomic law code in Deuteronomy 12–26 represents a seventh- and sixth-century revision of earlier laws for the new social, economic, and political conditions of that era. The laws reflect the critique of the eighth-century prophets and their call for justice. The laws are more humane, more sensitive to the needs of the poor, and reflect a more complex society than that reflected in Exodus 21–23.

The Deuteronomic movement retrieved old traditions and old laws and recast some of them in its redaction. Hence, many laws are old and unchanged from the earliest periods, but others are more updated. Comparison with the book of the covenant reveals that the same situations are discussed; sometimes no appreciable change occurs in the legal formulation, but at other times the law is expanded to cover new situations. Comparison between the book of the covenant and Deuteronomy is a cornerstone for evaluating the development of the legal heritage of Israel.

 Many ancient cultic and civil laws are contained in the holiness code of Leviticus 17–26. Though ancient in formulation these laws did not come into written form until the disaster of the Babylonian exile (586 B.C.). Priestly editors during the exile and perhaps in the postexilic period wove them together into the book of Leviticus lest these laws and directives be forgotten in the social upheavals of that era. Some of the material is ancient, with the result that the relationship to other legal corpora is difficult to ascertain. Scholars are not agreed on whether the formulation of material on civil matters occurred before or after Deuteronomic material and whether Levitical legislation is dependent upon Deuteronomic material or ignores it.

Taken all together, the total legislation of the law codes of Israel is idealistic. Religious imperative undergirds all the laws and specific religious imperatives permeate them. Laws favoring the weaker members of society demonstrate the ethos of the exodus experience wherein Yahweh delivers helpless slaves. Justice was part of the legal ethos, and laws addressed attitudes as well as situations. Poor and weak Israelites were given the identity of brothers and sisters to encourage society to care for them.[16] Thus, as George Ernest Wright observes:

> Justice was not to be administered solely in accordance with the importance of a man's stake in the community. . . . The principle behind the law was not "to every man his due according to his importance," but rather, "to every man his due according to his need" ["Deuteronomy," 427].

Israel was to keep these laws not merely for the sake of law and order in society, but in response to the divine love that brought slaves out of Egypt. Laws were obeyed out of love. This explains the deep humanitarian concern in the laws—one's neighbor was to be treated with love and the laws were to be kept out of a spirit of love, not merely a sense of legalistic obligation.

This creates a problem for the scholar. The laws have been preserved for us by theologians, and various laws are deeply embedded in the theology of divine love and human response. How can we be sure these laws were enforced in the courtrooms and villages in this fashion? At times the laws seem too idealistic to have been practiced. Deuteronomy in particular appears to be preaching about commandments rather than laying down laws and commandments. But scholars agree that these laws reflect the ideal toward which the Israelites strived, and even if they do not reflect the actual practice in courts at all times, they demonstrate the ideals of reformers who strove to put them into practice and at times succeeded.[17] As such they serve to inspire us in our own process of legal development.

Simple Theft

The covenant code contains a number of laws that pertain to simple theft of common goods. The basic principle is restitution: the thief shall repay the victim in a greater amount than was stolen. Thus the laws provide not only for simple justice but also offer a deterrent against theft by demanding fourfold and fivefold restitution. This principle, rather than mere punishment, reflects an attitude of respect for persons (Rushdoony, 458, 514–20).

A comparison of Israelite laws on theft with Mesopotamia shows that Israel regarded theft of property as a much less serious crime. In Babylon theft could be a capital offense, but not so in Israel where the value of persons was much higher.[18] A law from Hammurabi's code prescribes:

> If a man has stolen an ox, or a sheep, or an ass, or a pig, or a boat, either from a god or a palace, he shall pay thirty-fold. If he is a plebian, he shall render ten-fold. If the thief has nothing to pay, he shall be slain (Code of Hammurabi #8) [Edwards, 29].

The biblical version would have the thief sold into slavery, but not killed (Exod. 22:3). Rates of restitution were much higher elsewhere than in Israel. The restitution rates in Babylon and in Hittite laws were tenfold and thirtyfold, as compared with the Israelite rate of twofold, fourfold, and fivefold. The other nations had far more laws regulating different situations of theft than did Israel, because the Israelite ethos did not place so much importance on the protection of property. Because Israelite laws centered on the needs of the group rather than of the individual, the property of an individual was subordinate to the needs of the group. Israel was lenient on the issue of theft because persons were too sacred to be sacrificed for the sake of property.[19]

Particular laws regarding theft are found primarily in the book of the covenant and in Deuteronomy. Exodus 22 contains basic guidelines in matters of common theft. A very basic law is that of Exodus 22:1, 4:

> If a man steals an ox or a sheep, and kills it or sells it, he shall pay five oxen for an ox, and four sheep for a sheep. He shall make restitution; if he has nothing, then he shall be sold for his theft. . . . If the stolen beast is found alive in his possession, whether it is an ox or an ass or a sheep, he shall pay double.

Possession of stolen goods rates twofold restitution; actual theft demands more. Slaughter of the animal may also reflect the deliberate intent to steal, and hence the penalty is also higher. Because the ox is more valuable as a work animal, and its value as a draft animal makes it more likely to be stolen, the restitution rate is higher than for a sheep (Rylaarsdam, 1002; Hyatt, *Exodus*, 236). Livestock was the heart of a poor villager's possessions; its theft endangered his or her livelihood, and the deterrent had to be forceful.

Laws also cover property damage:

> When a man leaves a pit open, or when a man digs a pit and does not cover it, and an ox or an ass falls into it, the owner of the pit shall make it good; he shall give money to its owner, and the dead beast shall be his. When one man's ox hurts another's, so that it dies, then they shall sell the live ox and divide the price of it; and the dead beast also they shall divide. Or if it is known that the ox has been accustomed to gore in the past, and its owner has not kept it in, he shall pay ox for ox, and the dead beast shall be his [Exod. 21:33–36].
>
> When a man causes a field or vineyard to be grazed over,[20] or lets his beast loose and it feeds in another man's field, he shall make restitution from the best in his own field and in his own vineyard. When fire breaks out and catches in thorns so that the stacked grain or the standing grain or the field is consumed, he that kindled the fire shall make full restitution [Exod. 22:5–6].

Restitution is made for careless destruction of another's property, and as with the ox the penalty is stiffer if the owner has been irresponsible with a dangerous ox.

There were laws designed to cover the damage or loss of borrowed objects; a list of examples is provided in Exodus 22:

> If a man delivers to his neighbor money or goods to keep, and it is stolen out of the man's house, then, if the thief is found, he shall pay double. If the thief is not found, the owner of the house shall come near to God, to show whether or not he has put his hand to his neighbor's goods. For every breach of trust, whether it is for ox, for ass, for clothing, or for any kind of lost thing, of which one says, "This is it," the case of both parties shall come before God; he whom God shall condemn shall pay double to this neighbor. If a man delivers to his neighbor an ass or an ox or a sheep or any beast to keep, and it dies or is hurt or is driven away, without anyone seeing it, an oath by the Lord shall be between them both to see whether he has not put his hand to his neighbor's property; and the owner shall accept the oath, and he shall not make restitution. But if it is stolen from him, he shall make restitution to its owner. If it is torn by beasts, let him bring it as evidence; he shall not make restitution for what has been torn. If a man borrows anything of his neighbor, and

it is hurt or dies, the owner not being with it, he shall make full restitution. If the owner was with it, he shall not make restitution; if it was hired, it came for its hire [vv. 7-15].

The rationale is that if borrowers have not acted responsibly, they must make restitution. If there are mitigating circumstances, borrowers need not repay. When defendants "came near to God," they probably swore an oath before a house god (we have parallels at Mari) or at a local shrine (we have parallels in the Eshnunna laws ##36-37) (Fensham, "Eshnunna," 160-61; Loretz, 167-75). In Hammurabi's laws the borrower was always liable for damage; in the laws of Eshnunna the borrower was exempt only if his house were totally destroyed (Eshnunna laws ##36-37). With characteristic leniency Israel permits other exceptions. If the owner is with the livestock, the borrower is not liable, for the owner could stop any misuse. There is debate on the meaning of "it came for its hire." Some believe the hired man's wages go to the owner, others believe the owner bears the loss because that is the risk of renting out one's livestock, or it may mean the hired hand rather than the borrower pays the owner.[21]

Later legislation found it necessary to address the problem of dishonest business practices (such legislation is lacking in the book of the covenant because early Israel did not have developed business practices):

You shall not have in your bag two kinds of weights, a large and a small. You shall not have in your house two kinds of measures, a large and a small. A full and just weight you shall have, a full and just measure you shall have; that your days may be prolonged in the land which the Lord your God gives you. For all who do such things, all who act dishonestly, are an abomination to the Lord your God [Deut. 25:13-16].

You shall do no wrong in judgment, in measures of length or weight or quantity. You shall have just balances, just weights, a just ephah, and a just hin; I am the Lord your God, who brought you out of the land of Egypt [Lev. 19:35-36].

Such legislation provides protection especially for the poor in dealings with crafty merchants. Hammurabi also had to prevent the use of such false scales—either the use of two standards of measurement or two different sets of weights. When buying, a merchant might use heavy weights to purchase more for his money, and when selling he could use a lighter weight to sell less for the unit price. Such activity is criticized especially by the prophet Amos (Amos 8:5).[22]

Theft laws also cover various complicating factors that might arise. Exodus 22 treats of the homicide of a thief:

If a thief is found breaking in, and is struck so that he dies, there shall be no bloodguilt for him; but if the sun has risen upon him, there shall be bloodguilt for him [vv. 2-3].

In the first instance there is no bloodguilt, because the householder could not be sure of the burglar's intent in the dark. In the second instance the rights of the burglar are protected from unnecessary vindictiveness of the householder. Though the laws of Eshnunna distinguish between daytime and nighttime crimes, this law is unique in its forthright protection of a burglar's rights. The code of Hammurabi prescribes the execution of a thief for breaking into another person's home through the wall.[23]

Finally, the theological idealism of Israelite law codes surfaces with the demand to assist neighbors with what belonged to them:

> If you meet your enemy's ox or his ass going astray, you shall bring it back to him. If you see the ass of one who hates you lying under its burden, you shall refrain from leaving him with it, you shall help him to lift it up [Exod. 23:4–5].
>
> You shall not see your brother's ox or his sheep go astray, and withhold your help from them; you shall take them back to your brother. And if he is not near you, or if you do not know him, you shall bring it home to your house, and it shall be with you until your brother seeks it; then you shall restore it to him. And so you shall do with his ass; so you shall do with any lost thing of your brother's, which he loses and you find; you may not withhold your help. You shall not see your brother's ass or his ox fallen down by the way, and withhold your help from them; you shall help him to lift them up again [Deut. 22:1–4].

One is reminded of Luther's explanation for the commandment against stealing: we should help our neighbors protect and improve their property and business. Some commentators believe the reference to "your enemy" in Exodus 23:4–5 may refer to someone with whom one has a legal dispute pending. If so, the later reformulation in Deuteronomy widens the concept to include fellow Israelites of whatever status. Others feel that this means reading something into the Exodus text, and as it stands the text merely proclaims a humanitarian concern that extends to all. The laws of Eshnunna call for the return of an animal lest the individual be charged with theft, but the Israelite motivation seems to originate from humanitarian concerns. Persons should not shirk personal responsibility for the things that happen around them; rather positive action must be taken for the sake of others.[24]

In conclusion, the laws regarding theft of common goods in Israel are fairly similar to other laws in effect in the ancient Near East. But Israel regards the person as more important than property, and special concern is shown for poorer classes.

Interest on Loans

The interest laws in Israel diverged from accepted practice in the ancient world. Laws of Hammurabi and Eshnunna have provisions for fixed rates of interest lest interest become prohibitive for debtors. In both codes interest rates were set at 20 percent for money loans and 33 percent for grain investments. Assyrian rates were 25 percent for money and 50 percent for grain. These rates frequently led to bankruptcy and debt-enslavement for borrowers. By law creditors could seize the pledge of a debtor or debtors themselves, and the law codes gave little protection to poor debtors. Only reformers such as Urukagina and Gudea of Lagash and the law code of Ur-Nammu made efforts to protect widows and orphans of deceased debtors.[25]

The laws of Israel stand in vivid contrast, for Israel alone condemned interest:

> The prohibition against interest in the Bible is a reaction against the Babylonian system that laid the foundation for the financial structure of a capitalistic economy [Gordon, "Life," 54].

Ancient near eastern laws were created for settled, developed society; loans were for commercial purposes. But Israelite laws were developed out of a pastoral ethos; interest-free loans were to be given to assist others. The community was established on a kinship model, so that the neighbor was seen as part of an extended family, and loans were given to reduce poverty. Interest was therefore condemned because it destroyed borrowers and reduced them to debt-slavery. The debtor was described as being "in the hand of" the creditor, for hand symbolizes the power or control the creditor has on the debtor. The creditor was to "release" the debtor as well as the debt. In the less developed pastoral economy of Israel, those who needed to borrow were usually poor and unable to pay interest, whereas in more developed society borrowers were often merchants.[26]

The basic laws include:

> If you lend money to any of my people with you who is poor, you shall not be to him as a creditor, and you shall not exact interest from him [Exod. 22:25].
>
> You shall not lend upon interest to your brother, interest on money, interest on victuals, interest on anything that is lent for interest. To a foreigner you may lend upon interest, but to your brother you shall not lend upon interest; that the Lord your God may bless you in all that you undertake in the land which you are entering to take possession of it [Deut. 23:19–20].
>
> And if your brother becomes poor, and cannot maintain himself with you, you shall maintain him; as a stranger and a sojourner he shall live with you. Take no interest from him or increase, but fear your God; that your brother may live beside you. You shall not lend him your money at interest, nor give him your food for profit. I am the Lord your God, who brought you forth out of the land of Egypt to give you the land of Canaan, and to be your God [Lev. 25:35–38].

Two words used for interest are *neshek* and *tarbith*. The former means "bite" and refers to the sum extracted from the loan by the creditor before the borrower receives it. When the debt is due, the borrower pays the full amount. The latter word refers to the increased amount the debtor has to repay when the loan is due. Other interpretations view *neshek* as interest on money and *tarbith* on produce, or *neshek* as a regularly paid interest and *tarbith* as a lump sum.[27] The rabbinic commentator Rashi said of *neshek*, "it resembles the bite of a snake . . . inflicting a small wound in a person's foot which he does not feel at first, but all at once it swells, and distends the whole body up to the top of his head" (Childs, 479).

As the Israelite economy developed from a barter economy to a trade economy, changes came about. At times the laws were ignored. Exceptions were made: Deuteronomy 23:20 permits interest to be imposed upon a foreigner (*nokhri*). Inasmuch as the foreigner was probably a merchant, such an imposition would not reduce him to debt-slavery, as it would a poor person.[28] Some scholars believe loans were permitted to Israelites who were not poor according to the Exodus law, which prohibits the charging of interest only vis-à-vis the poor, and the later law in Deuteronomy forbade interest on loans for all Israelites. Later Levitical legislation closes loopholes by forbidding specific practices and various forms of loans.[29] Other scholars believe all these laws were early, total in their prohibition, idealistic, and all were ignored by Israel in later historical periods.[30]

Laws were later circumvented in various ways. A legal fiction arose whereby the debtor would offer to pay the debt, the creditor would politely refuse, but then accept money. Economic reality demanded some form of interest.[31] The prophets Amos and Ezekiel criticized the charging of interest, but the lack of references elsewhere makes one wonder about the seriousness of abuses. Papyrus records of Jews in Egypt indicate that interest was charged from 456 B.C. to 221 B.C., but after 182 B.C. loans appear to be interest-free (Gamoran, 133–34). The removal of interest from loans was an ideal to which Israel aspired, and perhaps this ideal was achieved at certain times in history.

Legislation also regulated the use and abuse of the pledge or surety that was put up for a loan. The following examples can be cited:

> If ever you take your neighbor's garment in pledge, you shall restore it to him before the sun goes down; for that is his only covering, it is his mantle for his body; in what else shall he sleep? And if he cries to me, I will hear, for I am compassionate [Exod. 22:26–27].
>
> No man shall take a mill or an upper millstone in pledge; for he would be taking a life in pledge. . . . When you make your neighbor a loan of any sort, you shall not go into his house to fetch his pledge. You shall stand outside, and the man to whom you make the loan shall bring the pledge out to you. And if he is a poor man, you shall not sleep in his pledge; when the sun goes down, you shall restore to him the pledge that

he may sleep in his cloak and bless you; and it shall be righteousness to you before the Lord your God [Deut. 24:6, 10–13].

Unlike other ancient near eastern laws, Israelite law restricted the right of creditors to seize property. The coat and the millstone are necessary for life— warmth at night and the baking of daily bread. The use of these items as surety may be a fiction, for if the person is so poor as to have only one of these items, then the creditor must be giving a loan out of compassion with no expectation of return. Nevertheless, the laws serve to limit oppression of the poor by protecting basic necessities of existence. The poor are also provided with the dignity of being able to select the object that they give as pledge. This contrasts with Hammurabi's laws wherein sanction may be given even to seize a *person* as pledge; this may be paralleled in 2 Kings 4:1–7 when the widow's sons are almost seized.[32]

Finally, the theological imperative of the legislation surfaces in the command in Deuteronomy 15:

If there is among you a poor man, one of your brothers, in any of your towns within your land which the Lord your God gives you, you shall not harden your heart or shut your hand against your poor brother, but you shall open your hand to him, and lend him sufficient for his need, whatever it may be. Take heed lest there be a base thought in your heart, and you say, "The seventh year, the year of release is near," and your eye be hostile to your poor brother, and you give him nothing, and he cry to the Lord against you, and it be sin in you. You shall give to him freely, and your heart shall not be grudging when you give to him; because for this the Lord your God will bless you in all your work and in all that you undertake. For the poor will never cease out of the land; therefore I command you, you shall open wide your hand to your brother, to the needy and to the poor, in the land [vv. 7–11].

One can legislate economic reform, but the theologian realizes that true success in the economic sphere must be motivated by an appeal for correct attitudes. The theological paradox of reality is readily seen here, for the divine promise that poverty will cease (found throughout Deuteronomy, e.g., 15:4–5) is counterbalanced by the admission of its continued existence. But this is the nature of the religious imperative.[33]

Slavery

Slavery and interest on loans are closely connected, for the latter frequently leads to the former. Our discussion must include slavery, inasmuch as slaves are property, and their freedom entails the loss of property for someone.

Israel had slaves, but in contrast with the rest of the ancient Near East,

Israel offered the slave greater protection and more opportunity for release. The ethos produced by the exodus and Yahweh's liberation of slaves created this attitude. Laws challenged the power of creditors to reduce persons to debt-slavery by denying the right to charge interest and by providing for the release of slaves. If an Israelite sold himself or herself into slavery, the relatives had the right of redemption, and if there were no relatives, the slave could demand his or her own release when means were available. The Old Testament is the first ancient document to protest the given assumptions of slavery.[34]

Israelites could become slaves in several sanctioned ways. They could be sold as minors: young girls might be sold (Exod. 21:7-11) and children might be seized for debts (2 Kings 4:1, Neh. 5:5). They could be enslaved for debts incurred either involuntarily (1 Sam. 22:2; Amos 2:6; Isa. 50:1) or voluntarily (Exod. 21:5-6; Deut. 15:16-17).

Once enslaved, the Israelite was to be treated with respect. Slaves would share in the family religious life—Sabbath (Exod. 20:10, 23:12), sacrificial meals (Deut. 12:12, 18), festivals (Deut. 16:11, 14), and Passover (Exod. 12:44). Ideally the Israelite slave was to be treated like a wage-earning guest (Lev. 25:40). Finally slaves were to be released after either six years (Exod. 21; Deut. 15) or fifty years (Lev. 25).

Exodus 21:2-6 provides the norms for the release of a slave:

> When you buy a Hebrew slave, he shall serve six years, and in the seventh he shall go out free, for nothing. If he comes in single, he shall go out single; if he comes in married, then his wife shall go out with him. If his master gives him a wife and she bears him sons and daughters, the wife and her children shall be her master's and he shall go out alone. But if the slave plainly says, "I love my master, my wife, and my children; I will not go out free," then his master shall bring him to the door or the doorpost; and his master shall bore his ear through with an awl; and he shall serve him for life.

The *ibri*, the word for "Hebrew," probably refers to a disadvantaged social class at this time; only later would it come to mean Israelite. Then legislation would be limited to freeing the Israelite but not the foreigner or Canaanite. *Hophshi*, or "free person," is also a class term; the equivalent, *huphshu*, is used at Nuzi and in Assyrian texts to describe free men.[35]

The voluntary enslavement mentioned in Exodus 21:5-6 was probably done before the household deity (there is a parallel at Mari) or in the local shrine (there is a parallel at Eshnunna). By piercing the slave's ear the master avoided punishment from Yahweh, who desired the freedom of all slaves, for in this act the slave declared before Yahweh that he relinquished his freedom voluntarily. A ring or card may have been placed in the ear with a tag of clay or metal. This marked the slave as permanent and corresponded to the branding or tattoos used in Babylon.[36]

Release of slaves is not simultaneous throughout the country, but occurs in the seventh year of the individual slave's service. The released slave may take his wife with him, but if he married while in slavery, his wife stays, for at this stage in Israel's legal development the woman was still at times viewed as property.[37]

The slave-release legislation is later revised, as found in Deuteronomy 15:

> If your brother, a Hebrew man, or a Hebrew woman, is sold to you, he shall serve you six years, and in the seventh year you shall let him go free from you. And when you let him go free from you, you shall not let him go empty-handed; you shall furnish him liberally out of your flock, out of your threshing floor, and out of your wine press; as the Lord your God has blessed you, you shall give to him. You shall remember that you were a slave in the land of Egypt, and the Lord your God redeemed you; therefore I command you this today. But if he says to you, "I will not go out from you," because he loves you and your household, since he fares well with you, then you shall take an awl, and thrust it through his ear into the door, and he shall be your bondman for ever. And to your bondwoman you shall do likewise. It shall not seem hard to you, when you let him go free from you; for at half the cost of a hired servant he has served you six years. So the Lord your God will bless you in all that you do [vv. 12–18].

This later legislation shows development beyond the covenant code legislation. Now women receive the same right to freedom, nor are restrictions placed on allowing the slave's family to be released. Slaves are to receive provisions from their master to survive as free persons, lest they be forced into debt-slavery again, and they deserve something for their years of labor. No other nation enacted such legislation.[38]

Other changes are also evident. The reference to piercing the slave's ear before God is omitted, because the Deuteronomic reform did not acknowledge the legitimate worship of Yahweh at shrines other than Jerusalem (Phillips, *Deuteronomy*, 107; Mayes, 252). The voluntary slave is now given a title, "perpetual slave," *'bd 'lm*, which was a title of distinction for a vassal to the king at the Canaanite city of Ugarit (Gray, *Text*, 52; Craigie, 238). Most important of all, the year of release may now be seen as an all-inclusive, simultaneous year of release for slaves throughout the land. Inasmuch as Deuteronomy 15:1–11 describes such a recurring year of debt release, the position of this legislation (vv. 12–18)—directly following it—implies that slave release is now part of that fixed pattern.[39] Perhaps the older legislation of Exodus was not being kept, and it had to be revived in this new form.

Unfortunately we have no evidence that this law was ever enforced. Jeremiah 34:8–16 implies that it was not observed, and his reference to the "covenant with your fathers" may allude to this very same Deuteronomic reform. Nehemiah 5:5 likewise indicates that the law had not been kept. Failure of this

Deuteronomic reform may have prompted the development of jubilee legislation in the book of Leviticus, which envisions slave release every fifty years.[40]

The Levitical legislation comes from the chapter on the jubilee year and is found in Leviticus 25:

> And if your brother becomes poor beside you, and sells himself to you, you shall not make him serve as a slave: he shall be with you as a hired servant and as a sojourner. He shall serve with you until the year of jubilee; then he shall go out from you, he and his children with him, and go back to his own family, and return to the possession of the fathers. For they are my servants, whom I brought forth out of the land of Egypt; they shall not be sold as slaves. You shall not rule over him with harshness, but shall fear your God. As for your male and female slaves who you may have: you may buy male and female slaves from among the nations that are round about you. You may also buy from among the strangers who sojourn with you and their families that are with you, who have been born in your land; and they may be your property. You may bequeath them to your sons after you, to inherit as a possession for ever; you may make slaves of them, but over your brethren the people of Israel you shall not rule, one over another, with harshness. If a stranger or sojourner with you becomes rich, and your brother beside him becomes poor and sells himself to the stranger or sojourner with you, or to a member of the stranger's family, then after he is sold he may be redeemed; one of his brothers may redeem him, or his uncle, or his cousin may redeem him, or a near kinsman belonging to his family may redeem him; or if he grows rich he may redeem himself. He shall reckon with him who bought him from the year when he sold himself to him until the year of jubilee, and the price of his release shall be according to the number; the time he was with his owner shall be rated as the time of a hired servant. If there are still many years, according to them he shall refund out of the price paid for him the price for his redemption. If there remain but a few years until the year of jubilee, he shall make a reckoning with him; according to the years of service due from him he shall not rule with harshness over him in your sight. And if he is not redeemed by these means, then he shall be released in the year of jubilee, he and his children with him. For to me the people of Israel are servants, they are my servants whom I brought forth out of the land of Egypt: I am the Lord your God [vv. 39–55].

Jubilee legislation was the most extensive attempt to restore economic equality in society by canceling debts, freeing slaves, and restoring land. In respect to slave manumission, this text moves beyond the book of the covenant and Deuteronomic legislation by adding property restoration to debt release and by elevating the quality of treatment for the slave. This particular legislation is added somewhat mechanically at the end of other jubilee legislation.

This legislation betokens the failure of previous slave-release laws: it settles for a longer, more practical, cycle—fifty years rather than six.[41] But in return the Levitical legislation sought to make slavery less degrading by increasing the quality of treatment. However, a person enslaved early in the fifty-year period would never live to see the end of servitude. A parallel may be found at Nuzi where an individual could sell himself as *ditennu*, slave, in a *ditennūtu*, slave transaction. He served for fifty years, which was also a legal fiction, for it virtually entailed the entire life of an adult (Mendelsohn, *Slavery*, 31–32). The jubilee legislators may have drawn upon this motif as well as others.

From another perspective, however, aspects of slave release are further developed. The ideology of the law clearly implies that no one may be kept in slavery forever. This may be the only legislation to free, after six years of debt-bondage, the voluntary slave who had committed himself or herself to permanent slavery. Finally, this legislation provides for the manumission of slaves held by non-Israelites. Because foreigners do not observe the laws of jubilee, the slave must be repurchased (Mendelsohn, "Slavery, ANE," 143; Noth, *Leviticus*, 192).

There were other ways for an Israelite slave to obtain freedom. Breach of contract could provide an opportunity. Exodus 21 outlines such examples in regard to slave girls:

> When a man sells his daughter as a slave, she shall not go out as the male slaves do. If she does not please her master, who has designated her for himself, then he shall let her be redeemed; he shall have no right to sell her to a foreign people, since he has dealt faithlessly with her. If he designates her for his son, he shall deal with her as with a daughter. If he takes another wife to himself, he shall not diminish her food, her clothing, or her marital rights.[42] And if he does not do these things for her, she shall go out for nothing, without payment of money [7–11].

The law simply states that the owner must either marry the girl, marry her to a son, keep her as a concubine, or let her be redeemed. Failure to abide by these stipulations means the girl may go free. At Nuzi the owner had to marry her, or marry her to his son, or a free man. But there was no freedom for her if he defaulted. In Babylon the woman would go free only if she had borne the master children and then if he tried to sell her (Code of Hammurabi #119). Thus the status of the Israelite girl was better. However, it becomes apparent that such distinctions were ignored, for Exodus 21:2–6 acknowledges that (male) debt slaves could marry another slave of the master, and no provision is made in the legislation for a slave girl to be married to another slave.[43]

Another situation that could bring freedom for a slave was mistreatment. Exodus 21 provides examples:

> When a man strikes his slave, male or female, with a rod and the slave dies under his hand, he shall be punished. But if the slave survives a day

or two, he is not to be punished; for the slave is his money. . . . When a man strikes the eye of his slave, male or female, and destroys it, he shall let the slave go free for the eye's sake. If he knocks out the tooth of his slave, male or female, he shall let the slave go free for the tooth's sake [20-21, 26-27].

These laws reflect the tension between viewing the slave as a person and as property. But as it stands, this law is very humanitarian, for the life of a slave is placed on a par with that of a free Israelite.[44] The Code of Hammurabi makes a distinction according to the birth of a slave:

If the distrained die in the house of the distrainer through blows or ill-treatment, the distrainer shall call his trader to account. If he be freeborn, his son shall be slain; if a slave, he shall pay a third of a mina of silver; and all that he should have received he shall lose (Code of Hammurabi #116) [Edwards, 43-44].

The biblical text makes no such distinctions, and it goes to the extent of granting freedom in cases of bodily injury.

Hebrew slaves could be released by reason of breach of contract, purchase, reparation for physical abuse, or according to a planned program of slave release. The earliest legislation proposed release after six years of labor, later legislation decreed general release of slaves every seven years, and finally jubilee legislation proposed slave release every fifty years.

Some scholars do not accept this idea of development and propose instead that the legislation in Exodus, Deuteronomy, and Leviticus was simultaneous and harmonious. Such a scheme suggests that Exodus 21:2-6 and Deuteronomy 15:12-18 refer only to involuntary debtor slaves who work six years and are released in the seventh (Deuteronomic release is independent of the Sabbath year debt release mentioned in Deut. 15:1-11). Leviticus 25:39-55 applies only to slaves who went into slavery willingly.[45] The chief problem with this view is that Leviticus seems to concern itself with debt slaves rather than voluntary slaves. It is also more logical to accept the historical development that elsewhere is so evident in the biblical text.

The radical nature of biblical slave laws is exemplified in the fugitive slave law of Deuteronomy 23:

You shall not give up to his master a slave who has escaped from his master to you; he shall dwell with you, in your midst, in the place where he shall choose within one of your towns, where it pleases him best; you shall not oppress him [vv. 15-16].

Most commentators assume this refers to slaves who flee from a foreign country into Israel for asylum. If domestic slaves are included, then the institution of slavery and debt enslavement in Israel would disappear.[46] If so, this would imply that Israel refused to acknowledge extradition procedures for slaves, which were generally included in all treaties made between nations. Inasmuch as the treaty-making process involved the recognition of the other deities of the other nation, Israelite theologians condemned the thought of establishing a treaty with any other nation, for Israel had a treaty or covenant with Yahweh alone. It is therefore logical to assume that Israelite theologians would also reject the extradition laws of such treaties and that rationale may underlie this legislation (Loewenstamm, "Law," 252; Craigie, 300–301). Thus any foreign slave could flee to Israel, the nation of ex-slaves, and there find sanctuary.

Some commentators believe the law refers only to Hebrew slaves who have now returned to Israel. Some parallel legislation is given for Babylonian slaves who return to Babylon (Code of Hammurabi ##280–81). Because the slave may choose the community in which to live, he or she may have familiarity with the land, thus indicating Hebrew origin.[47] However, the former option is more probable, because it is difficult to concede that the theologians of Israel would permit the return of any slave to a foreign taskmaster, especially with the ethos in Deuteronomy, which envisions Yahweh as a liberator of slaves.

The humanitarian nature of this law contrasts vividly with the laws of the ancient Near East, where fugitive slave laws were harsh. Sumerian law would fine a person twenty-five shekels of silver for harboring a fugitive slave. Nuzi legislation also imposed fines. The Code of Hammurabi demanded the death penalty for the same offense (Mendelsohn, *Slavery* 58–59, 63). The following excerpts illustrate the harshness of these laws:

> If a man has harbored in his house a fugitive male or female slave of the palace, or of a plebian; and has not brought them to the order of the commandment, that householder shall be slain (Code of Hammurabi # 16).
> If that slave be hidden in his house, and be arrested in his hands, that man shall be slain (Code of Hammurabi # 19).
> If a man has bought a male or female slave of the palace, or the male or female slave of a plebian, to pass out of the gate, he shall be slain (Code of Hammurabi # 15) [Edwards, 30–31].

Not only was the death penalty invoked for hiding a slave seeking his own freedom; there was a reward for those who captured slaves:

> If a man has seized in the field a fugitive slave, male or female, and has brought him back to his lord, the owner of the slave shall pay him two shekels of silver (Code of Hammurabi # 17).
> If a slave has escaped from the land of his captor, the latter shall swear by the name of God to the owner of the slave, and shall be guiltless (Code of Hammurabi # 20) [Edwards, 31].

By inference the captor was liable for the death penalty if the slave were deliberately allowed to escape. Furthermore, any owner could appeal to the government for assistance in recapturing a slave and the police would help (Mendelsohn, *Slavery*, 58–63).

In contrast, Israel has no such provisions for returning slaves, either domestic or foreign. It would seem preferable to conclude that the passage in Deuteronomy is a blanket statement covering all foreign slaves who fled to Israel, whether they were foreign-born or Israelite. Israel recognized the harshness of slavery and did much to lessen its impact, including passage of legislation to deny foreign slavemasters their "property."

Finally, Israel proposed very strong legislation against those who would capture and reduce another person to slavery:

> Whoever steals a man, whether he sells him or is found in possession of him, shall be put to death [Exod. 21:6].
>
> If a man is found stealing one of his brethren, the people of Israel, and if he treats him as a slave or sells him, then that thief shall die; so you shall purge the evil from the midst of you [Deut. 24:7].

Whereas the Exodus law seems to forbid kidnapping any individual, Deuteronomy specifies Israelites.

The same act was punishable by death in Babylon: "If a man has stolen a man's son underage, he shall be slain" (Code of Hammurabi #14) [Edwards, 30]. However, in Babylon the law covered the kidnaping of minors only. The text uses the expression *mar-awelum*, "son of a free man." The law in Israel was more comprehensive: the children of all people were included, and the prohibition was extended to also include all adult males. Again, the ethos of a nation freed from slavery affected Israelite legislation.

Gleaning Rights

Israel proposed laws that cut deeply into the modern notion of the sanctity of private property. Gleaning legislation gave the poor the right to share the harvest with those more fortunate than themselves:

> When you reap your harvest in your field, and have forgotten a sheaf in the field, you shall not go back to get it; it shall be for the sojourner, the fatherless, and the widow; that the Lord your God may bless you in all the work of your hands. When you beat your olive trees, you shall not go over the boughs again; it shall be for the sojourner, the fatherless, and the widow. When you gather the grapes of your vineyard, you shall not glean it afterward; it shall be for the sojourner, the fatherless, and the widow. You shall remember that you were a slave

in the land of Egypt; therefore I command you to do this [Deut. 24:19–22].

When you reap the harvest of your land, you shall not reap your field to its very border, neither shall you gather the gleanings after your harvest. And you shall not strip your vineyard; you shall leave them for the poor and for the sojourner: I am the Lord your God [Lev. 19:9–10].

And when you reap the harvest of your land, you shall not reap your field to its very border, nor shall you gather the gleanings after your harvest; you shall leave them for the poor and for the stranger: I am the Lord your God [Lev. 23:22].[48]

These gleaning laws may have had their roots in the ancient pagan rites of leaving crops for the spirits of the land. But for Israel the custom is adapted to serve humanitarian purposes. The laws declare that the land is for all Israel, and everyone must benefit from its produce. The poor, who are especially vulnerable, are protected by this legislation. They may now work out their own living without being forced to survive by begging. The story of Ruth gleaning in the fields of Boaz is a classic example of this custom in narrative literature.[49]

More radical legislation permits the poor to enter the fields of a farmer even before the harvest in order to satisfy their hunger:

When you go into your neighbor's vineyard, you may eat your fill of grapes, as many as you wish, but you shall not put any in your vessel. When you go into your neighbor's standing grain, you may pluck the ears with your hand, but you shall not put a sickle to your neighbor's standing grain [Deut. 23:24–25].

This is a humane custom rather than a law, a courtesy extended to the hungry poor and travelers. It may have had its roots in the ancient neighborhood rights between landlords and serfs in Canaanite culture or between settled peasants and private stock breeders in the Israelite milieu. As the custom is here articulated, it serves to check the greed of property owners and the avarice of the disadvantaged. The hungry may satisfy their need, but they should not take advantage of the generosity of others.[50]

Though the gleaning laws are not extensive, they provide us with significant insight into the command against theft. What the modern mind might call theft was not so defined in the Old Testament. Human need had a right of access to the basic essentials of life—for example, food. For the poor to take food from another person's land was not theft, but it was wrong for the more affluent person to withhold it. Theft is not defined strictly according to ownership; right of access to satisfy human need is also part of the definition.

Poverty Tithe

A number of institutions were proposed by Israelite reformers to alleviate economic imbalance between social classes. The three-year tithe, the fallow year, the Sabbath year release, and the jubilee year were institutions designed to redistribute wealth and thus promote economic harmony in the land of Israel. The creation of these institutions indicates that Israel would not interpret the amassing of wealth in the hands of a few as something justified by the commandment against theft. Rather, the understanding of the command as seen in view of these institutions appears to be, "You shall not take away or withhold from others those things (food, money, freedom, or land) that are necessary to their existence as independent and contributing members of society."

The first of these institutions is the tithe for the poor, which is mentioned only in the book of Deuteronomy:

> At the end of every three years you shall bring forth all the tithe of your produce in the same year, and lay it up within your towns; and the Levite, because he has no portion or inheritance with you, and the sojourner, the fatherless, and the widow, who are within your towns, shall come and eat and be filled; that the Lord your God may bless you in all the work of your hands that you do [Deut. 14:28–29].
>
> When you have finished paying all the tithe of your produce in the third year, which is the year of tithing, giving it to the Levite, the sojourner, the fatherless, and the widow, that they may eat within your towns and be filled . . . [Deut. 26:12].

Commentators are divided over whether this custom was actually practiced in some form, or whether it was an innovative proposal by the Deuteronomic movement—one that was never really practiced.[51] The creation of this custom would make sense in the historical context of the seventh-century Deuteronomic reform in Judah (622–609 B.C.). The movement closed local shrines in order to emphasize the importance of the temple in Jerusalem. The normal tithe for that year, which would have gone to the local shrines, would be distributed to the poor. The Israelite would then swear an oath in Jerusalem, on one of the three pilgrimages ordained by Deuteronomy, to the effect that the tithe had been deposited locally for use by the poor. The oath is found in Deuteronomy 16:13–15. Thus it was not a new tithe but an old tithe put to new use in the reform movement, and it is not listed in the other law codes in the Old Testament.

If this custom was regularly practiced, it would be logical to assume it was not practiced simultaneously for all farm lands, but a rotating basis provided provisions for the poor every year. Thus a systematic program of distribution provided for the welfare of all.[52]

Summary

Consideration of Israel's legislation concerning simple theft, loans, slaves, gleaning, and tithing reflect a strong concern with human need. Unlike neighboring cultures Israel tended to place the priority on people rather than property. Legislation frequently provided for the restoration of status, people received their freedom after debt slavery, and property returned to its original owner. In this way the egalitarian nature of society was maintained.

Chapter 3

Reform Legislation

Fallow Year—Sabbath Year

In addition to individual laws Israel's reformers also proposed more comprehensive legislation. Sabbath year and jubilee represent later attempts to create economic justice. The Sabbath year release developed out of the older custom of the fallow year. The fallow year legislation is found in two law codes:

> For six years you shall sow your land and gather in its yield; but the seventh year you shall let it rest and lie fallow, that the poor of your people may eat; and what they leave the wild beasts may eat. You shall do likewise with your vineyard, and with your olive orchard [Exod. 23:10-11].
>
> When you come into the land which I give you, the land shall keep a sabbath to the Lord. Six years you shall sow your field, and six years you shall prune your vineyard, and gather in its fruits; but in the seventh year there shall be a sabbath of solemn rest for the land, a sabbath to the Lord; you shall not sow your field or prune your vineyard. What grows of itself in your harvest you shall not reap, and the grape of your undressed vine you shall not gather; it shall be a year of solemn rest for the land. The sabbath of the land shall provide food for you, for yourself and your male and female slaves and for your hired servant and the sojourner who lives with you; for your cattle also and for the beasts that are in your land all its yield shall be for food [Lev. 25:2-7].

The original purpose of the fallow season was to appease the gods of the land, but Israel adopted the custom and gave to it a new sacral interpretation. The land is left unplowed because Yahweh is the owner of the land, and Yahweh gives it in grace to all Israel. The poor now share in the produce of the land, because the land is for everyone.[53]

Scholars offer different opinions as to how the fallow period functioned. Many believe the fields were not actually left unplowed; rather, their owners refrained from using them, and the poor could use the land to farm. Perhaps various plots of ground were rotated to provide land for the poor. This would provide the poor with the most practical relief. Maybe they rented the land at a low rate. Other scholars believe the produce of the land was given to local communal granaries for use by the poor: this is the interpretation provided by the rabbinic source Tosefta 8:1. Nor can it be discounted that the land was actually left unplowed. Perhaps the land was left for two months during the fall growing season without any planting, at least in the preexilic era. Postexilic sources imply that the land was left unplowed for the whole year and this caused economic hardships (300 B.C. to 150 A.D.). But this represented an attempt in a later era to understand and literally comply with the legislation.[54]

Though most commentators believe the early Exodus legislation was actually practiced, many feel that the Leviticus version was an idealistic projection. Whereas Exodus 23:10–11 permits land rotation, Leviticus implies a universal fallow year for all fields simultaneously every seven years. Reference to the land producing food sufficient for the next year indicates that the fallow land in Leviticus was unplowed land. The sign of divine blessing would be the presence of food that accidently grew on the land. The attempt of postexilic generations to follow this directive literally explains the hardships they experienced.[55]

Somehow connected to the fallow year is the Sabbath year release of debts legislated in Deuteronomy 15:

> At the end of every seven years you shall grant a release. And this is the manner of the release: every creditor shall release what he has lent to his neighbor; he shall not exact it of his neighbor, his brother, because the Lord's release has been proclaimed. Of a foreigner you may exact it; but whatever of yours is with your brother your hand shall release [vv. 1–3].

This command is somehow related to slave release in the seventh year and the fallow year. By placing slave release in the following verses, the author connects slave release to a seven-year cycle, so that all slaves are released in a seventh year of universal slave and debt release, rather than at the end of seven years of indentured service for each slave. Though many favor this interpretation, some scholars believe the slave-release material is here just by coincidence, and only debts were released on a fixed, universal, seven-year cycle.[56]

Because debt release came for everyone after seven years, temptation might exist not to extend loans, and to this Deuteronomy 15 speaks:

> If there is among you a poor man, one of your brethren, in any of your towns within your land which the Lord your God gives you, you shall not harden your heart or shut your hand against your poor brother, but you shall open your hand to him, and lend him sufficient for his need, what ever it may be. Take heed lest there be a base thought in your heart, and you say, "The seventh year, the year of release is near," and

your eye be hostile to your poor brother, and you give him nothing, and
he cry to the Lord against you; and it be sin in you [vv. 7-9].

If the debt release were fixed ahead of time, credit would dry up as the year
approached. So the Deuteronomic theologian issues this theological imperative rather than legislation. Loans were to be given out of charity, and the
Lord would bless the giver.

The theological impact of the passages is as significant as the actual en-
forcement of the legislation. The texts affirm that human society does not
rest on buying and selling. Persons cannot be managed like property; debt
release frees persons to be themselves, and slave release is an extension of
debt release. That is why both forms of legislation may be placed together
here.

Scholars dispute the nature of debt release. Some believe the debt was completely forgiven; others feel that payments were suspended for that year only.
If the fallow year was connected with debt remission, it would be logical to
suspend payments, because farmers would have no profit for that year. If so,
the foreign merchant or *nokhri* would still pay, for he did not abstain from
use of the land as did the Israelites. If the fallow year is unconnected with debt
remission, however, the remission might still be merely a suspension in which
debtors are allowed to keep their profit for that year and resume payments
the next. Some argue that if the fallow year fell simultaneously throughout
the land, it would be necessary to cancel debts completely. If debts were
merely suspended for a year, the text would more clearly state this. The
weight of the argument favors total cancelation. Later generations had to
devise stratagems by which creditors could maintain payments and not lose
their investment, and this implies that debts were canceled.[57]

Did this legislation become the working norm in Israel, or was it the idealistic vision of the Deuteronomic reformers? Was the Sabbath year ever practiced, and if so, in what form? Were land rest, debt remission, and slave
release all observed together, or was just one aspect obeyed in various eras of
Israelite history? Most commentators feel the Deuteronomic reforms were
never really put into effect.

Some scholars hypothesize the circumstances under which this legislation
might have functioned. Suggestions include: (1) the early period before the
tribes actually settled the land and in the earliest years of settlement; (2) the
northern kingdom of Israel prior to 722 B.C. for the Deuteronomic legislation, and the southern kingdom of Judah during the divided monarchy for
the Levitical legislation, both of which were derived from Exodus legislation
in use during the early settlement period; and (3) the northern kingdom of
Israel, 841-722 B.C., for the Exodus legislation; the material in Deuteronomy
and Leviticus is idealistic and was never put into practice.[58] Historians will
probably never determine the answer.

Interesting parallels are drawn with ancient near eastern sources that affirm the historicity and plausibility of debt-remission aspects of the Sabbath

year. Mesopotamian kings often issued decrees of debt remission and land restoration (the latter will be discussed under the jubilee year). In the first year of their reigns kings issued *mešarum* decrees to remit the obligations of debtors and thus establish control over the economy. Kings spoke of how they thus did justice in the eyes of a god. In fact, the old Babylonian word for such debt release is *šudûtu*, which may bear some relationship to the Hebrew word for release, *šemittah*.[59] However, this may be mere coincidence. Though kings remit debts, there is no reference to a fixed date or cycle of debt remission. Nor may the existence of the custom elsewhere verify its practice in Israel. Perhaps Israelite theologians merely borrowed the idea for their utopian vision.

Better evidence is adduced by those scholars who note the observation of Sabbath-year customs by postexilic Jews.[60] Evidence that this custom was observed after 539 B.C. includes the following: (1) 330 B.C.: Alexander the Great exempted Jews from taxes during their Sabbath year, according to Josephus. (2) 163/162 B.C.: 1 Maccabees 6:49–54 states that Judas Maccabeus lost the fortress of Beth-Zur because of a famine caused by the Sabbath year. (3) 135/134 B.C.: John Hyrcanus failed to avenge the death of Simon Maccabeus because it was a Sabbath year, according to Josephus. (4) 37/36 B.C.: Herod and his general, Sossius, were able to take Jerusalem by seige because of a food shortage caused by the Sabbath year, according to Josephus. (5) A.D. 41–42: King Agrippa I read Deuteronomy 7:15 at the festival of booths, which indicates observance of the custom. (6) A.D. 55/56: A papyrus note of indebtedness was written during the Sabbath year under Nero's reign. (7) A.D. 68–69: Seder Olam, a rabbinic tract, implies that Jerusalem was destroyed the year after a Sabbath year. (8) A.D. 132/133: Contracts at Murabba'at in Palestine imply a Sabbath year at the beginning of the Bar-Cochba revolt. (9) A.D. 433/434 and 440/441: Jewish tombstone inscriptions refer to the Sabbath year. (10) In the *Histories* of Tacitus there is reference to the Jewish custom of abstaining from work in the seventh year.[61]

All of the years mentioned fall mathematically into a seven-year cycle, so taken cumulatively the evidence is respectable. These references show that at least one aspect of the fallow year was observed, as the frequent reference to food shortage implies. Hence some scholars believe only the fallow year legislation of Exodus and Leviticus was kept, whereas Deuteronomic observations were ignored. However, the act of debt remission must have been in force, because it had to be circumvented. Rabbi Hillel, a contemporary of Jesus, created the prosbol clause whereby a debtor promised to pay regardless of the intervention of a Sabbath year. The above-mentioned contract of A.D. 133 had such a prosbol clause.[62] Finally, it is hypothesized that the concept of debt release and Sabbath year gave rise to messianic expectations, for these were things associated with the coming Messiah. The appearance of John the Baptist (perhaps A.D. 28), a reputed messiah in Egypt (A.D. 56), and the Bar-Cochba revolt (A.D. 133) all seem to fall on Sabbath years. The practice must have been observed to generate such hopes.[63]

Impressive though this data may seem, it does not prove that the Sabbath year was observed in the biblical period before the exile. It merely indicates the seriousness with which the later Jewish community understood this legislation, after 330 B.C.

The best evidence for establishing the existence of the Sabbath-year practice would come from the biblical text itself. The references adduced are as follows: (1) The three-year tithe of Deuteronomy 14:28, 26:12 implies a corresponding seven-year pattern. (2) Leviticus 26:34, 43 and 2 Chronicles 36:21 state that the exile was punishment upon Israel for not observing the Sabbath year. (3) 2 Kings 8:6 describes how Joram restored property to the Sunnemite woman. (4) Jeremiah 34:8 declares that slave release has not been observed as it should. And (5) Nehemiah 5:3 and 10:31 observe that the custom of debt release has not been observed and should be restored. The problem is that none of these texts really offers solid proof. The references in Deuteronomy are idealistic legislation, Joram's act may be unrelated to the Sabbath year, and the other references admit that laws have not been observed. Biblical data is lacking.

In conclusion, the Sabbath year (and its predecessor, the fallow year) were idealistic legislation proclaimed by the theologians of Israel to remedy the woes of the poor. This legislation was promulgated at various times in Israelite history for humanitarian reasons. However, it cannot be proven that it was the standard legal practice during the biblical period. More likely it was ignored, much to the chagrin of the prophets and reformers. Nevertheless they kept up their demand and call for reform, and history records that at least in one stage of Jewish history the ideals did become practice, if only in part. The modern reformer must be led by the ethos that inspired those prophets and reformers so as to champion the cause of the poor today.

Jubilee Year

The most comprehensive vision of reform is presented in the laws concerning the jubilee year in Leviticus 25. This material encompasses slave release, but goes beyond previous legislation by demanding the restoration of property to its original owners. The theologians utilized ancient concepts as they articulated this new manifesto for reform in the exilic period (586–539 B.C.). As it stands in the biblical text, the jubilee legislation is an assault upon any understanding of the commandment against stealing that tries to justify the aggrandizement of wealth in the hands of an elite few.

The jubilee laws reflect a courageous vision for society by theologians who have understood the depth of their religion. They declare that Yahweh is the owner of the land, and Yahweh would assure the people its place on it. Land was given to families and clans, and it would stay with them forever. It gave hope to the impoverished by offering a promise of return to their land and a place of equality in the community. It became an aid to prevent the breakdown of the family as a social element.[64]

The laws seek to alter radically the structure of society to preserve economic equality among all Israelites. The equality of the settlement period had given way to wide class distinctions in the monarchical era, and now this exilic legislation sought to restore the balance between classes. The jubilee sought to prevent wealth from remaining in the hands of a few. By blocking speculation in landed property the laws ensured to the peasant class, which springs from the soil, the right to preserve its identity. Not only did the jubilee restore land and give hope to the impoverished; it also reminded the rich that one day their own slaves and poor around them could stand before them as equals and free landholders in society. Perhaps they might even seek redress in the courts for mistreatment received, when they were debt slaves, at the hands of the rich.[65] As Karl Elliger states, "the laws were designed to hinder the tendency toward excessive capitalism and the rise of a proletariat by preserving the traditional settling of families on their own piece of land" (*Leviticus*, 349).

The spirit of the jubilee laws reminds the reader of the reforming tendencies of the Deuteronomic movement. Though that movement provided many different measures for reform, the jubilee legislation was one sweeping attempt to radically transform society by means of land distribution. Ironically, it was the usually conservative priests—not the prophetically inspired Deuteronomic movement—who proposed this solution (Sloan, 12). One must also respect the courage of the Levitical legislators to propose a model of society that differed so completely from that obtaining in the rest of the ancient world (Ring, 70; Eichrodt, I, 96–97).

The jubilee legislation is found in Leviticus 25:1–55 and 27:16–24. Much of the material is concerned with the Sabbath year and slave release, but it has now been absorbed by the institution of jubilee. This may imply the failure of the earlier legislation and the need to revise it in a new and radical form. The parts of the text that are the core of land restoration in the jubilee laws are the following:

> And you shall count seven weeks of years, seven times seven years, so that the time of the seven weeks of years shall be to you forty-nine years Then you shall send abroad the loud trumpet on the tenth day of the seventh month; on the day of atonement you shall send abroad the trumpet throughout all your land. And you shall hallow the fiftieth year, and proclaim liberty throughout the land to all its inhabitants; it shall be a jubilee for you, when each of you shall return to his property and each of you shall return to his family. A jubilee shall that fiftieth year be to you; in it you shall neither sow, nor reap what it grows of itself, nor gather the grapes from the undressed vines. For it is a jubilee; it shall be holy to you; you shall eat what it yields out of the field. In this year of jubilee each of you shall return to his property. And if you sell to your neighbor or buy from your neighbor, you shall not wrong one another. According to the number of years after the jubilee, you shall buy from your neighbor, and according to the number of crops he shall

sell to you. If the years are many you shall increase the price, and if the years are few you shall diminish the price, for it is the number of crops that he is selling to you. You shall not wrong one another, but you shall fear your God: for I am the Lord your God. . . . The land shall not be sold in perpetuity, for the land is mine; for you are strangers and sojourners with me. And in all the country you possess, you shall grant a redemption of the land. If your brother becomes poor, and sells part of his property, then his next of kin shall come and redeem what his brother has sold. If a man has no one to redeem it, and then himself becomes prosperous and finds sufficient means to redeem it, let him reckon the years since he sold it and pay back the overpayment to the man to whom he sold it; and he shall return to his property. But if he has not sufficient means to get it back for himself, then what he sold shall remain in the hand of him who bought it until the year of jubilee; in the jubilee it shall be released, and he shall return to his property. If a man sells a dwelling house in a walled city, he may redeem it within a whole year after its sale; for a full year he shall have the right of redemption. If it is not redeemed within a full year, then the house that is in the walled city shall be made sure in perpetuity to him who bought it, throughout his generations; it shall not be released in the jubilee. But the house of the villages which have no wall around them shall be reckoned with the fields of the country; they may be redeemed, and they shall be released in the jubilee. Nevertheless the cities of the Levites, the houses in the cities of their possession, the Levites may redeem at any time. And if one of the Levites does not exercise his right of redemption, then the house that was sold in a city of their possession shall be released in the jubilee; for the houses in the cities of the Levites are their possession among the people of Israel. But the fields of common land belonging to their cities may not be sold; for that is their perpetual possession [Lev. 25:8-17, 23-34].

If a man dedicates to the Lord part of the land which is his by inheritance, then your valuation shall be according to the seed for it; a sowing of a homer of barley shall be valued at fifty shekels of silver. If he dedicates his field from the year of jubilee, it shall stand at your full valuation; but if he dedicates his field after the jubilee, then the priest shall compute the money-value for it according to the years that remain until the year of jubilee, and a deduction shall be made from your valuation. And if he who dedicates the field wishes to redeem it, then he shall add a fifth of the valuation in money to it, and it shall remain his. But if he does not wish to redeem the field, or if he has sold the field to another man, it shall not be redeemed any more; but the field, when it is released in the jubilee, shall be holy to the Lord, as a field that has been devoted; the priest shall be in possession of it. If he dedicates to the Lord a field which he has bought, which is not a part of his possession by inheritance, then the priest shall compute the valuation for it up to the year of jubilee, and the man shall give the amount of the valuation on that day as a holy thing to the Lord. In the year of jubilee the field shall return to him from whom it was bought, to whom the land belongs as a possession by inheritance [Lev. 27:16–24].

The trumpet was sounded on the tenth day of Tishri, the old New Year's Day, which was celebrated in the fall. How the number fifty was arrived at remains an issue of debate. The jubilee may have really been the forty-ninth year, and by counting the previous jubilee year, the next jubilee would be the fiftieth year. The jubilee would be the seventh Sabbath year. However, some scholars believe it actually was a separate year that followed the seventh Sabbath year. If so, the burden of two such years in succession would have been unbearable. A third option sees jubilee as limited to just the fall months or as a short intercalary period.[66] However, if the jubilee legislation is interpreted as idealistic projections of exilic theologians and never actualized as historical reality, then there is no problem.

More important are the provisions for proper land transferral. The legislation admits that land could be sold in dire necessity, an act that would have appalled Naboth (1 Kings 21), for he refused sale of his inherited property even to the king. But now the land that may be sold by an owner must ultimately be returned. Thus the strong may not oppress the weak by holding their land from them.

To ensure fairness very specific details had to be developed. Guidelines were devised for the proper sale of land—guidelines that recognized depreciation in view of the impending jubilee (taking jubilee as a fixed, general release, not varying with each piece of property, as fallow-year and Sabbath-year releases may have been). The best calculation would have been that based on the number of crops available to the new buyer. Not only was this convenient for calculation, but it preserved the underlying ideology in the transaction: one would deduce that the buyer did not really purchase the land but rather the crops. Theoretically land was not sold but only loaned to the buyer, and at the jubilee it returned to the full usage of the true owner.[67]

This new legislation could not, however, ignore existing legislation. The possibility of redemption by relatives was an ancient custom, and it is reflected in the book of Ruth. The Levitical legislator had to work this old material into his land-restoration scheme.

Special consideration had to be given concerning houses in walled cities. This reflects the difference in Canaanite and Israelite economic practice. Land in walled cities could not be repurchased or restored: it fell under old Canaanite law, which was based on capitalistic principles of private ownership. Unwalled cities or villages tended to fall into the Israelite economic and cultural sphere of influence, so they could be redeemed. Also, the house in an unwalled city is more visibly part of the land than one in a walled city.[68]

Further exceptions are granted to the Levites, especially in the Levitical cities; they may repurchase houses at any time. Special consideration for the

Levites was prompted by concern for this landless group of religious servants, and it may reflect the respect of the priestly school for earlier Deuteronomic legislation.

Further recognition of previous Deuteronomic material may be reflected in the lack of reference to debt release in Leviticus 25. The material covered in Deuteronomy 15 on debt release may still have been seen as binding, and so there was no need to repeat or clarify it. However, some scholars feel that Leviticus respected only the material in the book of the covenant (Exod. 21–23) and not the Deuteronomic laws, because the latter were relatively recent (North, *Jubilee*, 31–32; Westbook, 224).

Finally, norms for dealing with dedicated land had to be devised. Some might take advantage of the laws and sell land that had been donated to the priests or the temple. If people do this, the land is forfeited. This might have been done because the land thus dedicated was still the responsibility of those who gave it. Not only would they absolve themselves of responsibility, but they would receive credit from the priests as well as financial profit.[69] This and other practices, such as repurchase of dedicated land, had to be discussed in Leviticus. The jubilee legislators had to think out the possibilities that might arise with their new institution, just as they had to respect previous legislation.

Historical Background of Jubilee Legislation

The most significant question discussed by commentators is whether jubilee legislation was an ideal projected by exilic theologians though never practiced or whether jubilee laws were observed in some fashion during Israelite history.

Most commentators believe jubilee was a utopian vision of hope projected by exilic priests who used motifs and ideas current at that time.[70] Several cogent arguments are presented: (1) No clear reference occurs in biblical literature to jubilee practice. According to 2 Chronicles 36:21, it was not observed before the exile, and later rabbis admit it was not observed after the exile. Ezekiel 46:16–17 and Isaiah 61:1–3 mention a year of emancipation (*deror*), but both are exilic documents contemporaneous with Leviticus, and they see this release as a vision of hope for the future. The only other allusion to land restoration, Numbers 36:4, refers to property inherited by the appropriate clan when there are no male heirs. (2) The jubilee legislation contradicts earlier laws in Exodus and Deuteronomy on slaves and the fallow/Sabbath year. Only if the earlier laws had failed would these idealistic projections be needed. (3) The legislation is economically impractical. Two fallow years in succession on the forty-ninth and fiftieth year would be self-destructive. Wholesale exchange of property every fifty years would produce chaos in the land.

Thus jubilee legislation appears to represent late and idealistic attempts to restore the Sabbath year and debt remission. These laws were inspired by ancient ideals, but they failed in the postexilic era. Ironically, the postexilic Jews observed laws connected with the Sabbath year.

Defenders of the historicity of jubilee practice often adduce ancient Near Eastern parallels, arguing that if the custom was observed elsewhere, then it could have been practiced in Israel. In the Akkadian period (2400-2200 B.C.) and the Old Babylonian or Amorite period (1900-1600 B.C.) Mesopotamian kings could proclaim a *mišhnarum*, a royal edict that would cancel debts, suspend taxes, release debt-slaves, return land seized by creditors, and enact other economic reforms.

These proclamations were made at irregular intervals, but they usually came in the first year of a king's reign. We have reports of such proclamations for the twenty-sixth, thirty-fifth, and forty-first years of the reign of Rim Sin; the first and perhaps the twelfth, twenty-second, and thirtieth years of Hammurabi; the eighth or ninth year of Sinmuballit, the first and eighth year of Samsuiluna, the first year of Abiesuh, the first and twentieth or twenty-first year of Ammiditana, and the first year of Ammisaduqa (Finkelstein, "Mishnarum," 243; Westbrook, 216–17). Ammisaduqa permitted an original owner to repurchase land upon demand, even if the first buyer had resold it. This created a reluctance among buyers to buy such property on a second sale, and in the Eshnunna laws a house cannot be resold a second time, unless the original owner has a chance to repurchase it (Finkelstein, "Edict," 91–104; "Mishnarum," 240–42).

When the king made this proclamation he could claim to have done "justice in the eyes of Marduk," which reminds us of a similar biblical theme. When the king in Israel did "justice" or when the laws demand justice, the defense of the poor and oppressed was the usual reason given. Another word for such proclamations was *anduâru*, a word similar to the biblical word for "release" in Leviticus 25, *deror*. Many scholars assume the two institutions were historically related. Scholars note the similarity between the Babylonian word for release, *šudûtu*, and the Hebrew word *šemittah*, used for debt release in Deuteronomy 15. Thus *anduâru* corresponds to jubilee and *šudûtu* corresponds to Sabbath, and because *anduâru* occurs less frequently in the Babylonian texts than does *šudûtu*, this reinforces the connection with the less frequent jubilee and the regular Sabbath year in the Old Testament.[71]

This argument has weaknesses. Customs in effect elsewhere in the ancient Near East do not necessarily prove that the same customs were practiced in Israel; they may only indicate the source of inspiration for Leviticus. *Mišhnarum* edicts are irregular in their proclamation, and they are emergency measures to restore economic equilibrium, unlike biblical measures that apply every seven or fifty years. The *anduâru* proclamations are now thought to be general references to any release of debt, slaves, taxes, or land.[72] These proclamations are really "administrative acts" that reverse political or economic situations once a crisis has been reached. "Laws" prescribe behavior on a regular basis, and an effective law is one that cannot be evaded. The *anduâru* edicts, if they were laws that took effect on a regular basis, would be evaded by merchants and businessmen; they are effective because they come by surprise, at irregular intervals. Jubilee legislation could not function as law; it would be impractical. Merchants could evade the responsibilities of restoration with advance warning, credit would dry up prior to jubilee, and the poor would bear a greater burden. Jubilee laws could function as irregular edicts, but not as laws (Westbrook, 216–21). Comparison between jubilee legislation and other ancient Near Eastern material may disprove the historicity of the jubilee rather than reinforce it.

Advocates of the historicity of jubilee legislation often point to internal biblical data. Advocates may defend any one of a number of different theories.

(1) Though some admit the jubilee laws to be exilic and utopian, they maintain that a historical kernel lies behind them. The idea of land redistribution comes from the early settlement period when the economy was simple and land reapportionment would not have caused social and economic upheaval. Israelite clans and tribes conquered the land and it was turned over to large family units. The ethos behind such legislation assumed communal ownership, and redistribution was not hindered by the idea of the private ownership, a concept that would develop only later.[73] *Mišhnarum* proclamations were made by kings in the ancient Near East, but because Levitical legislation was not proclaimed by a king, the custom must have originated in the early settlement period—before Israel had kings. Hence the cycle is fixed rather than spontaneous.[74]

Advocates of this theory also maintain that the laws in Leviticus do not overlap or contradict legislation in Exodus and Deuteronomy. Slave-release laws in Exodus and Deuteronomy apply to Israelites in debt enslavement for up to six years, whereas Leviticus applies to voluntary slaves who continue service after six years and to non-Israelite slaves. Exodus and Deuteronomy deal with private slave release, whereas Leviticus treats public release. The motivation for restoration of land in Leviticus 25 differs from that in Deuteronomy 15, and the recipient of land is not necessarily a slave in Leviticus.[75] (Though such views are more typical of those who defend Mosaic authorship of the Pentateuch, some critical scholars have advanced interesting historical reconstructions for the development in the early period.)[76]

Weaknesses arise in any theory that projects the jubilee institution back into the early settlement period. There would be no real need for reform legislation in an early period, for the problems would not arise until the monarchical era. Legislation to meet the specific problems cannot be so carefully detailed before legislators are confronted by the problems (Westbrook, 212). There is no concrete evidence in the early period for such practices. To place jubilee in early Israelite history merely avoids the difficulties of accommodating its existence to postexilic times by placement in the shadowy early history.

Furthermore, scholars who associate the jubilee with the early period because of communal ownership in that era make an incorrect association.

Leviticus 25 refers to the return of inherited property, which implies the selling of property such as one would find in the monarchical era. Leviticus makes no mention of communal property. The legislation in Leviticus accepts the fact that land is sold out of economic necessity, and this reflects the later exilic mentality, which would not have been present in the early period.

(2) Some scholars propose that the fiftieth year was really an intercalary year—a shorter period of time inserted into the year in order to bring the calendar up to date with the seasons.[77] This avoids the difficulty of positing two consecutive fallow years. The jubilee "year" was really forty-nine days in length, and the reference to "forty-nine" in the text was originally a reference to days, not years. The text originally read, "the forty-nine days . . . shall be for you a year." The Jewish calendar was 364 days in length, comprising four seasons of ninety-one days each. After forty-nine years the calendar was short forty-nine days, and the fall growing season would be dislocated into the hot summer. The jubilee year of forty-nine days filled out the season, and the fiftieth year merely completed the forty-ninth year. Because the forty-ninth year was a sabbatical year, which meant no fall planting, and the jubilee year coincided with that fall season, only one planting was missed. The fallow land could be returned to the original owners in the forty-nine-day period with minimal social dislocation. The original owner could then plant in the spring, which was in a new year.

This intercalary year of forty-nine days was a preexilic invention to balance a shifting calendar. However, one-fourth day of every year was still unaccounted for, so that every fifty years there was a twelve-day discrepancy. The Israelites in exile were forced to change their calendric system to that of the Babylonians. The second century B.C. Book of Jubilees complains about this Babylonian calendar and calls for a return to the old calendar of jubilee cycles, which were forty-nine years in duration.[78]

This very creative theory has a major flaw. If there was a discrepancy of twelve days, why did the Israelites not make the intercalary month sixty-one days in duration? The theory is too hypothetical and elaborate.

(3) Some theories propose that the fiftieth year symbolically coincided with the forty-ninth year. One possibility is that jubilee year begins with the trumpet blast in the seventh month, a fall month. The jubilee then is a liturgical year that overlaps two civil years. The jubilee year runs from the fall of the forty-ninth year into the spring of the next year, which is then counted as the first year after jubilee. Only one growing season would be affected by both the Sabbath year (forty-ninth in the civil cycle) and the jubilee year (fiftieth), which would be the fall of the forty-ninth year. Land restoration would occur in this fallow season (North, *Jubilee*, 122–24).

Another solution is even more simple. The fiftieth year is only a symbolic way of describing the forty-ninth year. One may derive the figure of fifty by counting the previous jubilee as year number one. Thus jubilee is the seventh Sabbath year, and the fallow season lasts only one year (or season), not two. This may be reflected in the Book of Jubilees and later by Rabbi Judah, for they reckoned jubilee cycles to be forty-nine years in duration (Van Selms, 496).

These theories are semantic games. The text speaks of a forty-ninth and a fiftieth year as separate years. Why introduce fifty as a number if the cycle is forty-nine years in length? If the seventh Sabbath year is the important year, it is a forty-ninth year, not a fiftieth.

(4) A final attempt seeks to make jubilee institutions conform to existing social practices. Parcels of land may have had a fifty-year lease, and jubilee restored land that the creditor held by "lease" on a debt forfeiture. The creditor would use the land for produce, but after seven Sabbath years the land reverted to the original owner. Jubilee came on a rotating basis for different parcels of land; every year a few parcels were returned to their original owners, and the economy did not suffer massive dislocation in any one year. Because this legislation was preserved in cultic texts, it was made to appear as a simultaneous, universal, and cyclic act.[79] This view posits the same rotating pattern for individual debts and slave release. (North adds the suggestion that perhaps on the fiftieth year the original owner might be permitted to work the land and keep the profit, and with this he could repurchase part of the land. Gradually the poor peasant would have been able to repurchase all the land [North, *Jubilee*, 188]).

This theory, too, has weaknesses. The prorating system for purchase in Leviticus 25:16 implies that the jubilee year is fixed for all the land. If an individual buys land when only a few years remain until jubilee, then there certainly is no fifty-year contract for that land. Advocates of this theory usually consider this passage to be a gloss. But they merely manipulate the text to get an interpretation coherent with their theory.

North's suggestion that the peasant slowly repurchases the land removes the radical reform implicit in the text. If the peasant lost land due to an unfairly competitive economy, how could he or she repurchase the land with yearly profits from only a portion of the original plot?

In conclusion one must admit that a great deal of uncertainty has arisen over the practical nature of the jubilee institution. Whether jubilee was ever practiced and how it functioned are questions of extensive debate. But ultimately that is not as important for us as the ethos that inspired such legislation. As Pixley says, "We do not know how these prescriptions were put into practice, but their intention to make real a society without poverty is clear" (*Kingdom*, 35).

For the purposes of our study the actual historicity of jubilee practice would make little difference. If the jubilee was practiced at some point in history, it is a testimony to the modern era that social reform can be undertaken successfully. If we side with the majority of scholars in affirming that the jubilee legislation was of later origin and utopian in character, there is still a message. While in the throes of Babylonian exile, Israel could have a vision of a restored egalitarian society. Despite centuries of failure the idealistic vision of reformers endured. Such tenacious hope speaks a word of encouragement to social reformers today who are tempted to despair when the odds seem overwhelming and the progress minimal.

The following synopsis of Israelite legislation provides a simplified overview of the periodicity of four types of reform measures:

	Fallow Year	Slave Release	Debt Release	Land Restoration
Exod.	7 years	7 years		
Deut.		7 years	7 years	
Lev.	7 and 50 years	50 years		50 years

Economic Rights of the Poor

A final category worthy of mention has to do with the laws that seek to preserve the general well-being of the weaker members of society. They could easily be victimized by the powerful and influential. Any move to oppress them is considered to be an instance of theft.

Special laws in both the early and later legislation sought to ensure daily workers of fair wages:

> You shall not oppress a hired servant who is poor and needy, whether he is one of your brethren or one of the sojourners who are in your land within your towns; you shall give him his hire on the day he earns it, before the sun goes down (for he is poor, and sets his heart upon it) lest he cry against you to the Lord, and it be sin in you [Deut. 24:14–15].
>
> You shall not oppress your neighbor or rob him. The wages of a hired servant shall not remain with you all night until morning [Lev. 19:13].

The word for oppress, '*ašak*, implies extortion or tyrannical behavior, and its use would impress the Israelite that to withhold such wages is a criminal offense, not merely an administrative misdemeanor. The day worker is among the more disadvantaged, for he has no land of his own, he is vulnerable and, if he receives no wages for that day, he will suffer.[80] Wright makes the following observation on the text from Deuteronomy:

> The whole economy existed not for the special benefit of the strong, but for the purpose of supplying need, which meant that special attention must be given to the welfare of the weak. Hence the focus of attention in the law is not on the rights of the strong but on those of the weak which the strong are inclined to neglect or deny to their own profit [*Deuteronomy*, 476].

Another area where the rich and powerful could lean their influential weight against the poor and helpless was the court of law—either the local elders at the gate or the more established judges in courtroom setting. All three law codes proclaim strongly to judges and all Israel the need for fairness in the courts:

> You shall not pervert the justice due to your poor in his suit, keep far from a false charge, and do not slay the innocent and righteous, for I will not acquit the wicked. And you shall take no bribe, for a bribe blinds the officials, and subverts the cause of those who are in the right [Exod. 23:6-8].

> You shall appoint judges and officers in all your towns which the Lord your God gives you, according to your tribes; and they shall judge the people with righteous judgment. You shall not pervert justice; you shall not show partiality; and you shall not take a bribe, for a bribe blinds the eyes of the wise and subverts the cause of the righteous. Justice, and only justice, you shall follow, that you may live and inherit the land which the Lord your God gives you [Deut. 16:18-20].

> You shall do no injustice in judgment; you shall not be partial to the poor or defer to the great, but in righteousness shall you judge your neighbor [Lev. 19:15].

The development of the Israelite court system is perhaps reflected in the difference between the Exodus and Deuteronomy texts. In the early period the judges were the elders at the gate in all the local villages. The Deuteronomy text may reflect the more organized court system of the monarchy, which may have arisen with the reform of Jehoshaphat described in 2 Chronicles 19:5-11.[81]

These texts call for justice that goes beyond similar demands found in other law codes from the ancient Near East. The Israelite call for justice is not only a demand for a radical impartiality that surpasses other legal traditions; it makes a special appeal for consideration of the needs of the poor and oppressed in particular. The Talmud interprets the passage in Leviticus to mean that the Israelite must judge with mercy rather than with impartiality vis-à-vis both rich and poor (Wright, "Deuteronomy," 436; Brueggemann, *Land*, 131). This contrasts vividly with Babylonian laws, which recognize distinctions between classes in society and legislate stricter punishments for crimes committed by the poor against the rich. And Leviticus seems to universalize this imperative to include all Israelites, not simply judges.

Finally, there are legislative imperatives of a very general nature, demanding justice for the poor classes of society in all aspects of economic and legal involvement:

> You shall not wrong a stranger or oppress him, for you were strangers in the land of Egypt. You shall not afflict any widow or orphan. If you do afflict them, and they cry out to me, I will surely hear their cry; and my wrath will burn, and I will kill you with the sword, and your wives

shall become widows and your children fatherless [Exod. 22:21–24].

You shall not pervert the justice due to the sojourner or to the fatherless, or take a widow's garment in pledge; but you shall remember that you were a slave in Egypt and the Lord your God redeemed you from there: therefore I command you to do this [Deut. 24:17–18].

These same themes may be found throughout the ancient Near East. The law codes of Ur-Nammu of Ur III and Hammurabi of Babylon and the wisdom literature all proclaim the need to protect widows and orphans.[82]

The recurring use of the word "stranger" or "sojourner" (Hebrew, *ger*) deserves some explanation. Though debate persists concerning the exact meaning, the *ger* is some sort of resident alien or guest who temporarily resides in the land either as a refugee or a wandering pastoralist. Such persons were free but owned no land. As such they were economically vulnerable. They are to be distinguished from the foreigner, or *nokhri*, who may be either a merchant or a traveler.[83] One could charge interest to a foreigner but not a sojourner. The Israelites probably identified more readily with sojourners, for they themselves had once been landless slaves in Egypt.

Summary

Significant institutions such as the Sabbath year and the jubilee were instituted to provide economic balance and harmony in Israelite society. Individual laws concerning interest, slavery, and property were united together in more comprehensive legislation. By such activity Israel's legal guardians further demonstrated their zeal to provide for economic equality.

Summary of Part One

The legislation of Israel adds a new perspective to the concept of theft. Laws and moral imperatives about loans, interest, debts, slaves, land, wages, and justice in general indicate that the first concern of Israel was for human need, not ownership. Laws mandated the relinquishment of wealth by the rich for the sake of the poor. Laws called for the economic restoration of individuals who had suffered economic reversal. The ancient Israelite legislator realized what too few of our contemporaries are willing to acknowledge: if a healthy society prioritizes the economic integrity of its citizens, it will stay a healthy society. The maintenance of property and possessions must come second to human need.

Israelite law favored persons over property and possessions. Loans had to be provided interest-free (Exod. 22:25; Deut. 15:7-11, 23:19-20; Lev. 25:35-38). A pledge or surety on a loan could not be arbitrarily taken nor could it be an item necessary to the welfare of the individual (Exod. 22:26-27; Deut. 24:6-17). Debt had to be canceled after six years or in the seventh (Deut. 15:1-3). Fair wages had to be paid on time to poor laborers (Deut. 24:14-15; Lev. 19:13).

Slaves had to be freed after six years of labor (Exod. 21:2-6), or in the seventh (Deut. 15:12-18) or fiftieth year (Lev. 25:39-55). Slaves were also freed by reason of breach of contract (Exod. 21:7-11) or mistreatment (Exod. 21:20-27), and foreign slaves were not to be returned to their masters (Deut. 23:15-16).

In the seventh year the poor had a right to what grew in fields lying fallow (Exod. 23:10-11; Lev. 25:1-7), and at all times they had gleaning rights (Deut. 24:19-22; Lev. 19:9-10, 23:22; Ruth 2:1-23) and hungry travelers' rights (Deut. 23:24-25). Land restoration was envisioned every fifty years (Lev. 25:8-17). Legislation called for honest judges (Exod. 23:6-8; Deut. 24:17-18) and justice for all members of society (Exod. 22:21-24; Deut. 24:17-18).

Many of these provisions would infringe upon modern property rights granted by law in contemporary society. But the ancient Israelite would respond that some of our laws infringe upon human rights granted by God.

The critical mind may object that many of these laws were idealistic. If they were ever put into practice, they were frequently disobeyed. So often did infractions occur that successive generations of theological lawgivers had to reissue the laws. Increased needs in society, especially as provoked by the oppression of the weak by the strong, demanded new law codes with greater elaboration. Thus the book of the covenant or covenant code (Exod. 21–23) was followed by the Deuteronomic legislation (Deut. 12–26) and the priestly legislation in Leviticus. Even then many of the new laws were largely ignored and they failed to completely reform society.

What does this failure say to us? It tells us that, in this respect, ancient Israel was no different from our own society. Legislation and reform to help the poor and oppressed often fails today in the labyrinths of bureaucracy and the streets of the city. But just as our ancient spiritual forebears in Israel did not despair, neither should we. They are inspired by a God of love and a vision of hope, as we can be. The God of the exodus and resurrection is a just and loving God who calls us to participate in meeting the spiritual and physical needs of others.

Perhaps we should not say that the Israelite theologians failed. After all is it not their literature that informs and supports our religious institutions and communities? Has not their literature been read more than any other work for the past two millennia of Western history? Does not their ethos influence and inspire the social and political ethos of our modern society? We, their spiritual offspring, live on under their aegis.

The conflict between the ideal vision of the theologians and lawgivers stood in tension with the reality of Israelite history. I turn now to sketching a brief history of the Israelite ethos as it related to property and theft in order to perceive that tension in its historical context.

PART TWO

History of an Ideal

Chapter 4

Canaanite Ethos versus Israelite Ethos

Throughout the history of Israel up to the Babylonian exile (1200–586 B.C.), we note a conflict of ideology among Israelites. The traditional Israelite ethos that produced the humanitarian legislation described in the previous two chapters found itself in conflict with an ethos already established in the land of Canaan prior to the arrival of Israel. Until the exile Israel engaged in political, cultural, economic, and religious conflict with this Canaanite ethos, and frequently Israelites were tempted to compromise and create a syncretistic blending of the two worldviews or even to capitulate totally. When the Deuteronomistic historians (620–550 B.C.) wrote their grand history of Israel (Joshua, Judges, Samuel, and Kings), they were well aware of the continuing conflict with Canaanite culture, and they lamented the Israelite failure to exterminate the Canaanites in the very early days of the nation.

Radical Opposition

The religious values of the two societies were diametrically opposed.[84] Israel affirmed Yahweh as the one God, who had acted in history to deliver oppressed slaves from Egypt. As liberator of slaves Yahweh demanded equality of all Israelite males before him. (Later the tradition would also seek to elevate the status of women in the Deuteronomic movement.)

The equality of all believers is typical of monotheistic religions. Polytheistic religions have many gods varying in degrees of importance, and just as there resides a hierarchy in the heavens, so there is a hierarchy or class system on earth. Monotheistic religions (Judaism, Zoroastrianism, Christianity, and Islam) proclaim the equality of fellowship of all believers under the aegis of one supreme deity.

This equality was mandated in Israel by the creation of laws that formed the structure of the community and preserved political and economic equality. As a result the observance of law and a corresponding emphasis upon social ethics and morality took precedence over sacrifice and cult in the tradition. Yahweh was seen as the deliverer of Israel—Yahweh had acted once in the exodus and would continue to act for Israel in the future. Yahweh's mighty deeds were recalled in the great festivals of Passover, the spring festival of Weeks, and the fall festival of Tabernacles. Although these originally were agricultural festivals, they took on a dimension of historical commemoration under the influence of the Israelite ethos. The Israelite view of reality was linear, and the historical dimension began to prevail in the articulation of faith. To be sure, it was not the exclusive principle of faith, for some material in the Old Testament (Psalms, Wisdom) does not conform to the pattern of a "God who acts in history." But the emphasis upon divine actions of Yahweh contrasts with the conceptualizations found in the rest of the ancient Near East.

Canaanite religion was rooted in the same ethos as was religion in the rest of the ancient Near East. Canaanites worshiped many gods, among whom the most important was El, Baal, Anat, and Asherah. These deities were associated with the forces of nature rather than with history, and overtones of fertility and sexuality were strong in the makeup of each of these gods. The myths that speak of the activities of the gods portray them as violent and sexually active. Chief among the myths are those that record Baal's combat with Yam and Mot. This combat may reflect the cycle of the Palestinian year with its rainy winters (Yam) and its dry summers (Mot), which threatened fertility and crops (Baal). Or it may reflect a cycle of famine and agricultural success over a period of years.[85] In either respect the myths reflect agricultural concerns and view the divine reality as cyclic. Nature, with its changing pattern of seasons, is cyclic, and this is the central concern for Canaanite religion. As such it contrasts with the Israelite linear view and its emphasis on the historical.

The gods were important for bestowing fertility, and for this reason sacrifice was offered to them. Devotees would engage in sexual activity of various sorts (with humans and animals) in sympathetic imitation of the gods, so as to release latent powers for the fertility of the land and the people. This emphasis on sacrifice and fertility contrasted with the Israelite emphasis on laws, morality, and ethics in the social sphere of human activity, deemphasizing the sphere of nature.

The result in the Canaanite religion was an increased concern for cult, with little concern for human needs and rights. Protection of the weaker members of society had no roots in cult or religion. However, El is sometimes seen as a kind and gracious deity in his dealings with human beings, and perhaps Israelites could identify El with Yahweh.

In the Aqhat epic the judge Dan'el is portrayed as fair and just to widows, orphans, and the poor, and this probably reflects the ideal king in Canaan (as well as in the rest of the ancient Near East) (Fensham, "Widow," 161–71). But in practice Canaanite society fell short of these lofty ideals, for they were not rooted in the heart of Canaanite religion. The central cultic affirmation of Israel, on the contrary, was the memory of the exodus wherein Yahweh had liberated oppressed slaves.

Just as the Canaanite pantheon contained many gods in a hierarchy, so human society exhibited clearly established class structures. At the top was the king and his retainers, the *maryannu* or warriors, perhaps descendants of Aryan invaders in the eighteenth century B.C. This hereditary class was exclusivist; the racially distinct lower class could not enter its distinctive aristocracy. The king was controller and distributor of the wealth, which was amassed and maintained by taxation. His power was legitimated by a religious appeal; he styled himself a "son of the deity," usually El. His position was consolidated by the warriors and their monopoly on weaponry—chariots, steeds, bronze and iron weapons. The king and his soldiers resided in a fortified city or citadel in the plains and they controlled the surrounding territory with its unwalled villages. Canaanite cities were organized as small feudal states along territorial principles; their borders marked geographical divisions.

The middle class was composed of merchants, craftsmen, and freemen called *aweluti ḥupsi*. They were five times as numerous as the *maryannu*, and they provided the economic resources of the city-state through trade. They paid the taxes and in hard economic times they could be reduced to serf or slave status. The Egyptian campaigns in Palestine imposed heavy taxes on all the city-states (1500–1200 B.C.); the Canaanites had to pay tribute to the pharaoh, and the middle class was decimated by it. This may have prepared the way for the ultimate downfall of their cities to the Israelites.

At the bottom were the peasants who worked the farmland around the walled city and the unwalled villages. They also paid taxes, were subject to military conscription, and generally were at the mercy of the upper classes. In hard economic times they would lose their land to the merchants, and the king had the power to obtain land whenever he wished. The concept of private property and the right of kings took precedence over the need of poor villagers. According to documents from the Phoenician city of Alalakh, the king sold and bought entire villages. Records from the reigns of Niqmadu II and Niqmadu III of Ugarit (fourteenth and thirteenth centuries B.C.) demonstrate the royal right to buy and sell land. Frequently landless or even landed peasants fell into slavery, and their misery might force them to flee to the highlands or to Transjordan to escape the control of the lords in the cities. They were called *'apiru* or *'abiru* (*hapiru* or *habiru*) by the city dwellers. Doubtless many of them joined Israelite tribes.[86]

The economy of Canaan was similar to that of the river civilizations, Egypt and Mesopotamia. There the rulers collected crops, barter, and other forms of wealth in central storage places, and from their vantage point of power they could redistribute the food or wealth according to their own desire. This central storehouse economic system could produce inequitable distribution as the powerful members of society obtained more than their fair share. This system has been called a "redistributive" economy by economic historians

(Polanyi, 12–26; Oppenheim, 27–37). This system evolved along the river valleys of Egypt and Mesopotamia where strong central control was necessary to create organized cooperation among the people in order to master the rivers and produce irrigation for agriculture (Davisson and Harper, 30–31, 38–56; Carney, 21–22). For this reason the entire social-economic system has been termed a "hydraulic economy" or "hydraulic society" (Wittfogel, 1–449). As the first economic system to move beyond simple reciprocation, or trading barter, redistributive economies were responsible for producing a harmonious society and the first true civilization in human history (Carney, 66–70, 109–15).

The principle of redistribution was designed to provide for human need in an egalitarian fashion. But in Egypt and Mesopotamia, and other areas to which this system spread, inequity of distribution quickly arose. The trader-priest-kings responsible for collecting the wealth often redistributed it to themselves and their friends. Hence, some economic historians refer to this system as a "status-distributive" economy (Davisson and Harper, 38–71), "oriental despotism" (Wittfogel, 1–449), or "aristocratic empires" (Kautsky, 3–376). The powerful rulers forced out any free market exchange, and not until the rise of Greek culture did an open market develop (Carney, 36–37). In the "status-distributive" economy goods were collected by priests (Mesopotamia) or pharaohs (Egypt) in a central storehouse system built around the temple or palace. The system was essentially "oppressive, wasteful, and destructive of economic innovation" (Davisson and Harper, v). The bureaucracy created to administer this hoarded wealth became an upper class of power and prestige which could oppress the lower classes and use the wealth for personal gain. These bureaucrats have been described as officials "with a punishment orientation toward their subject populations," who were treated "as milch cows, to be carefully milked for maximum returns" (Carney, 36). This economic system spread to Syria, Canaan, and the Aegean islands (Minoan and Mycenaean cultures), and even Israel would begin to adopt this "status-distributive" or "aristocratic" tradition (Davisson and Harper, 67–71, 79–85; Kautsky, 64). However, Israel was the first culture to raise a voice of protest against the tyranny of this system (Davisson and Harper, 84–85).

The social structures of Canaanite society differed from those of Israel. The Canaanites were sedentary; they lived either in cities or on farmland around the cities and villages. The cities and the best farmland were found in the low plains; few Canaanites lived in the highlands and their military and political strength was weak there. Their economy was based on trade and commerce, which favored the accumulation of wealth. Taxes were collected, the right of private property prevailed, traveling merchants paid tariffs, and a wide gap developed between upper-class rich and lower-class poor. Land proprietors did not forgive debts, slaves were retained permanently, and the whole economy functioned smoothly with urban/rural interdependence.

The dispossessed had the option of becoming slaves or of fleeing to the highlands and forming a new group with other refugees. For this reason the city would seek to expand control over those who had escaped to the highlands and resettle them. Records show a continual movement of persons between a settled agricultural and a pastoral lifestyle in Canaan and elsewhere.[87]

The social structures of the Israelites were radically different. Their monotheism prompted the creation of an egalitarian society, and the emphasis on the exodus event made concern for the poor and oppressed an issue for cultic remembrance. The Canaanite sedentary urban ethos contrasted with their strong pastoralist ethos.

Whether the Israelites were pastoralists when they entered Canaan from the wilderness is debated. We know from ancient history and the general lines of human development that groups moved from the hunting and food-gathering state into small villages and nonmigratory agricultural lifestyles. Pastoralism or transhumance then developed out of the village population. Pastoralists moved with their flocks of cattle, sheep, and goats from one pasturage to another according to the seasons of the year. In Mesopotamia and elsewhere, pastoralists or seminomads (the term formerly in use) came into existence when village life engendered surplus population.

Pastoralists maintained connections, including mercantile ties, with urban and village settlements. Individuals and groups might alternate between sedentary and pastoral lifestyles depending on economic and social conditions. Urban populations often sought to resettle pastoral populations for economic reasons, but the latter often moved away from the security and control of urban structures in the pursuit of their freedom. Pure nomadism was the last lifestyle to develop. Not until after 1000 B.C., with the domestication of the camel, did true nomads come upon the scene. Hence the old theory, that nomads came out of the desert periodically to conquer fertile areas and evolve from nomadism to seminomadism and finally to a settled way of life, is false. The de facto process may have been exactly the reverse.[88]

Israel may have been primarily composed of persons who were sedentary at some earlier point in history. Certainly the wilderness traditions in Exodus and Numbers reflect their discomfort and unfamiliarity with life in the wilderness. Many who became Israelites may have been Canaanites who withdrew from sedentary life to join pastoralist Israel. If this is the case, then the Israelite pastoralist ethos is knowingly affirmed by later theologians, and not simply inherited by virtue of being from the wilderness.

Whether they inherited the ethos or adopted it is irrelevant, for the fact remains that the Israelites' pastoral ethos contrasted with that of the Canaanites. In Israel all were equal before God, and the structuring of society was based on kinship models. Social units were tribal or extended families. They could transcend the territorial states of the Canaanites, for tribal bonds could transcend geographic barriers. As with other pastoralists, wealth tended to be shared with the community as a whole. Flocks were held in common by the group, and land was viewed as the property of the entire clan or tribe. There were no professional soldiers: all able-bodied men were warriors when needed. There was no job specialization as in urban society, hence no particular trades or skilled professions arose to groom entrepreneurs who could monopolize wealth. Some social historians believe that Canaanites who joined Israel simply retribalized and became part of this democratic ethos.[89]

The Israelite worldview, thus, was radically different from the Canaanite in terms not only of religious values but also of social structures. As Israel settled the land and more Canaanites joined Israel, a certain aloofness was evident among the Israelites. Even when they settled in villages and adopted an agricultural lifestyle, they tried to maintain their pastoral identity. They continued to use kinship terminology to describe their social structures ("tribes of Israel"), they lived primarily in unwalled villages instead of cities, they maintained an anti-urban polemic, and—most important of all—their legislation reflected the pastoralist goal of political and economic equality for all.

The anti-urban motif is found not only in the prophetic diatribes of the Old Testament but even in narrative material. Sodom and the other cities of the plain (Gen. 18–19) symbolize Canaanite cities with their class oppression and sexual fertility rites, which led to gross immorality and the treatment of persons as objects. Cain the farmer (sedentary lifestyle) kills Abel the shepherd (pastoralist lifestyle) and must leave the countryside and live in a city (Gen. 4:12). Even after settlement the Canaanite culture remained alien to the Israelites and they continued to struggle against it.[90] The history of Israel reflects this ongoing struggle, with results noted by R. B. Y. Scott:

> No compromise between absolutism and fraternal democracy could be worked out easily in the atmosphere of Canaan, where the example of divine right was set by local tradition and by the practice of surrounding nations. The clan brotherhood of Israel was rent permanently into the powerful and the oppressed, the rich and the poor. Once a people loses its organic relationship, its means of subsistence, the herds of the nomad, or the fields and vineyards of the farmer; once individual wealth and power become the accepted goal of endeavor within the community—poverty, injustice, and social strife have come to stay [Scott, *Prophets*, 31].

Conquest and Settlement

There is considerable debate among scholars as to the nature of the Israelite conquest and entry into the land of Palestine. Three major theories have been proposed.

The earliest modern theory proposed was that by Albrecht Alt and Martin Noth in the 1920s and 30s. They believed the settlement of the land proceeded in two stages. At first there was peaceful infiltration as pastoralists moved into the land. For years these pastoralists had moved their flocks into the land for part of the year then returned to the Transjordan periphery. But with the breakdown of the Canaanite city-states under the rule of Egypt, pastoralists began to reside in the land, and their transhumance came to an end.

The second stage occurred as the pastoralists increased in number. They undertook territorial expansion, and conflict between them and the Canaanites ensued. This conflict was remembered and glorified in the books of Joshua and Judges. Cities such as Hazor and Luz/Bethel were taken. But for the most part the settlement was peaceful, gradual, and sporadic. Israelites moved slowly into spheres of Canaanite influence. Only gradually did the tribal sense of unified Israel take shape and confer on all the tribes a common identity. The final unification did not come until the rise of David.[91]

This view of the German scholars was challenged by American archeologists William Foxwell Albright, Nelson Glueck, George Ernest Wright, and others in the 1940s and 50s. They believed the conquest was unified, systematic, military, and very effective. They discovered that Canaanite cities at Debir, Lachish, Luz/Bethel, and Hazor had been destroyed in the late thirteenth century B.C., and successive occupation had been that of early iron-age Israelites.

Their conclusion was that the campaign led by Joshua had been primarily responsible for the swift and violent conquest of the land, and that even more land and cities had been taken than the biblical text records. They criticized the German school for its reliance on the biblical text, and they touted archeological findings as the way to reconstruct the history of Israel.[92]

The debate between these two positions lasted an entire generation. But more recently the American or "Albright" school has come under greater criticism. The use of archeology to verify data in the Bible can be questionable, for data are often ambiguous, and archeologists may bring their own prejudices into consideration. It has not been shown convincingly that the cities in question were destroyed by Israelites rather than by Egyptians or the "people of the sea," both of whom caused great destruction in this era. Nor have the archeologists explained why certain sites (Jericho, Ai) show no signs of destruction in the era when Joshua supposedly conquered them. Scholars are less inclined to follow this position in recent years.[93]

Finally, there is a third position, which has gained great respect and acceptance in recent years. George Mendenhall, Norman Gottwald, and others believe that the conquest of the land was primarily a social revolution, wherein Canaanites rejected their social system, joined the Israelite cause, and made war on the Canaanite city-states. Severe economic difficulties, high interest rates, and social oppression forced persons to become parasocials, *hapiru/ habiru*. They retribalized in the wilderness as pastoralists. (Sociologists call this "enclosed nomadism": the formation of villages, usually in the highlands, free from the control of a city-state.)[94] The highland population increased in Iron Age I (after 1200 B.C.) because of the iron plowshare, which made it possible to farm rocky land, and the invention of the lime-coated cistern, which permitted deeper wells. When the cities attempted to reestablish control over highland villages, conflict ensued.

With the arrival of a core of escaped slaves from Egypt who worshiped a god named Yahweh, who liberated slaves, resistance crystalized. Canaanites in the cities revolted and joined with the parasocial Canaanite elements and the newly arrived Israelites to overthrow the city-states. A new egalitarian society was created, which called itself Israel (the use of the name of the god El reflects Canaanite influence). It continued to wage religious, psychological, and military combat against those remaining elements of the old Canaanite culture in the land until the rise of the monarchy.[95]

This theory has several advantages to it. It builds upon many of the ideas advocated by the Alt school concerning pastoralists and combines them with the latest archeological discoveries. Contemporary studies of pastoralism and transhumance in the ancient and modern world are utilized. The theory explains why Israelites were able to settle in villages and farm the land so quickly—they had experience. It also explains why foreigners were more readily amalgamated in the early period of Israelite history, whereas in later periods there was xenophobia due to the continued conflict with Canaanite and other cultures.[96] It would also explain the easy incursion of Canaanite religious ideas into Israel, for a Canaanite might join Israel for social and political reasons, but see no real need to give up religious practices. The paradigm of the Gibeonites (Josh. 9) may have been common in the early period.

Among advocates of this viewpoint there are varieties of opinion. Some believe that the withdrawal from the cities did not involve conflict or a peasant uprising. It was a peaceful withdrawal concurrent with the gradual decline of the city-states. The withdrawal was psychological and socioeconomic rather than violent. The peasant society simply took the old Canaanite values and reintegrated them into a new value system. Hence, they continued their sedentary existence, and now they dwelt in unwalled villages rather than cities. They continued to use Canaanite technological skills, for they built homes in the highlands like the Canaanites in the lowlands, and they terraced the hills with the same farming techniques.[97] But this position does not radically depart from that of Mendenhall.

Despite the differences between these three theories of peaceful infiltration, military conquest, and peasant withdrawal and revolution, all three agree on one point. The value system of the Israelites differed from that of the Canaanites, and the result was cultural conflict. The Mendenhall theory, more than the other two, would tend to emphasize this aspect. As this model gains increased respect among scholars, more attention will be paid to the social, political, and economic differences between Israelites and Canaanites. All three theories would agree, however, that the Israelites sought to reject the value system of the Canaanites, but as they settled in the land, created their own institutions, witnessed the rise of an established state, they gradually succumbed to Canaanite ways.

The Concept of Property

The traditions about the conquest in Numbers 26:55–56, 33:54, and Joshua 13–19 recall a massive land distribution program. Land was distributed by lot to the various clans in what would seem to be a very democratic fashion. Whether this was actually done or whether these texts are an idealized vision created by later Israelite theologians is debated. Nevertheless, later prophets described the casting of a lot (*goral*) as an accepted institution. Isaiah 34:17 and Micah 2:5 allude to its existence, and Ezekiel 45:1 and 47:22 speak of it as a future activity that will occur when the Jews return from exile. If land distribution did not occur in Joshua's day, there seems to be evidence that it did occur at later periods. Modern Palestinian Arabs (prior to the expansion of Israel) would redistribute common village lands on a rotating basis to individual families (Lowenstamm, "Law," 165–66).

Archeologists have determined that as Israelites occupied old Canaanite sites that had been destroyed (by Israelites or others), they lived in simple egalitarian fashion. They moved into old patrician homes in Tell Beit Mirsim and Bethel and lived on the first floor, the old slave quarters, rather than the second floor of the patrician dwellings. The size and quality of buildings decreased in this period in all Israelite settlements, probably because they lacked forced labor or corvée (Albright, *Archaeology*, 119). Other archeological work has disclosed that the homes built by Israelites at Tirsah were all the same size. This appears to indicate a general parity in the distribution of wealth (Davisson and Harper, 80).

The undergirding basis for the distribution of land and general economic equality was the view of Yahweh as owner of all the land. Yahweh was the true lord of the manor, who distributed the land to the people; the people lived on it, but Yahweh continued to own it. Land was never to be sold: the people could not sell the land that belonged to Yahweh. Land was kept in the hands of the same families and equality of distribution was maintained. Israelites were one with their land, and they would never part with it. The poor peasant remained a truly free individual by virtue of owning a parcel of land. This ideal protected small farmers against the growth of large estates or latifundia, as experienced under the Canaanites.[98]

The ideal may have grown out of ancient Near Eastern concepts. Feudalism was the usual system found in Mesopotamia and Canaan. The king, lord of the manor, or temple priests usually owned the land, and the farmers worked on it as serfs, virtual slaves. But in Israel Yahweh was the lord of the manor who let the people work the land. Yahweh was the God who liberated slaves from Egypt; and so Yahweh's land was given to the poor and oppressed (Van Selms, 498).

Some scholars believe this idea was not rooted in the feudal model, but rather in the West-Semitic pattern of tribal resistance to the creation of latifundia. The strong concept of familial ownership resisted creation of large estates. Perhaps the ideal of divine ownership and concomitant legislation (esp. in Lev. 25) were the theological brainchild of this West-Semitic ideal (Andersen, 49). Even so, the result is still the same: Yahweh is the true owner of the land, and poor farmers should not be displaced.

This explains why so much legislation was designed to protect the poor in relationship to the land. Laws discussed in the previous chapters—gleaning rights, tithes for the poor, travelers' rights, and jubilee—are grounded in this ideal. By way of contrast, Israel lacked laws designed to protect private ownership, provisions for renting the land, and land tenancy laws found so frequently elsewhere in the ancient Near East.[99]

The well-established institution of kinship redemption was rooted in this pattern of ownership. If a person became poor and lost property, it must be bought by a family member or the nearest relative, and a breach of land would occur if a non–family member purchased it (Lev. 25:25). Examples include Jeremiah's purchase of land (Jer. 32:6–9) and Boaz's purchase of the land of Naomi (Ruth 4:1–10) (Kippenberg, 30–31).

Property redeemed by a relative did not really belong to that person. We are not sure of the details concerning this institution, nor do we know if the practice varied in different eras. But the principle is rooted in the ideal of divine ownership, which mandates that property belongs to the original owner, even if he becomes poor and loses it by legal measures (Pedersen, I, 83–93; Noth, *Leviticus*, 51).

This contrasts with the rest of the ancient Near Eastern world. In the great river civilizations of Egypt and Mesopotamia the centralization of property in the hands of a few was necessary for social control. The irrigation of large tracts of land was necessary to produce sufficient food for the large numbers of persons who lived in the confined area of the river plains. Strong central governments arose to administer public works and possess the land as early as the third millennium B.C. The pharaoh in Egypt and the temple priests in Mesopotamia claimed the land by sheer force and legitimated their seizure by theological understandings. In Egypt the pharaoh was a god, and in Mesopotamia the masses were slaves of the gods, destined to work forever on the temple manor that served as the link with the divine realm. The small property owner in Mesopotamia was protected by legislation occasionally proposed by reform-minded kings, such as Urukagina. The *mushkenum* in Mesopotamia was protected by laws, for he was liable to great exploitation in this system. But his protection fell short of what his Israelite counterpart received.

Outside the great river civilizations this centralized control of property was not so extreme. At Nuzi and Mari (both in northern Mesopotamia on the periphery of the temple state system) and even in Canaan the sale of land was more difficult. Private ownership was respected by law, and this probably reflected the conservative tribal nature of West-Semitic peoples. But even in this area the influence of the river civilizations led many individuals to carve out large estates.

Property could be wrested from the hands of individuals or families by ruse. A rich person could be adopted by a poor person as a family member and thus inherit the land in return for "financial assistance" given to his or her "family." Or land might be obtained by a "gift exchange" or a "land exchange," which left the dispossessed family with something else perhaps not as valuable as the family land had been. Thus even though laws might have been designed to protect poorer individuals, the rich and powerful found ways to circumvent them.

Israel, however, rooted the defense of the poor but free landowner in religious values rather than in laws. Legislation then developed out of theology. Israelite laws were more than humanitarian; they were theological. By grounding laws in an appeal to religious authority Israel sought to afford greater protection for poor landowners. In fact, all Israelite laws seem to be rooted in divine authority, for they are placed in the context of the revelation at Sinai. This attempt to ground all legislation in a more binding authority surpasses what the rest of the ancient Near East intended with its more secular law.

This understanding came into conflict with the Canaanite views of land possession. During the period of the judges Israel resisted the Canaanite economic state system. The Israelites remained in the highlands in unwalled villages, where there was economic equality, communal ownership, self-sufficiency in the production of goods, and social structures built upon kinship models. But gradually the influence of Canaanite economics penetrated Israelite communities.

Though Israel frequently defeated Canaanites in battle, the organized force of the Philistines was too much for them. The social structure of the Philistines was an effective variation on the Canaanite state system, and their military prowess made them virtual rulers of Israel prior to the rise of David. In response to the Philistines the Israelites had to develop organized leadership under their own kings—Saul, David, and Solomon. The Philistine threat left Israel no other alternative: it had to resort to the hated institution of kingship. Thereafter, the process of the Canaanization of the economy of Israel began to accelerate seriously (Pixley, 32–33; Dietrich, 21–31).

The compromise with Canaanite values concerning property began at an early stage. Once the Israelites began to settle in villages they started to follow the pattern of Canaanite city life. Leviticus 25 contains legislation from the sixth century B.C., but it reflects this early compromise. The distinction between the repurchase of land in walled and unwalled cities reflects this conflict between the two systems: the land in walled cities could not be repurchased. Walled cities were strongholds of Canaanite culture, and the old laws were based on principles of capitalism and private ownership.[100]

Laws in the book of the covenant (Exod. 21–23) reflect the model of limited private ownership of land and livestock, and if the book of the covenant is early, this process must have begun in the settlement period (1200–1050 B.C.). Even in Israelite villages the pattern changed. The houses at Tirsah were all the same size early in Israelite history, but by the eighth century B.C. there were larger and smaller homes, reflecting the increasing gap between the rich and the poor (de Vaux, *Israel*, 72–73; Boecker, 93). Chiefly responsible for this change from the old Israelite value system was the rise of the monarchy (Davisson and Harper, 80).

An interesting discussion has arisen concerning the nature of landowner-ship in early Israel. Many scholars believe the early Israelites were communis-tic or at least communalistic in their shared possessions of land and livestock.[101] Pastures and watering places were held in common by tribes, and when they settled in villages, the arable fields were held in common. R.B.Y. Scott makes the following observations:

> Certain consequences of this family-tribal organization of society are to be noted. The first is that the economic wealth of the community was actually community wealth; though vested in the head of the family or clan, it was held in trust for all. Personal property was confined to personal items such as ornaments, dress, and weapons, and there was no individual private property, as a rule, in the flocks and herds upon which the community as a whole depended for its existence [Scott, *Prophets*, 23].

The same sociological practices can be observed in other similar societies, including those contemporaneous with Israel. The Arameans practiced com-munal ownership of land, which was sectioned into areas called *kudurrus*. Even among modern Palestinians the practice of common property and its redistribution was still observed prior to Israeli occupation (de Vaux, *Israel*, 165). The same phenomenon is found among village communities in India and was practiced among the villages of Western Europe prior to the indus-trial age. In East and West, communal plots administered by particular fami-lies may not be sold. The land was regularly distributed to other families on a rotating basis. The typical Teutonic, Irish, or Indian village and the sur-rounding land would be laid out in concentric circles. The land nearest the village would be property periodically redistributed to individual families every three, five, or seven years; the next region would be the "arable mark" or common pasture lands for the entire village; the outermost region would be the undeveloped lands, which were also owned communally (Maine, 41–42, 77–113; Fenton, *Life*, 25–30). The early Israelite village may have paralleled this pattern.

The periodic redistribution of lands allotted to individual families may be reflected in the later laws of the jubilee year.[102] Other laws that may reflect this early communal ownership include: (1) responsibility to protect one's neighbor's livestock—Exod. 23:4–5; Deut. 22:1–4; (2) joint responsibility for the murder of a stranger on the land between two villages—Deut. 21:1–9; (3) protection of fruit trees—Deut. 20:19–20; (4) protection of bird's nests—Deut. 22:6–7; (5) Sabbath release—Deut. 15:1–3; (6) gleaning rights—Deut. 24:19–22; Lev. 19:9–10, 23:22; and (7) travelers' rights—Deut. 23:24–25.

If this model were applied to Israel, one could reconstruct the following economic history. In the first stage of settlement, land and flocks were held in common by the family, clan, or tribe. Only family property and moveables were privately owned, just as in India the property of the "house community" was privately owned. This would include ornaments, clothing, weapons, and jewelry—items that would have particular meaning for specific individuals. The land allotted to families would be periodically redistributed to other families (though some scholars doubt this and think it was merely restored to the original families). As the transition from pastoral to settled life came about, communal ownership was replaced by private ownership: families subdivided and farmed separate tracts of land.

In the early period economic surplus went to the clan as a whole, for it was community wealth vested in the clan leader who distributed it according to need. But with the rise of the monarchy this surplus wealth was taxed and removed to support the royal court, and villagers were slowly reduced to poverty.[103]

Some historians question this reconstruction. They believe that private property *and* communal ownership were in effect from the very beginning. Others maintain that a system in which land is owned by families is not communalistic but rather a form of private ownership. Thus from the beginning the land was owned by individual families, but never by the entire community. The land ownership was familial, not communal, and the "portion" or "heritage" (*heleq* or *nahalah*) refers to land inherited by families—land that could never be relinquished by them.[104]

These observations are well taken. But the disagreement may be more semantic than real. The first group interprets familial ownership on a permanent basis as communal ownership because it rejects the right of individuals to aggrandize property in their own name. The second group defines familial ownership as private because it rejects the right of the state to own and administer land, which these scholars see as the de facto practice of modern communism. The two groups may differ only in that the first group believes there was periodic redistribution, whereas the others see no evidence of such practice.

The Israelite pattern was familial ownership, a system that aimed to keep property in the hands of the common people and opposed the attempts of rich individuals or city-states and their ruling monarchs to appropriate land. The land policies of Israel opposed both extremes. Whether it be called communalism or private property, the point is that the rights of poor but free peasants were protected. It is called communalism if the "enemy" is seen to be rich individuals; it is called private property if the "enemy" is the powerful city-state. For Israel, the voracity of both groups was to be thwarted.

Summary

The Israelite ethos was formed in the crucible of slavery in Egypt and of conflict in Canaan. Regardless of which model is used to describe the conquest, the constituent members of Israel were either escaped slaves from Egypt or lower-class Canaanites in revolt against Canaanite city-states. They viewed Yahweh as the liberator of slaves who willed a society in which all members (adult males at first, then later all persons) were politically, socially, and economically equal. The entire legal tradition reflects this religiously inspired ideal.

The contrast between Israel's ideals and the reality of Canaanite society is striking. Though Israelites settled in the land of Canaan (or withdrew from Canaanite cities to join the Israelite movement) and eventually adopted many Canaanite ways and customs, they still sought to maintain the high ideals inspired by their Yahwistic faith. A key concept was their view of property as the possession of all. This particular ideal was vital for the maintenance of a free and equal society.

Chapter 5

Monarchy and the Decline
of the Israelite Ethos

In its early years, Israel viewed kingship as a Canaanite institution. Yahweh was their king; other kings, with their standing professional armies, were not only alien but representatives of a hateful institution. However, survival in the face of the Philistine threat was impossible for an army of free but militarily unsophisticated peasants. Their only alternative was leadership by a king who could command the continued respect of trained soldiers. David answered these qualifications. In fact, David was prepared for successful rule by his years living in the wilderness with renegade mercenaries. These mercenaries, especially Joab, enabled him to unite Israel, defeat the Philistines, withstand the revolution of Absalom and others, so that the royal crown could be transferred to his son Solomon. Thus kingship was cemented.

With the rise of the monarchy Israel came into closer contact with urban Canaanite culture. Central control was administered from cities such as Jerusalem and Samaria, local government was weakened, and familial structures faded in the presence of bureaucratic officials and impersonal governmental districts. Tribal structures were replaced by tax districts, central courts, and all the machinery of state politics. Families of wealth were created by a new mercantilism in the cities. These families engaged in trade, reaped the benefit of taxes, disarmed the peasants in favor of a professional army, and engaged in politics and war.

These new ventures were legitimated by a syncretistic religion sponsored by the royal court, merging Israelite and Canaanite elements. The result was a deemphasis on law, morality, justice, and equality in exchange for a religion of cult and sacrifice that could ignore the oppression of the poor. Kingship brought a return to bronze-age paganism, class structures, and city-state control—the old oriental despotism revisited. A great gap widened between rich and poor in the following two centuries, and the rural poor were victimized again and again by the urban rich. From the time of David onward, there would be a struggle between monarchical criteria and old traditional Israelite values.[105]

Saul, David, and Solomon

Saul's attempt to establish a kingship pattern had failed, for he lacked the broad base of support and the dedicated cadre of mercenaries commanded by David. Nevertheless, Saul demonstrated some of the characteristics of later kings. He owned much land (2 Sam. 9:9–10) and was able to distribute vineyards to his officers (1 Sam. 22:7). Land aggrandizement had begun.

David was the true creator of kingship; he defeated the Canaanites with their own weapon—the organized state. He was king of the city-states of Ziklag and Hebron before he assumed rule over all Israel. After David became king over both the north (Israel) and the south (Judah), he conquered the Jebusite city of Jerusalem (2 Sam. 5), situated between Israel and Judah. He made this well-fortified city his capital and gave it theological legitimation by moving the Ark of the Covenant there (2 Sam. 6). When David took the city he did not kill the inhabitants or destroy the site. He took over a ready-made administrative center and absorbed the Jebusite inhabitants into his empire. Gradually other Canaanite cities surrendered to him because of this nonaggressive policy.

With Jerusalem established as the capital of the new empire, the process of the Canaanization of all Israel began. Jerusalem had been a Jebusite city with Egyptian political structures and a social ideology inherited from Syria and Mesopotamia. One author describes Canaanization as the transformation of the community of the people of Yahweh into a typical Syro-Hittite state, in which the Mt. Zion theology of Jerusalem became merely a variation on the theme of the Canaanite god El who dwells on Mt. Zaphon (the sacred Canaanite mountain in the north). Another author sees this as the beginning of a struggle between the Canaanite "state" party and the Israelite "land" party, which would consume the ensuing political history of Jerusalem.[106]

It is with Solomon that the traditional Israelite kinship system was almost abolished in favor of a royal despotism and monopolistic state capitalism or "status redistributive" system that virtually reduced the people to slavery (Davisson and Harper, 79–85). The court history of King Solomon in 1 Kings 3–11 records his accomplishments and portrays them in a positive light. But as we read the text the autocratic transformation is evident. The accounts laud Solomon for his wisdom, wealth, glory, and building projects. But these achievements were bought at the price of Israelite suffering.

Corvée was the most notorious of his oppressive measures. Israelites were forced to work several months out of the year on the royal building projects in the same way that pharaohs had forced free Egyptians to build the pyramids (2800–2500 B.C.). Though the court history implies that only slaves and Canaanites did corvée (1 Kings 4:6, 9:15–22; 2 Chron. 2:17–18, 9:7–9), later texts (1 Kings 12:1–4) indicate that free-born Israelites were also forced into such service, and King Asa later forced all Judah to perform such labor (1 Kings 15:22). The irony is that such hated labor was what the Israelites had left behind in Egypt.[107]

For purposes of taxation, which was heavy, according to the lament of the elders in 1 Kings 12:1–16, Solomon created new tax districts. His twelve tax districts ignored and perhaps sought to abolish the old tribal structure. As these districts are outlined in 1 Kings 4:7-19, they follow the same territorial patterns as the old Canaanite city-state system prior to the Israelite arrival in the land.[108] What better indication of the royal tendency to adopt Canaanite culture? To add insult to injury, the territory of Judah and Jerusalem, the base of support for Solomon, was exempt from the system of twelve tax districts. Israelites were slaves to King Solomon and his city-state fortress of Jerusalem. The tribal system was now insignificant in comparison with Solomon's dynastic power (Alt, "Gaue," 89).

A bureaucracy was created (1 Kings 1:4–6), displacing the authority of the local tribal leaders. Many of these royal administrators in Jerusalem were probably from the Canaanite aristocracy. Their new position of power enabled them to pursue their old mercantilistic business practices and set a model for Israelites in communal practice (Boecker, 92).

The new economic practices included new policies regarding landowner-ship. If there had been any communal ownership in the villages, or land resto-ration, those practices waned when the new policies of landownership were put into effect. The king could now buy and sell land (2 Sam. 24:24; 1 Kings 16:24), receive the land of those who were executed or exiled, and land could be given and received as a gift in dealings with other kings (1 Kings 9:10-17). Such were the practices of Canaanite or Phoenician kings such as Niqmadu II and Niqmadu III of Ugarit. Solomon could even surrender the territory of Israel to a foreign king when debt forced him into such straits. What an insult this must have been for Israelites who viewed the land as a divine gift that they should keep forever (1 Kings 9:10-14)! With Solomon the creation of latifun-dia or large estates was begun, a practice that would reach its zenith in the social oppression of the eighth century B.C.[109]

Solomon's building projects were his claim to fame and glory. But they were also a form of social control. By keeping his subjects, whether Canaan-ites or Israelites, active on building projects, Solomon kept them under the watchful eyes of his own authority, and their propensity to rebel was stifled. His father David had faced such rebellions led by Absalom and Sheba (1 Sam. 15-20). The forced labor spent on building projects also impressed upon the laborers the importance of Solomon and his authority. Most fa-mous of his projects was the temple in Jerusalem, a religious as well as politi-cal symbol of the new centralized rule (1 Kings 5-8). In addition Solomon built a palace for himself and a house for his wife, the Egyptian daughter of a pharaoh (1 Kings 7:1-12). He strengthened fortifications at Jerusalem and built powerful cities for military purposes. Chariots, horses, and supplies were kept at Hazor, Megiddo, and Gezer (1 Kings 9:15-19).

The building of these and other cities demonstrated the royal policy of Canaanization and the aggrandizement of power. They were a form of control against revolution and they linked outlying rural areas to the central monarchy. The soldiers in them were mercenaries, many of them foreign. Uriah the Hittite and other foreign mercenaries (1 Sam. 23:8–39 provides a list of them) served David and later Solomon. Thus the chariot knights and mercenaries once opposed by free Israelites now became their army, and the masses were in effect disarmed. These old Canaanite cities once again became administrative and military centers designed to create a unified nation. From their inception they would receive taxes, perform bureaucratic administration, serve as cultic centers with the erection of shrines, and function as a refuge for country dwellers in times of war.[110] Rural Israelites were drawn into the Canaanite sphere of urban culture.

The temple was a special symbol of the new state cult. It was created with the aid of Phoenicia; King Hiram supplied raw materials and craftsmen (for which Solomon even gave him Israelite cities—1 Kings 9:10–14). Canaanite art forms were so extensively introduced that the shape of the temple resembled that of a Canaanite shrine.[111] Solomon was the chief priest in the dedicatory service (1 Kings 8), something that should have astounded traditional Israelites, for the assumption of priestly prerogatives led to Saul's downfall (1 Sam. 13:7–14). By this act Solomon presented himself as the semidivine priest-king of the Israelites.

Canaanites were servants in the temple precincts, and the Canaanite (or Jebusite) Zadok replaced the Israelite Abiathar as high priest. The temple became a center for syncretistic worship of both Yahweh and the gods of Canaan, and this may have been an attempt by Solomon to rule both peoples effectively. Foreign cults abounded in Jerusalem (1 Kings 11:1–13); Baal, Moloch, and Astarte had their place there.

All this was done in an attempt at political and religious unification and control of the land.[112] This "exploitation of the religious tradition for the purpose of maintaining political solidarity" ultimately would fail because it had become so thoroughly pagan (Mendenhall, *Generation*, 181).

Alliances were created with surrounding nations. Such alliances in the ancient Near East meant that both parties would make a covenant or treaty involving the reciprocal recognition of the deities of both nations. Traditional Israelites made covenants with no one save Yahweh, for their allegiance to Yahweh as their religious and political suzerain was total. Later prophets condemned foreign treaties because they involved the worship of foreign gods. Such alliances usually involved the intermarriage of royal houses and the reception of princesses into the royal harem. Solomon had many wives and concubines by reason of political marriages. The biblical text condemns these activities (1 Kings 11:1–8) when it recalls that the entrance of foreign princesses into Jerusalem meant the introduction of foreign cults. Solomon even built shrines for these women. Religious apostasy was furthered by power politics.

Political alliances also entailed commercial and cultural interchange. Solomon's commercial dealings with Hiram of Tyre were extensive (1 Kings 5:1-11, 9:26-28), and much of Solomon's wealth came from tariffs, taxes, trade, and commerce. All this betokens the rise of a new mercantilistic ethos that probably crushed the old tribal communalism and corporate economic responsibility on the local level. With the new commercialism, much of which was imported from Phoenicia, came a corresponding cultural exchange. The chief architect was Phoenician (1 Kings 7:13-14) and with him were many craftsmen from Phoenicia and elsewhere. Their presence was probably part of a greater cultural influx into Jerusalem. Traditional Israelite culture was being drowned (Heaton, 29–42; Brueggemann, *Imagination*, 28–43).

Biblical egalitarianism would have been lost forever by this development, except that the paganization was so extreme that reactionary forces were set in motion. The Solomonic empire could not hold together the disparate highlanders and plains dwellers, the north and the south, the Israelites and the Canaanites. Shortly after his death the northern tribes broke off and formed their own kingdom (Mendenhall, *Generation*, 180; Marfoe, 33).

The Kingdom Divided

When Rehoboam, the son of Solomon, became king, he was asked to be more lenient than his father (perhaps he was called upon to deliver a *mišnarum*, a release of debts and slaves). His refusal caused the northern tribes, already oppressed by unfair taxes and corvée, to revolt. Their money had gone to adorn the lavish court in Jerusalem and the military defenses of Judah, and they would tolerate no more of this blatant sectionalism. The banner of revolt was carried by Jeroboam, a former official under Solomon in charge of corvée, and the northern state established its independence. The future years brought civil war and occasional peaceful alliance between Israel in the north and Judah in the south. Throughout most of the period Israel was the stronger nation.

The conflict between Canaanite cultural values and Israelite values continued, and ironically the nation of Israel in the north was more open to Canaanite and foreign influence. Its larger geographic area included more Canaanite population centers, and the national successes wrought by its kings brought stronger political and economic contacts with surrounding nations. Subsequent years (930–721 B.C.) witnessed conflict between the Canaanite ethos of the kings and urban classes, on the one hand, and the Israelite ethos of the prophets and Yahwistic countryside on the other.

Though Jeroboam opposed the statist policies of Solomon, he had to be open to the potential offered by the Canaanites when he created his own state. As a wise politician he accepted a broad base of support. Some historians believe the history of the northern state was that of a series of kings who vacillated between pro-Canaanite and pro-Israelite policy. The authors of the biblical books of Kings imply that all the kings of Israel were bad because they followed in the sin of Jeroboam by worshiping golden calves at Dan and Bethel. A closer reading of the text reveals that certain kings were more hostile than others in their dealings with conservative Yahwistic elements.

The same fluctuation between Canaanite and Israelite influence may have characterized royal decision-making in Judah also. Hezekiah (715–687 B.C.) and Josiah (640–609 B.C.) were praised by the authors of Kings for their strong devotion to Yahweh, which implies that the other kings may not have pursued an equally strong pro-Yahwistic policy.[113]

Ultimately the destruction of Israel by Assyria in 721 B.C. and of Judah by Babylon in 586 B.C. are attributed to religious causes by the authors of Kings. Both nations worshiped other gods and oppressed poor Israelites in their midst, and Yahweh raised up foreign nations to punish them. These indictments by the Deuteronomic theologians and the major prophets are their way of describing how large segments of the Israelite people incorporated the Canaanite ethos in their religious and economic dealings. Ultimately the royal policies of Israelite and Judean kings were responsible for this development and for the destruction of the nation.

Conflict between the two value systems is best exemplified in the rise of the Omride dynasty in the north, Israel (876–842 B.C.). Though the passage in 1 Kings 16:21–28 concerning Omri's reign is short, other material from the ancient Near East indicates that he was one of the more significant kings in the history of Israel.

The crowning achievement of his reign was the creation of Samaria as a new capital for Israel. Such a move was usually undertaken by the founder of a dynasty to assure political stability, for the new city would function as a base of support for the monarch and his successors. His choice of Samaria was wise, for the city continued to be the capital of Israel until the destruction of the nation in 721 B.C.

Advantages of the site were many: (1) Geographically, it was close to the sea (25 miles), on the main trade route in the center of the country. (2) As a newly created city it was free of old traditions and tribal structures. Both Omri and Ahab appear to have had their power limited by elders elsewhere in the country, but in Samaria they were free from such restraints. (3) The city prospered economically. Contact with trade routes brought business, and the strategic location enabled the king to levy tariffs on merchant caravans. By the time of Jeroboam II (750 B.C.) the prosperity had peaked with tremendous wealth in the hands of the citizenry. (4) The city was militarily defensible, and Omri's vision as a general can be seen in his choice. From his new position of power he was able to oppose Syria to the northeast and create a military and trade alliance with Phoenicia to the northwest. (5) The creation of the new city enabled the king to amass a large amount of private property. This not only brought him personal wealth, but enabled him to reward loyal confederates with tracts of land. Continued support was thus ensured for the dynasty in the form of a body of retainers.[114]

Omri embarked upon a grand expansionist policy to unify and modernize

Israel. His new city strengthened Israel militarily, politically, culturally, and economically, and Samaria compared favorably to Jerusalem in Judah. Archeology has confirmed its affluence, the presence of beautiful artwork, and the strength of its defenses. Some of the finest examples of Phoenician and Syrian art, a sign of extensive affluence, have been unearthed at Samaria.[115]

But the success of Samaria only further eroded the traditional Israelite ethos and increased Canaanite influence. The geographic location further exposed Israel to foreign cultural influence, the creation of a royal aristocracy paralleled the old Canaanite city-state models, trade opened the door to Canaanite commercial practices, and political treaties brought foreign influence (exemplified by the artwork) into the city.

Some scholars believe Omri tried to create a dual kingdom of Canaanites and Israelites. Samaria was the Canaanite capital and Jezreel was the Israelite capital. Religious syncretism was sponsored by the king in an attempt to merge the two peoples.[116] Omri bought the land for Samaria from a Canaanite—a transaction that recognized the Canaanite right to buy and sell land in opposition to the Israelite belief that Yahweh had given the land to Israel forever. He imported Phoenician builders and craftsmen to create the city. Samaria became a separate independent city-state within Israel, for the elders and the inhabitants of Samaria later are referred to as being separate from the elders and inhabitants of Israel. In 2 Kings 9 Jehu was confirmed as king separately by the elders of both Israel and Samaria.

Canaanite religion was introduced into Samaria on an official basis. Omri had his son Ahab marry Jezebel, the daughter of Ethbaal, the Phoenician king of Tyre. According to legend she was a priestess of Astarte. The biblical text implies that she brought into Samaria the cult of Baal Melqart of Tyre, along with the notion of divine kingship.[117] The religious and political synthesis was part of Omri's grand plan to unify the entire population under his rule. The result was the creation of a strong Canaanite party that lasted until the fall of the city in 721 B.C.

The Omride dynasty collapsed much sooner (842 B.C.). Opposition came from rural Yahwists who were led by the prophets Elijah and Elisha. Ahab called Elijah the "troubler of Israel" because he opposed the dualism instituted by Omri (1 Kings 18:17). Gradually resistance against the Omrides grew, probably as the gap between rich and poor widened, and more elements of Israelite society joined the popular resistance.[118] When finally the army joined the resistance movement, the Omride dynasty collapsed. Jehu the general seized power with the help of the prophetic and Yahwistic parties (842 B.C.)

Ironically, Jehu could not reverse the pattern set by Omri. Though he put to death the family of Omri and the Baal worshipers, he was able to control Samaria only by compromise. The independent status of the city and the separate power of the elders and landed aristocracy was guaranteed in return for Jehu's ascent to the throne. Samaria became the sole capital of Israel and Canaanite influence continued in a covert fashion to influence the popular mind. The rich and powerful families of Samaria increased under the rule of Jehu's family until the time of Jeroboam (786–746 B.C.). At that time Israel was at its pinnacle of power and prosperity, and Samaria was the center of tremendous affluence. But by then the gap between rich and poor was at its widest, and the Yahwistic religion had been subtly transformed into a syncretistic Baal cult under the royal patronage of shrines at Bethel and Dan.

The Naboth Incident

The incident of Naboth's vineyard (1 Kings 21), during the era of the Omrides and the reign of Ahab, typifies the conflict between the Israelite and Canaanite ideology vis-à-vis property.

The story as we have it is primarily a rhetorical creation of the Deuteronomistic historian (620–550 B.C.) for the purpose of condemning the Omride dynasty and its policy of syncretism. The story confirms the suspicion of the Deuteronomistic historian that kings are evil, and even good men are corrupted by the office. Calling Ahab the king of Samaria rather than the king of Israel may be a subtle hint that he was not truly king in the hearts of the people; he ruled only in his little city-state. The text in chapter 21 reflects later revision portraying Ahab in a reprehensible light.

Most commentators concur on the historicity of the basic kernel of the account. It fits the ethos of the era. The curse of Elijah is probably an authentic memory, for it did not come true exactly as Elijah had predicted. (Elijah said the dogs would lick Ahab's blood at Jezreel, but Ahab was killed in battle, and the dogs licked blood from the chariot in Samaria—1 Kings 22. It was Jehoram [Joram] who died near Jezreel—2 Kings 9.) The historian included these stories in an effort to relate them to the curse of Elijah.[119]

According to 1 Kings 21, Ahab wished to obtain the vineyard of Naboth in Jezreel and he was willing to give another vineyard or cash in exchange.[120] But Naboth adamantly responded, "The Lord forbid that I should give you the inheritance of my fathers" (1 Kings 21:3). Commentators agree that Naboth's statement reflected the traditional Israelite view of the land as Yahweh's gift to the clan or family—a gift that should remain in their possession forever. Naboth thought of himself as an heir to a gift, not as an owner of property. By surrendering the ancestral land he would have forfeited his status as a freeman; he would have become a royal dependent and would have betrayed his descendants.[121]

Israelite ideals prevailed in Jezreel: land remained in the possession of the common families. Ahab had different economic ideas: he believed in buying and selling property according to Canaanite principles of mercantilism. Just as his father Omri purchased Samaria, so he wished to buy the vineyard of Naboth. But the mercantilistic economic principles observed in Samaria were invalid in Jezreel, and Naboth was within his right by Israelite law to reject the king's offer. Ahab knew this, so he went home dejected. His attempt to apply Canaanite business practice had failed in this instance.[122]

Jezebel could not understand Ahab's attitude, for she was a Canaanite, daughter of the king of Tyre and perhaps a priestess to Baal (according to Josephus). In her country kings had the right and the power to rule with authority, the power to buy land, and they were above the law. So Jezebel scolded Ahab for being a weak monarch, and then she took matters into her own hands.

A fast was proclaimed for a day of repentance, but whether this was due to the famine in the land or because Naboth had supposedly committed a crime is unclear. Naboth was "set on high" among the people. This may mean any one of the following: (1) he was appointed leader of the people in the prayer service; (2) he was accused of the crime of blasphemy; (3) he was called as litigant in the debate over who rightfully owned the vineyard; or (4) he was merely seated at the forefront because he was a leader in the community.[123]

Two false witnesses accused him of blasphemy against Yahweh and the king, but what does that mean? Perhaps the witnesses construed Naboth's statement to Ahab as blasphemous and disrespectful toward Yahweh. Naboth's forthright statement of refusal to Ahab was perhaps interpreted as a curse, and this could be viewed as blasphemy toward Yahweh's anointed servant, the king. The witnesses might have interpreted Naboth's statement to be exactly the opposite of what he really said, so that Naboth was pictured as blessing the new owner, Ahab, and uttering a curse upon himself if he reneged on the agreement. Another possibility is that Naboth's declaration was an "oath of the king" (*niš šarri*), an appeal to the royal records to verify his true ownership. But Jezebel sent falsified records indicating that Naboth had earlier sold the vineyard to Ahab. Naboth would then have been found guilty of deceit and perjury. A final theory proposes that Naboth's death by stoning at the end of his "trial" was vicarious. He was a substitute for the king (hence, Naboth was "at the head of the people"), and his death was offered to Yahweh to relieve the famine.[124] No real consensus exists among experts on the charges brought against Naboth.

By what right did Ahab seize the vineyard? Perhaps the state received property of those executed for a capital crime, but we have no real textual evidence for that practice. Some believe it may have been a simple act of confiscation, or the king may have applied Canaanite mercantilism by brute force in the face of little or no opposition from the intimidated townsfolk. Or if the witnesses stated that Naboth had sold the land, and (forged) documents of sale were introduced, Ahab received the land "by right."[125]

Only Elijah spoke out against the king. Most commentators view Elijah as the advocate of traditional views concerning property. Angered by Ahab's new social and economic policies, the prophet announced doom for Ahab and his family. However, some scholars believe Elijah criticized Ahab not for his economic policies—because Elijah did not care whether Ahab obtained the land or not—but for the cruel way in which he accomplished his ends (Hammershaimb, 95-96; Frick, 109). Most scholars, however, believe this confrontation reflects the conflict of two socio-economic worldviews.

The Message of the Prophets

The affluent period of Jeroboam II, with its religious syncretism and ever-widening gap between rich and poor, witnessed the strident criticism of reform-minded prophets.

The older peasant economy with familial ownership of the land and economic autonomy of individuals was eclipsed by the rise of an urban culture in Samaria, which created commerce and an affluent upper class. Small farmers were displaced to become dependent workers. Urban merchants manipulated peasants by stockpiling grain, buying crops at low prices, and then offering loans at high interest rates to nearly bankrupt farmers—loans they could not repay. Finally, small landholders were forced off their land, and the merchants then purchased it, grew crops with debt slaves, and sold grain at high prices to the landless peasants who had been displaced into the cities. Some peasants stayed on the land as tenants, paying rent to the new owners as they worked the land their families had owned for generations. Often the rent absorbed the major portion of their crops.

Local courts, composed of tribal elders, were the only institution capable of stopping this outrage. But they were replaced by new administrators and courts created by the king and located in the urban administrative centers. These new courts were subject to bribes from rich landowners. Courts may even have charged small landholders with capital crimes and confiscated their land (as with Naboth).

When the poor were pushed off their land by this economic manipulation, they lost their status in the community. Loss of land meant loss of representation in the community. If they did not become debt slaves at the outset, due to loans with high interest rates, eventually they would fall into debt slavery, for without land their means for economic survival were diminished radically. The eighth century B.C. saw this process at its peak; the feudalism of Canaanite culture was in full effect, and the erosion of the class of free farmers threatened the destruction of the state in the face of foreign aggression.[126]

Prophets arose in this era to voice their religious and social criticisms of society. They believed themselves called and set apart as spokesmen for the divine will of Yahweh. Their motivation was religious—to bring a message from Yahweh to the people. Only secondarily were they social critics and reformers, and their vision for society was therefore very idealistic. The practical application of their vision would be left to others, such as the Deuteronomic reformers.

When they attacked the sins of the people, the prophets issued two indictments: (1) Israel has worshiped other gods, and (2) rich Israelites have oppressed their weaker brothers and sisters. The indictments are intertwined. Worship of other deities, especially the Canaanite gods, made it easier for the Israelites to ignore the ethos of Yahwism and the laws of Moses with their demand for the democratic treatment of all Israelites in political, legal, and economic matters. Even to worship Yahweh *in conjunction with* other deities permitted the impact of these laws to be weakened. Eventually the prophetic critique and the Deuteronomic reform would seek to restore the imperative of these laws in heightened form (Deut. 12–26).

The prophets spoke a twofold message. Destruction and doom were forthcoming for unrepentant Israelites, if they did not return to the old ways of the Mosaic community. Yahweh would come as a warrior to attack, not defend, the people on the Day of Yahweh. Nations such as Assyria and Babylon would be used to punish the people. Ultimately the destruction of the state of Israel by Assyria in 721 B.C. and of the state of Judah by Babylon in 586 B.C. was seen as vindication of these prophetic warnings and premonitions.

The other side of the prophetic message was hope. If the people repented, Yahweh would be merciful, and would forgive and restore the people. In their oracles of hope (esp. Isa. 7–11—oracles addressed to Judeans, in the south) the prophets spoke of a new age in which Israelites would keep the laws in love, peace would reign, and an ideal and just king would rule them.

For the most part prophets such as Amos, Hosea, Micah, and Isaiah had to proclaim stern warnings in the eighth century B.C. Though prophets saw themselves as messengers of Yahweh rather than as spokesmen of oppressed classes in a struggle of rural poor against rich urban oppressors and a despotic king, their message is as virulent as any marshaled by modern social critics, and it has been the inspiration of modern reformers and social critics. The rich, powerful classes of Samaria and Jerusalem were accused of oppression, which defied the will of Yahweh. Prophets were advocates of the dispossessed and exploited against the injustices perpetrated and perpetuated by the wealthy. The prophets argued passionately for the benefit of the weak and hurled wrathful curses against the great and rich.[127] However, they never gained a large popular following (as with Elijah and Elisha), because they also attacked the superstitions and religious abuses prevalent among the people.

R. B. Y. Scott summarizes the period well:

All confronted a society where a period of prolonged prosperity for the ruling classes had absorbed their interest and established new standards of luxury and social power; as a corollary, the old sense of kinship among members of the community was lost, the poor were exploited and oppressed, and justice was no longer administered in accordance with the old standards of right. At the same time, the meaning of religion itself was changed; worship became an occasion of display, and the worth of sacrifices was measured by their costliness. The forms and ceremonies adopted from Canaanite religion had become dominant, and the living relationship to the Lord as the covenant God peculiar to Israel was now a fading tradition [Scott, *Prophets*, 199].

It is interesting that the socio-critical aspect of the prophetic phenomenon arose in Israel but not in the rest of the ancient near east where cultic prophets or divinators were to be found. Sociologists point out that the great river civilizations, such as Egypt and Mesopotamia, required the rise of centralized control, complex bureaucracies, division of labor, the collectivization of peasants, the divinization of the king, and the suppression of dissent simply for society to survive (Davisson and Harper, 84–85).

In a peripheral or marginal economic setting, such as that of Israel, which was not dependent on sophisticated river irrigation and complex social structures, the creative impulse would call forth the appearance of the critical prophetic figure (Weber, *Judaism*, xix, 206). The prophets in Israel arose to critique the very things that were imported from the river civilizations: polytheism, mercantilistic economics, loss of equality, class systems, extensive slavery, and powerful kings who claimed divinity for their person and immunity from the law for their actions.

The ancient Near East had laws for maintaining morality, and there was a strong tradition of the king as defender of the rights of the poor, widows, and orphans.[128] But its moral ethos did not enter into the practical governance of society, and the universe was seen as amoral in its relationship to human beings. The prophets, however, believed that a divine moral purpose permeated the universe. In Israelite traditions Yahweh had liberated the people from Egypt, Moses was the paradigm of a true leader, and Yahweh's will was that all persons be treated as equals. The laws of the land were the commands revealed by Yahweh; hence, a divine moral purpose, spelled out in the form of extensive Torah legislation, pervaded society at all levels. The many laws of Israel ensured the religious ethos of an impact on all facets of Israelite existence.

The first commandment, against worshiping other gods, had the practical result of limiting the king when he aspired to the semidivine or divine status claimed by non-Israelite kings. When kings failed to defend the rights of the poor, widows, and orphans, the prophets raised a voice of protest. Not only had the kings failed to respect deep-seated ancient near eastern traditions, but—more importantly—they had opposed Yahweh's will for a liberated and democratic society. The ideal king (Isa. 7–11) should be responsible for redeeming the poor from slavery and their property from confiscation. The prophetic ideal—Yahweh's will for an egalitarian society—eventually became a vision of Yahweh who would side with the oppressed to obtain justice from the rich and powerful.[129]

Many indictments of social oppression are to be found among the prophetic writings. For our purposes the statements that deal with property and land are most meaningful.

From Amos to Ezekiel

The most outspoken social critic of Israel was the prophet Amos. Speaking to the northern state of Israel around 750 B.C., he articulated a stern message of doom. The destruction of the northern state in 722 B.C. caused his oracles to be remembered. In a series of doom oracles he stated:

> Thus says the Lord: "For three transgressions of Israel, and for four, I will not revoke the punishment; because they sell the righteous for silver, and the needy for a pair of [sandals]—they trample the head of the poor into the dust of the earth, and turn aside the way of the afflicted [Amos 2:6-7].

This refers to selling persons into slavery because they could not pay their debts. The debt could even be as small as the price of a pair of sandals. The choice of sandals is appropriate, since people would symbolically exchange sandals after a major business transaction.[130]

The rich manipulated the poor so as to obtain their money and land. But Amos stated that this ill-gotten wealth would soon be lost:

> Therefore because you trample upon the poor and take from him exactions of wheat, you have built houses of hewn stone, but you shall not dwell in them; you have planted pleasant vineyards, but you shall not drink their wine. For I know how many are your transgressions, and how great are your sins—you who afflict the righteous, who take a bribe, and turn aside the needy in the gate [5:11-12].

Landed peasants were either driven from their homes or forced to become tenants and pay exorbitant rents to new landlords. Elders and judges who could have stopped such practices received bribes to ignore the injustice. Rich landowners built beautiful new homes made of hewn stone, the material normally used by Canaanites. The rich, in addition to following Canaanite economic policies, lived like them (Mays, *Amos*, 94, 97; Wolff, 247).

In his unrelenting attack upon the rich, Amos described the wives of rich merchants as "cows of Bashan" (4:1), cows bred for slaughter—an apt allusion to the impending destruction of Samaria and the slaughter of its inhabitants.

Amos said that the avarice of merchants was so great that they could hardly wait for religious festivals to end in order for business to begin:

> Hear this, you who trample upon the needy, and bring the poor of the land to an end, saying, "When will the new moon be over, that we may sell grain? And the sabbath, that we may offer wheat for sale, that we may make the ephah small and the shekel great, and deal deceitfully with false balances, that we may buy the poor for silver and the needy for a pair of sandals . . . and sell the refuse of the wheat?" [8:4-6].

The ephah is the measure by which grain was sold to the poor, and it was made smaller; the shekel was the weight by which merchants bought grain from the poor, and it was made larger. The chaff or "refuse" of the grain was sold at full price. The new urban class created by new Israelite foreign and domestic policies exploited the poor with ruthlessness, and the markets of Israel traded in human misery.[131] Against these social injustices Amos spoke boldly.

Hosea was a contemporary of Amos. He addressed the same issues and developed their religious dimensions. He portrayed the apostasy of Israel in deep emotional images; its infidelity was mirrored in Gomer, Hosea's unfaithful wife. Her desertion paralleled the Israelite religious syncretism in which the strict demands of the Mosaic legislation were ignored in favor of worship that centered on cultic concerns.

Hosea described the dishonest business practices that forced Israelites into poverty:

A trader, in whose hands are false balances, he loves to oppress. Ephraim has said, "Ah, but I am rich, I have gained wealth for myself"; but all his riches can never offset the guilt he has incurred [12:7–8].

The word translated "trader" in the RSV is really "Canaan," an obvious allusion to how Israel had assumed Canaanite business practices. Throughout Hosea's oracles we hear protest against the new way of life that has destroyed the ethical austerity of the Israelite origins in the wilderness. The widespread attitude of the people was that the presence of wealth must be a sign of divine blessing (an argument heard today). Hosea responds: "riches never offset guilt."[132]

A generation later the prophet Micah (fl. 710–700 B.C.) articulated the same concerns to the nation of Judah in the south. Coming from the rural town of Moresheth, he had observed firsthand the oppression of the rural poor by the urban patricians of Jerusalem. Like Amos he spoke fiercely to the oppressors. As in Israel, the rich in Judah, with the aid of royal policies, seized land from the poor and bribed judges. Taking land was bad enough, but the rich devised means of forceful eviction. Perhaps the poor were evicted after being found guilty of false charges in the courts. Bribery of judges is described in Micah 3:11 and 7:3. Power in the hands of the king and the rich classes led to the eventual loss of freedom for the poor, for the loss of land meant loss of free status:

But you rise against my people as an enemy; you strip the robe from the peaceful, from those who pass by trustingly with no thought of war. The women of my people, you drive out from their pleasant houses; from their young children you take away my glory forever [Mic. 2:8–9].

Young children sold into slavery meant a decreased population of free adults for the next generation. Not only were lands seized by the rich, but the rich may have hired brigands to rob travelers. The old clan structure and peaceful rural existence were under attack.[133]

Isaiah (735–690 B.C.) was a contemporary of Micah. Isaiah lived in Jerusalem and reflected a more positive hope for the monarchy and the future of the nation. He could envision an age of peace that would come after the Assyrian invasion of Judah (701 B.C.) when an ideal king would rule the nation. But he also had strong indictments against rich oppressors in his nation:

> Your princes are rebels and companions of thieves. Every one loves a bribe and runs after gifts. They do not defend the fatherless, and the widow's cause does not come to them [Isa. 1:23].
> Woe to those who decree iniquitous decrees, and the writers who keep writing oppression, to turn aside the needy from justice and to rob the poor of my people of their right, that widows may be their spoil, and that they may make the fatherless their prey! [10:1–2].

Widows and orphans are particularly vulnerable members of society, and when they have their land seized, they face slavery or starvation.

Isaiah vividly described land appropriation:

> Woe to those who join house to house, who add field to field, until there is no more room, and you are made to dwell alone in the midst of the land [5:8].

The peace and prosperity of Uzziah's reign in Judah helped introduce capitalistic conditions whereby the rich drove poor landholders out of existence. Isaiah described this process vividly. Landowners bought up common lands and the property of small farmers until they alone lived in "deserted territory"—a symbol for the destruction of the community they had effected. Their houses were now full of stolen treasures (Isa. 2:7), for they had attacked the sacred ordinance that the land was for the people. Yet Isaiah still had hope; he envisioned the Ideal king (Isa. 11:4) who would judge the poor with righteousness, render justice with mercy, and slay the wicked. But for the eighth century B.C. it remained only an ideal.[134]

The following century saw a continuing prophetic critique. Jeremiah (626/ 606–580 B.C.) upbraided his contemporaries for their social injustice. In one poignant passage he ruthlessly condemned king Jehoiakim (who ruled from 609 to 598 B.C.):

> Woe to him who builds his house by unrighteousness, and his upper room by injustice; who makes his neighbor serve him for nothing, and does not give him his wages. . . . But you have eyes and heart only for your dishonest gain, for shedding innocent blood, and for practicing oppression and violence [22:13, 17].

The king was meant to be an equal or neighbor to his fellow Israelites, but Jehoiakim had failed. He taxed his people to pay Egyptian tribute and used corvée labor to build his palace. The land and possessions of the poor were appropriated by his unjust decisions. The "upper room" may refer to a balcony from which he would appear to his subjects in regal splendor so as to impress upon them his semidivine royal status, for such was the custom among other ancient near east kings. Jehoiakim was the opposite of his father Josiah (640–609 B.C.), who had aspired to prophetic ideals and sponsored Deuteronomic reform.[135]

A contemporary of Jeremiah was Ezekiel, who lived among the exiles in Babylon. He described the exile as fitting punishment for the sins of Judah. By way of contrast he described the righteous man as one who oppressed no one, restored the pledge to the debtor, gave bread to the hungry, robbed no one, clothed the naked, and charged no interest, all of which reflect the laws of the Deuteronomic reform. In Ezekiel 48 there is a vision of the restoration. It brings to mind the plan of a communal village, and may be a recollection of the old communal property traditions (Fenton, *Life*, 77–80; Pedersen, I, 87).

The Deuteronomic Reformers

The voice of protest continued. The Deuteronomic reform movement (622–609 B.C.) was the culmination of two centuries of Yahwistic resistance to Canaanite ways. This theological tradition originated in Israel and came south to Judah after the destruction of Israel in 721 B.C. It was kept alive as an underground resistance movement during the long reign of King Manasseh (688–642 B.C.), who sought to destroy the prophetic movement. Manasseh was a vassal of Assyria and he willingly imported pagan religious customs into Jerusalem and Judah (McKay, 20–27; M. Coogan, 9–115). After Manasseh's death and the decline of Assyria, Josiah began to assert political independence from Assyrian vassalage, and eventually he included religious reform. At this time the Deuteronomic reformers came to power, and in 622 B.C. the "book of the law" (perhaps Deuteronomy 12–26) was promulgated. Eventually the movement produced the biblical books of Deuteronomy, Joshua, Judges, 1 and 2 Samuel, and 1 and 2 Kings.

The Deuteronomic reformers imbibed deeply of the prophetic movement. They saw Yahweh as the creator of Israel by the liberation of the slaves in the exodus. Yahweh called forth the people to enter into a covenant at Sinai; Yahweh would be its God and the people would keep the Sinai commandments in loving response. If Israel failed to keep the covenantal stipulations or the commands, the covenant would be broken and the nation would have to be punished by Yahweh. History records how Israel and later the divided monarchies of Israel and Judah repeatedly sinned and were punished, but also how the people repented and received deliverance from Yahweh. The lesson taught by history was that of moral encouragement to repent and obey Yahweh.

Two sins of the Israelites were singled out: (1) they had worshiped other gods, and (2) they had oppressed their fellow Israelites. These were the same indictments issued by the prophets. Deuteronomists called for repentance and reform: Israel must obey the laws that prescribe equality for all members of society. The emotional and theological appeal was to the exodus event that had created the nation. "You must take care of the poor, widows, orphans, and sojourners in the land; for once you were slaves in Egypt, but I brought you out with a strong arm and a mighty hand, says the Lord," would best sum up the appeal of the Deuteronomic preachers.

Deuteronomic reform and the laws promulgated in Deuteronomy 12–26 were humanitarian, but they were also directed toward correcting social abuses experienced in the previous two centuries. Though the laws cover many of the same situations treated by laws in Exodus, as we have seen in the previous two chapters, many of them deepen the requirements for society to provide for the weaker members of the community. The laws of Deuteronomy address a society that is more complex than that of Exodus.

The laws sought to redistribute wealth and property to the poorer members of society. Theft was defined as an act that deprives others of things necessary for a healthy and productive life, even if the deprivation takes place by legal means. Even the legal amassing of wealth must be followed by a form of redistribution to ensure a healthy society. Deuteronomic laws provided for freeing slaves, prohibiting interest, releasing debts, returning land, and extending welfare to the poor in the form of gleaning rights and poor tithes. Legislation was enacted to prevent abuse of the poor in judicial proceedings and with respect to loans.

The prophetic outcry against land aggrandizement in previous centuries was also echoed by the reformers. Ancient legislation concerning familial property rights was reaffirmed:

> In the inheritance which you will hold in the land that the Lord your God gives you to possess, you shall not remove your neighbor's landmark, which the men of old have set [Deut. 19:14].

The same imperative is also found in the wisdom literature (which may imply some connection between the wisdom and legal traditions of Israel):

> Remove not the ancient landmark which your fathers have set [Prov. 22:28].
> Do not move an ancient landmark or enter the fields of the fatherless; for their Redeemer is strong; he will plead their cause against you [Prov. 23:10].

The prophets deplored this recurrent activity (Hos. 5:10; Mic. 2:2; Isa. 5:8); it was the most blatant form of theft during the era of the divided monarchies.

The Deuteronomic reformers mandated that land would stay with family ownership; the rich could no longer carve out large estates. Perhaps the Deuteronomic reform also initiated land redistribution.[136] The reform attempted to translate the ideal vision of the prophets into a working reality.

Unfortunately the untimely death of King Josiah at Megiddo brought the movement to an end in 609 B.C. As the oracles of Jeremiah indicate, the nation returned to business as usual—Canaanite style. As the Deuteronomists had threatened, punishment was soon in coming. In 597 B.C. and 586 B.C. Judah was invaded, Jerusalem captured, and the people carried into exile.

In exile, awareness arose that their defeat had been punishment for sin. The traditions of the Deuteronomists and the prophets were kept alive so that Israelites would never again commit the sins of their forefathers. Further reform legislation, which dealt with both cultic and social reform, was proposed by priests in the exile. Legislation in Leviticus reflects this activity. Though the content of Leviticus is the object of debate in many respects, the consensus among scholars is that very early material has been incorporated and updated by exilic editors to meet new social needs of Israel (Micklem, 3-4; Noth, *Leviticus*, 10-15).

Summary

With the rise of kingship the Israelite ethos was repeatedly compromised by the political machinations of kings. The Canaanite ethos began to reassert itself in the whole fabric of Israelite life, with lip service paid to Yahweh. Canaanite social and economic policies eroded the base of free Israelite society and destroyed the middle class by reducing landholders to tenants, debt slaves, and urban proletarians. This was probably the chief cause for the inability of Israel and Judah to survive the onslaught of Assyrian and Babylonian armies. In a real political sense the prophets were correct when they maintained that the demise of the nation was caused by sin, for the worship of foreign deities and the accompanying oppression of the poor destroyed the soul of the nation and weakened the popular will to resist foreign invasion.

The voice of dissent was raised by prophets and the Deuteronomic reformers. They hearkened to the old Mosaic ideals of equality and exclusive allegiance to Yahweh. Though they were in the minority and were often persecuted, these dissenters were able for a time to seize the reins of power and put their policies into practice. Ultimately the objective historian would have to call them a failure. They were too often idealistic, too often in the minority, and they failed to avert national destruction. However, in another sense they were successful. They preserved an ideal born in the exodus and conquest experiences, and they brought it to fruition in the laws of the Pentateuch and the prophetic oracles. This corpus of literature preserved by the postexilic Jewish community has become the perpetuated heritage of Judaism, Christianity, and Western civilization. It has inspired not only religious beliefs but also political institutions and ideals that we cherish. These faithful few dissenters are our spiritual ancestors. Even an objective economic historian would admit,

> The normative rules of economic behavior transmitted from Judaism to Christianity and the European culture were so solid that nineteenth-century industrialism, capitalism, and free trade could not eradicate them (Davisson and Harper, 85).

The ethos of Israel called for a sharing of property according to human need. Theft was the deprival of things necessary for a meaningful life—it was the Canaanite way of doing business. Though the laws studied in chapter 2 were not always in effect during the era of cultural conflict, they were the ideal to which the "true" Israel aspired in its conflict with the Canaanite ethos.

Chapter 6

Beyond the Exile:
Judaism and the Rise of Christianity

With the Babylonian exile (586–539 B.C.) the history of Israel as a political unit came to an end. After the exile the people sought cohesion with a religious rather than a political identity, whether they lived in Judah or were scattered throughout the ancient world in diaspora. Historians signal this transformation by calling them Jews henceforth rather than Israelites.

This new religious self-identification affected the understanding of the ancient traditions. Though old ideas and themes concerning theft and property continued into the postexilic era, new developments and understandings arose in the social and religious matrix of early Judaism.

Postexilic Judaism, 539 B.C. to A.D. 70, comprised diverse theological trajectories, including priestly theology, the visions of prophetic-apocalyptic theology, and the intellectual pursuits of the wisdom tradition. Out of these traditions arose socio-political movements such as the Sadducees, Pharisees, Zealots, and Essenes. Christianity should also be seen as a movement within Judaism: it inherited many old traditional values and reshaped them for a new religious self-understanding.

There is continuity between postexilic Judaism and early Christianity vis-à-vis property and possessions. Hence early Judaism and the rise of Christianity will be considered together.

Postexilic Era

When the Jews returned from exile in 539 B.C., they brought with them not only their sacred traditions but also a desire to form a more just society. They were more faithful to monotheism, but whether they more faithfully preserved a fair and democratic society cannot be clearly determined. Our historical sources are limited, and a discussion of this topic would be too hypothetical.

The Jewish homeland was an occupied province of various empires: the

Persian (539–330 B.C.), that of Alexander the Great (330–323 B.C.), the Egyptian Greek or Ptolemaic (323–199 B.C.), the Syrian Greek or Seleucid (199–164 B.C.), and the Roman (63 B.C.–A.D. 70). (Only for a brief period was it independent, under Maccabean or Hasmonean rule, 164–63 B.C., but in the later stages these Jewish rulers were no better than were foreign powers.) Under foreign occupation, the preservation of a just and fair society was rendered very difficult if not impossible. During this period traditions were preserved and social ideals were transformed into eschatological visions of the future when God would save the people, send the Messiah, and establish an age of peace.

Definite references to economic injustice are infrequent. The prophet Malachi (450–400 B.C.?), in a sweeping catalog of vices, has Yahweh promise to be a witness "against those who oppress the hireling in his wages, the widow and the orphan, against those who thrust aside the sojourner" (Mal. 3:5). But there is no elaboration. The prophetic movement died by 400 B.C., and the corpus of postexilic literature is small.

Historical accounts of the postexilic era are limited to the books of Ezra and Nehemiah. In Nehemiah 5 there is an account of Nehemiah's social reform (ca. 440 B.C.). Citizens of Judea (the postexilic name of the province) complained:

> We are mortgaging our fields, our vineyards, and our houses to get grain because of the famine. . . . we are forcing our sons and our daughters to be slaves, and some of our daughters have already been enslaved; but it is not in our power to help it, for other men have our fields and our vineyards [Neh. 5:3, 5].

Laws against interest were being ignored, and Nehemiah criticized the officials for permitting interest (Neh. 5:6-9). Nehemiah instituted a program to lend money and grain, to remove the interest charge, and to return fields, vineyards, olive orchards, houses, and the previously charged interest fees to the victims of injustice (5:10–11). The oppressors agreed to do what Nehemiah demanded and everything was resolved (15:12–13). The resolution of this crisis may have been idealized by the author of the text. Nor can we be sure that this crisis was an isolated instance in the postexilic era created by a famine situation, or whether such economic oppression may have occurred more regularly. Having only one account, we cannot determine the events of half a millennium.

From outside historical sources we can glean other insights. The simple fact that Judea was ruled by foreign empires implies the presence of economic oppression of the poor by powerful individuals of foreign or domestic origin. During the Hellenistic era (after 330 B.C.) Judea, under the rule of Greeks and Romans, saw the rise of a latifundia system created by the ruling powers. The land system of the preexilic era was surpassed by the scope of the Hellenistic feudal estates. The number of landless peasants increased, especially after

Herod the Great (30–4 B.C.), and the misery of the rural poor increased until the days of Jesus and the final Jewish revolt against Rome (Hengel, 15).

Postexilic Literature

Poetic and didactic literature from this era reflects the classic theme of the oppressed poor. The Psalms speak of the wicked who oppress the poor (Pss. 10:2, 9; 14:4, 6; 15:5; 26:10; 37:14; 43:2; 55:3; 58:2; 71:4; 82:2–4; 94:4–7; 109:16). The texts refer to oppression in several ways. The author may lament the general oppression of the poor by evildoers, or call upon the Lord to prevent such oppression, or speak of himself as a poor person afflicted by evildoers. An example is Psalm 94:6–7: "They slay the widow and the sojourner and murder the fatherless; and they say, 'The Lord does not see; the God of Jacob does not perceive.' " The Psalms contain very stereotyped language. The reference to evildoers (Hebrew, *resha'im*) does not always imply they are rich; they are portrayed primarily as irreligious.

Psalms were written in the form of prayers and songs; they are worded to move the Lord to action, as the above passage illustrates. In hymns of lament the petitioner often bewails personal rejection by God, his or her own affliction, and the persecution of others in stereotypical expressions. The reference to evil ones falls into this third category. The evil ones may refer to rich oppressors, unbelievers, magicians who cast spells, or those acquaintances of the petitioner who now reject or ridicule him or her.[137] As a result it is difficult to draw social and historical conclusions.

A subtle tendency may be noted in the Psalms, especially in those which may be of postexilic origin. Psalm 37:14 states: "The wicked draw the sword and bend their bows, to bring down the poor and needy, to slay those who walk upright." Here and elsewhere the oppressed poor are imbued with a religious quality. Poverty and religious faithfulness begin to be equated in the postexilic era.[138]

Wisdom literature also addressed the issue of poverty and oppression. The book of Proverbs, compiled in final written form by 400 B.C., rejects prosperity obtained by oppression (14:31; 21:15; 22:22–23; 24:15) and forms of cheating and bribery (11:1; 15:27; 16:11; 17:15, 23; 18:5; 20:10, 23; 21:14, 28; 24:23–24). However, because many of the proverbs in chapters 10–31 may be preexilic in their original oral form, these references may not be helpful in assessing the postexilic situation. Several remind us of the prophetic critique—for example, Proverbs 22:22–23: "Do not rob the poor, because he is poor, or crush the afflicted at the gate; for the Lord will plead their cause and despoil of life those who despoil them."

The book of Job (ca. 400 B.C.) offers a classic description of the plight of the oppressed and poor (24:2–12). It speaks of appropriated land and livestock of widows and orphans, and how the poor must scrounge like wild animals for a little food and clothing, and how they are unfairly used for labor. This passage clearly describes social and economic oppression, and it may be descriptive of contemporary activity.

The book of Sirach, a work dated 200-150 B.C., speaks more frequently of economic oppression. Sirach admonishes his readers not to take advantage of the poor (4:1-6; 7:3, 20), or render unfair judgments against them (4:9; 42:1-4). Sirach appears to lament a society where the rich are respected, but the humble are ridiculed and ignored (13:21-23). The Lord will uplift the poor (11:12-13) and hear their prayer for justice vis-à-vis the rich (4:6; 21:5). A strong prophetic statement is made in Sirach 34:

> Like one who kills a son before his father's eyes is the man who offers a sacrifice from the property of the poor. The bread of the needy is the life of the poor; whoever deprives them of it is a man of blood. To take away a neighbor's living is to murder him; to deprive an employee of his wages is to shed blood [vv. 20-22].

Social offenses are described in hyperbolic fashion, the law is deepened to include social wrongs as forms of murder, and one is reminded of the sayings of Jesus.

The response required from the rich is almsgiving for the sake of the poor (17:22, 35:2; 40:17, 24). The reader senses that Sirach interprets poverty as an interior attitude at times: as in the Psalms, poverty and righteousness appear to be equated.[139]

The Wisdom of Solomon (150-100 B.C.) is caustic in its critique of rich oppressors. It even offers a parody on the words of evil ones:

> Let us oppress the righteous poor man; let us not spare the widow nor regard the gray hairs of the aged. But let our might be our law of right, for what is weak proves itself to be useless. Let us lie in wait for the righteous man, because he is inconvenient to us and opposes our actions; he reproaches us for sins against the law, and accuses us of sins against our training. He professes to have knowledge of God, and calls himself a child of the Lord [Wisd. of Sol. 2:10-13].

Here as elsewhere in this work, the real tension is between the godly and the ungodly. In Wisdom of Solomon 11-19 the history of Israel is reviewed in sermonic fashion. Israel is portrayed as godly and wise; the Egyptians epitomize godlessness and folly. The allusions in chapter 2 to the rich and the poor are also designed as a paradigm of the godly/wise and the ungodly/fools contrast, which pervades the work. Again the poor are associated with the righteous.

The most critical testimonies are found in apocalyptic literature (200 B.C.-A.D. 100). Apocalyptic works such as Daniel, Enoch, Testament of the Twelve Patriarchs, Book of Jubilees, and Revelation describe the plight of poor, oppressed saints who are persecuted for their faithfulness to God. The persecutors are unbelievers, both foreign and domestic (for Jewish apocalyptic), and the saints can only endure their tribulation and wait for God to overthrow their oppressors in a judgment hoped to be imminent. The oppressors are rich, powerful, and—most significant of all—godless. They are the allies of demonic forces that permeate the universe. The categories of religious faithfulness and piety underlie the expression "poor saints."

The Essenes at Qumran were related to the apocalyptic movement. They, too, viewed themselves as outcasts who were oppressed by the rich, powerful, and unrighteous leaders in Jerusalem and by demonic foreign powers. Though they did not characterize themselves as poor in financial terms, they called themselves poor in spirit or downtrodden. They viewed poverty in religious terms and equated it with humility. In real economic terms they shared their goods communally and thus alleviated the physical poverty others might have experienced.[140]

As this literature on poverty indicates, the term "poor" (Hebrew, *'ani*, *'anaw*, and *'ebyon*) underwent a change after the exile. It meant actual economic poverty in the preexilic era, but after the exile it gradually was understood in spiritual or religious categories. The poor person was the righteous or humble individual who remained faithful to God despite adversity and ill-treatment. Upon this faithful believer divine grace would be showered. Though economic poverty was a common characteristic, it was not a necessary precondition. True poverty or humility was primarily an interior attribute of those who obeyed the law and served the Lord.[141]

The origin and cause of this process is assessed differently. Gelin believes the equation of poor with righteousness began with the preexilic prophet Zephaniah. Others think it is a postexilic phenomenon that began with the Psalms or a postexilic prophet such as Trito-Isaiah (Isa. 56–66). The poor and afflicted are viewed as righteous believers (Isa. 61:1). In the postexilic era the entire nation experienced foreign oppression, and to be a believer in Yahweh was to be an oppressed Jew. This caused a basic identification of the two ideas. Furthermore, the preexilic prophetic critique of the rich convinced postexilic Jews that the fall of the nation was due to the sins of the rich. Ideally, Jews wished to view themselves as poor and therefore more righteous after the exile. Poverty and righteousness were twin virtues, and they eventually merged.[142]

This development continued into Jesus' era, and many religious movements claimed for themselves the virtues of poverty and righteousness. Originally, the Pharisees called themselves the pious and the poor in the second century B.C. as they opposed the ruling Hasmonean or Maccabean Jewish kings. Their writings, such as the Psalms of Solomon, reflect this. The later rabbis, who developed out of the Pharisees in the second century A.D., kept this concept. But they balanced it in tension with the idea that riches could also be a sign of divine blessing. Perhaps in Jesus' day some Pharisees were beginning to emphasize this distinction. In any case, Christians sought to define themselves as the righteous poor or "poor in spirit" (as in the beatitudes of Matthew) to distinguish themselves from the Pharisees.[143]

Thus the postexilic era saw a development that would have implications for early Christianity. The concepts of poverty and oppression evolved from social and economic categories. This has implications for the discussion of New Testament teachings.

Teachings of Jesus

The sayings and deeds of Jesus were committed to writing at a later date by the four evangelists: Mark (A.D. 65–75), Matthew (A.D. 75–85), Luke (A.D. 85–95), and John (A.D. 95–110). They each selected from oral tradition the sayings of Jesus that fitted into their own theological perspectives. Thus it is impossible to recreate an objective, balanced, and systematic presentation of Jesus' theology. But certain themes stand out, enabling us to discuss the teachings of Jesus in general categories. A number of well-known sayings by Jesus on property and possessions are remembered by the gospel writers.

The audiences addressed by Jesus were not composed of the extremely poor; they were the common country folk who lived a simple existence on the land. The development of latifundia in the Hellenistic period saw many of these persons displaced or absorbed into feudal estates. This process increased during Herod's reign, so that many of the Jews in Jesus' day must have been aware of a widening gap between rich and poor.

The poor were self-sufficient but did not observe all the rituals of Judaism. Thus they were regarded as unclean by those who were scrupulously religious, such as the urban priestly groups. Jesus' attack on Pharisees and other religiously self-righteous elements of society appealed to common folk. "Sinners" and tax collectors may have included the small businessmen and craftsmen in urban centers whose marginal work rendered them unclean by strict ritual standards. Jesus' followers were those middle- and lower middle-class persons who were pious, traditional, mainly rural, and marginal in terms of economic and religious status. These faithful Jews would consider themselves "poor" in the sense that the term had come to mean by that time: they were humble, faithful, and obedient to God, and they lacked the wealth of the rich and powerful.[144]

The sayings of Jesus appear to contain many critical statements about wealth and possessions. The popular modern mind easily remembers some of these maxims: "It is easier for a camel to pass through the eye of a needle than for a rich man to enter the kingdom of God"; "You cannot serve God and mammon"; "Lay not up for yourselves treasures on earth"; and others of similar bent. The parable of the rich man and Lazarus (Luke 16:19–31), the rich farmer (Luke 12:16–21), and the rich young man (Mark 10:17–31; Matt. 19:16–30; Luke 18:18–30) deepen the impression that Jesus was opposed to the rich in favor of the poor. Jesus' own lifestyle and ministry seem to reflect this commitment to poverty. He owned no tangible possessions; he said, "The Son of Man has nowhere to lay his head" (Matt. 8:20; Luke 9:58). He called his disciples to leave behind their families and possessions; when he sent them forth on a mission, they went as simple and poor preachers. Jesus called upon his followers not to worry about their own daily needs (Matt. 6:25–34), and to provide for the needs of others.

Reading these texts has led some to assume that Jesus was anti-rich and a revolutionary. However, most interpreters believe that Jesus did not condemn riches or the rich as such, but he criticized the love and attachment to wealth that led persons to ignore everything else, including God and God's requirements. One who is free from the desire for wealth (not necessarily wealth itself) is free to follow Jesus.[145]

A central theme in Jesus' teachings was the coming kingdom of God. This coming kingdom will be ushered in by God, not by human effort or human revolution. It is spiritual as well as physical; it is the dawning of a new age. In this new era all men and women will be brothers and sisters, children of God. Love will be shown by all God's children to each other, regardless of race, as the parable of the good Samaritan (Luke 10:25–37) demonstrates.

Many of Jesus' teachings and parables elaborate on the theme of the kingdom—how it will come quickly and violently, divine grace will be given to the pious and faithful, and it will be the fulfillment of Old Testament expectations. In this regard, Jesus referred to the concept of the jubilee release of captives in terms of a universalized liberation (Luke 4:18–19). It is very important to keep in mind that the parables of Jesus elaborate on the coming kingdom as a divine, not a human, creation.

The best known saying of Jesus on possessions is in the beatitudes:

Blessed are the poor in spirit, for theirs is the kingdom of heaven. Blessed are those who mourn, for they shall be comforted. Blessed are the meek, for they shall inherit the earth [Matt. 5:3–5].

Blessed are you poor, for yours is the kingdom of God. Blessed are you that hunger now, for you shall be satisfied. Blessed are you that weep now, for you shall laugh [Luke 6:20b–21].

The differences between Matthew and Luke are striking. Matthew uses the term "poor" in a spiritual sense ("poor in spirit"), linking it with the parallel term "meek," whereas Luke uses the same term in a socio-economic sense, as the parallel word "hunger" implies. Some believe Matthew's spiritual interpretation is closer to the original, because "poor in spirit" is closer to the Aramaic idiom Jesus spoke, and it corresponds to the postexilic Jewish understanding of poverty and piety (Dupont, *Béatitudes*, 214–17, 250–65; Gelin, 107). Others gravitate toward the Lukan version with its emphasis on literal poverty. The second person singular address of Luke seems more original to this era, and the Matthean version appears to have been influenced by Isaiah 61:2–3, which may have prompted the insertion of mourning into Matthew.[146]

Dupont believes both Matthew and Luke have modified Jesus' original saying, and both have an aspect of the truth. Matthew is closer to the idiom of Jesus' own day, in which "poor in spirit" implied both economic poverty and pious humility. Luke has caught the essence of Jesus' message, for the beatitudes are rooted in prophetic ideals, which included a strong emphasis on social justice. If Dupont is correct, the beatitudes emphasize both the religious and the social dimension, just as the general theme of the kingdom of God does (Dupont, *Béatitudes*, 214-98).

Equally well known is the story of the rich young man, which is concluded by the saying about the camel. A young man comes to Jesus seeking to be a disciple; he thinks he is worthy to be a disciple because he has kept the law. Jesus does not quibble with him on his past performances, though elsewhere from Jesus' teachings one would assume that keeping the law perfectly is impossible and especially in his understanding of the essentials of the law. In this instance Jesus takes a different approach. If the young man has kept the letter of the law, Jesus challenges him to keep the spirit of the law. For the rich young man, true obedience would entail the renunciation of his wealth. But it was his wealth that had enabled him to keep the ritual observances of the law, and not only gave him his confidence and place in society, it was his identity:

> And Jesus looking upon him loved him, and said to him, "You lack one thing; go, sell what you have, and give to the poor, and you will have treasure in heaven; and come, follow me." At that saying his countenance fell, and he went away sorrowful; for he had great possessions. And Jesus looked around and said to his disciples, "How hard it will be for those who have riches to enter the kingdom of God!" And the disciples were amazed at his words. But Jesus said to them again, "Children, how hard it is to enter the kingdom of God! It is easier for a camel to go through the eye of a needle than for a rich man to enter the kingdom of God" [Mark 10:21-25].
>
> Jesus said to him, "If you would be perfect, go, sell what you possess and give to the poor, and you will have treasure in heaven; and come, follow me." When the young man heard this he went away sorrowful; for he had great possessions. And Jesus said to his disciples, "Truly, I say to you, it will be hard for a rich man to enter the kingdom of heaven. Again I tell you, it is easier for a camel to go through the eye of a needle than for a rich man to enter the kingdom of God" [Matt. 19:21-24].
>
> And when Jesus heard it, he said to him, "One thing you still lack. Sell all that you have and distribute to the poor, and you will have treasure in heaven." But when he heard this he became sad, for he was very rich. Jesus looking at him said, "How hard it is for those who have riches to enter the kingdom of God! For it is easier for a camel to go through the eye of a needle than for a rich man to enter the kingdom of God" [Luke 18:22-25].

The command given to the young man is often universalized as a general command given to all Christians. But this is inaccurate. The command was a specific directive given to this arrogant young man because of his wealth, the source of his confidence. Jesus did not establish this as an imperative for all Christians, nor was it a prerequisite for becoming a disciple. Jesus calls upon no one else to renounce so radically personal wealth. Matthew's version even implies that he could keep his wealth and be saved, but that *perfection* would demand the extra step of total renunciation. Matthew has reinterpreted the passage to make it relevant for everyone, not just the young man in question.[147]

Even though the imperative is given to one individual, a message may be found for all. The young man was called upon to renounce what was central to his concerns. For him it was wealth; for someone else it could be a different "idol." The young man was called upon to transcend his wealth in a self-forgetfulness that would put Jesus and the needs of others first. It was not necessary for disciples to dispense with their possessions, but they should never let possessions take priority in their life.

Jesus thus rejected a contemporary trend in the Pharisee tradition that had begun to view wealth as a sign of divine blessing. Jesus affirmed the older value of pious poverty and humility of postexilic Judaism, which looked first to God and considered everything else secondary. Jesus would concur with the Pharisees and the rabbis, however, in that the duty of believers with possessions was to give alms to the poor (which one could not continue to do if all wealth were given away at one time). Jesus called his disciples to personal values; in itself the relinquishment of wealth was not as important as serving the needs of others (Taylor, 429–30; Danker, *Luke*, 188).

The saying, logion, about the camel and the eye of the needle has fascinated and haunted interpreters. One popular notion had it that there was a gate in Jerusalem called the eye of the needle through which a camel would pass only with great difficulty. The theory, first circulating in the ninth century A.D., proposes that Jesus was describing such a gate. But no such gate has ever been found. This theory represents a rationalization of the text to render the intent of the saying less scandalous. Likewise, the more scholarly opinion that the Greek word for camel (*kamelos*) is a corruption of the Greek word for rope (*kamilos*) is another attempt to lessen the severity of the statement. Commentators reject both of these interpretations.[148]

The passage is hyperbolic: it uses exaggeration to catch an audience's attention. Mark, the oldest version of the gospel, captures the spirit of this exaggeration, for the text records the disciples' amazement. A similar statement is found in rabbinic literature, which speaks of the difficulty an elephant would have to pass through the eye of a needle. Once he has shocked the disciples, Jesus makes the important observation: what is impossible for humans is possible for God. Both rich and poor are saved by divine grace.[149]

Combined with the earlier account of the rich young man, the saying takes on greater meaning. Persons enter the kingdom of God by grace. Jesus overturns the idea that wealth could be a sign of divine blessing. Divine blessing is a gift, and the appropriate response to it is relinquishment of other priorities in life, such as possessions. Jesus is warning his disciples not against riches as such but against the danger of riches, which may be tempting regardless of how poor a person may be. The important change is an interior disposition that no longer considers possessions important. Disciples may give away their wealth, but if there is no spiritual change of self-transcendence, if the old desires are still present, the renunciation of wealth is an empty gesture.[150]

Another passage that implies that renunciation is the primary virtue speaks about treasures in heaven:

> Do not lay up for yourselves treasures on earth, where moth and rust consume and where thieves break in and steal, but lay up for yourselves treasures in heaven, where neither moth nor rust consumes and where thieves do not break in and steal. For where your treasure is, there will your heart be also [Matt. 6:19–21].
>
> Sell your possessions, and give alms; provide yourselves with purses that do not grow old, with a treasure in the heavens that does not fail, where no thief approaches and no moth destroys. For where your treasure is, there will your heart be also [Luke 12:33–34].

The initial implication appears to be that the Christian should renounce wealth in this world for spiritual wealth in the next. The Lukan version (which modifies the Matthean) accentuates this idea with the imperative to sell one's possessions.

The Lukan version then immediately connects the idea of selling possessions with that of giving alms, which is an ongoing process. How can a person renounce wealth and still continue to give alms? For Luke the Christian ideal is the proper use of money in almsgiving, not ascetic rejection of material things. Luke addresses a Greek audience, some of whom are wealthy, and encourages them to share their wealth with the poor by almsgiving. This very important theme is driven home by Luke with the imperative "sell your possessions"—his modification of the Matthean text.[151] Luke seeks to build up a certain attitude among his readers.

There is another text that deals with this attitude:

> No one can serve two masters; for either he will hate the one and love the other, or he will be devoted to the one and despise the other. You cannot serve God and mammon [Matt. 6:24].
>
> No servant can serve two masters; for either he will hate the one and love the other, or he will be devoted to the one and despise the other. You cannot serve God and Mammon [Luke 16:13].

These passages imply that the attitude of the disciple is important; the amount of wealth, be it great or small, is unimportant. Even a meager sum greedily hoarded by its owner prevents true service in the kingdom of God.

The Lukan saying serves as a conclusion to the parable of the unjust servant—the story of a servant who forgives the debts of his master somewhat dishonestly in order to ensure his future welfare by the released debtors (Luke 16:1-8). Jesus does not praise the moral attitude or action of the servant, but he commends the wise use of wealth that the servant typifies. Luke uses this parable to call upon Christians with wealth to use it creatively and wisely to help the poor by almsgiving.[152] Thus the goal is not renunciation but a wise use of possessions with an attitude of self-detachment toward them.

Jesus more than once called for the positive use of wealth and commended the affluent for so doing. The well-off are to support their elderly parents and not give away what is needed for them (Mark 7:9-13). Possessions should be used to help the poor; loans should be given without interest or expectation of repayment (Mark 12:41-44; Matt. 6:2-4; 25:31-40; Luke 6:30; 10:30-37). Jesus associates with persons of wealth (Mark 14:3-9; Luke 7:36-40; 11: 37-41; 14:1-2). Zacchaeus gives away half of his wealth, and Jesus says nothing about the other half (Luke 19:8-10).

A frequently cited passage needs discussion in this regard. In Mark 14:7 Jesus says, "For you always have the poor with you, and whenever you will, you can do good to them; but you will not always have me." This passage has often been used to justify the continued existence of poverty in such a way as to permit apathy on the part of the affluent. But the middle part of the verse must not be forgotten. Jesus implies that after he is gone, his followers should meet the needs of the poor. Certainly the scene of the final judgment in Matthew 25:31-40, where the righteous ask how they have served the Lord, should reinforce the intent of the first passage.

Jesus' concern was not so much with the social effects of wealth, as the prophets had directed their invective, but with the effect on the moral and psychological attitude of the individual. This is not to say that Jesus ignored the social implications of the gap between rich and poor. In Matthew 6:20-21, 24-25 he could utter woes against the rich for being rich while others were poor. But he perceived that the problem involved something deeper than merely the maldistribution of wealth. The root of the problem lay in human hearts. Mere redistribution of wealth without a corresponding change of attitude permits the same problem to arise again. If you sweep a demon from your house, seven more will return, unless you take steps to prevent it (Matt. 12:43-45; Luke 11:24-26). Jesus wanted his followers to give undivided allegiance to God and the kingdom, and to renounce the desire for wealth. Only when values are rightly aligned may the kingdom come (Hyatt, *Religion*, 68).

James

The short epistle of James has interesting and critical observations concerning the rich and the poor. It makes one of the most vicious critiques of the rich:

Come now, you rich, weep and howl for the miseries that are coming upon you. Your riches have rotted and your garments are moth-eaten. Your gold and silver have rusted, and their rust will be evidence against you and will eat your flesh like fire. You have laid up treasure for the last days. Behold, the wages of the laborers who mowed your fields, which you kept back by fraud, cry out; and the cries of the harvesters have reached the ears of the Lord of hosts. You have lived on the earth in luxury and in pleasure; you have fattened your hearts in a day of slaughter. You have condemned, you have killed the righteous man; he does not resist you [James 5:1–6].

The passage reflects the classic imagery found in the prophets. It is eschatological in its view of the impending judgment to come upon the rich for their oppression of laborers and marginal workers. Though elsewhere in his letter James incorporates the traditional critique of the rich from wisdom or paranetic sources, this passage seems to speak of the rich in economic categories, as did the prophets. The rich are critiqued in economic terms, but James sees the poor and dispossessed in economic *and* religious categories. They are poor and righteous. James has been influenced by the contemporary image of the poor as righteous country folk oppressed by rich and powerful Sadducees, the priestly aristocracy, who had enough wealth to observe the law meticulously. But he merges this with older prophetic images of the rich as oppressors.[153]

To what does James refer? He may resonate the anger felt by rural Jews and Christians against the latifundia system in Palestine. Or he may simply have inherited traditional prophetic imagery and placed it into his wisdom collection as a wisdom teacher would place such paranetic material together. If so this would be merely a dispassionate process of collection on his part.[154]

Other passages indicate that James may not have equated the rich exclusively with the evil, as some believe.[155] There were rich Christians at this time, and James would not attack them. They were called upon to share their wealth, and passages in James reflect this:

If a brother or sister is ill-clad and in lack of daily food, and one of you says to them, "Go in peace, be warmed and filled," without giving them the things needed for the body, what does it profit? [2:15–16].

James seeks to implement the social teachings of Jesus (Adamson, 29–31, 123–24, 182–90).

Another passage implies that the category of evil oppressor should be narrowed from the rich in general to those rich and powerful individuals who persecute Christians:

But you have dishonored the poor man. Is it not the rich who oppress you, is it not they who drag you into court? Is it not they who blaspheme that honorable name by which you are called? [2:6-7].

Though it is difficult to determine whether the passage describes the rich who oppress the poor, or the rich and powerful Sadducees who oppress Christians, the reference to "that honorable name" leads us to conclude that the persecuted ones are those called by the name of Christ. If so, the rich and poor dichotomy is religious rather than socio-economic in James. But we cannot be certain.

Perhaps James was reacting negatively to the new class of wealthy Christians. Perhaps these Christians sided with rich nonbelievers against poor Christians. This would explain his hyperbolic prophetic invective against the rich, which was combined with the imperative for the rich to help the poor. Recourse to negative critique to motivate the rich would be modified in the second century A.D. to a positive exhortation for the rich to share their wealth (Dibelius, 44-45).

James represents early Jewish Christianity; his letter is dated somewhere between A.D. 40 and 100. James may have had some influence on the Jewish Christians in Palestine during the second century A.D. who were called the Ebionites, or "poor ones." James may represent the transition from the earlier prophetic critique and anti-Sadducean feeling of his own day to this latter movement with its ethos of simplicity. Unfortunately we know too little about the Ebionites. We do not know whether "ebion" refers to poverty (economic) or humility (religious) (R. Williams, 131-32; Keck, "Poor," 54-66). Jewish Christianity declined rapidly after the destruction of Jerusalem in A.D. 70, to be replaced by Greek Christianity, spearheaded by the missionary endeavors of St. Paul.

Summary

The experience of exile in Babylon (586-539 B.C.) caused a great transformation of the people of God. We call them Jews, not Israelites, after the exile, for they are no longer a socio-political entity. As a province in various empires they were able to keep their identity by clinging to religious values. This caused a change in many traditions, including concepts of property, possessions, and poverty.

Postexilic literature began to emphasize the concept of poverty as a virtue. Socio-economic categories were widened to include spiritual dimensions. When the Jews were ruled by foreign powers, most of them were poor. Given this circumstance and the faithful memory of the prophetic critique of wealth, religiously motivated Jews came to be characterized as "poor." Gradually "poor" came to mean "poor in spirit" or "humble," and it became a virtuous ideal. The ideal of physical poverty and spiritual humility was held in tension, and the early Christians would inherit this tension. It would influence their views about property and possessions.

At a first reading Jesus appears to be radical in his call for the renunciation of wealth and the creation of a strict economic order. A closer reading reveals that the message is really idealized exhortation designed to motivate Christians to act in love. The first priority is a change of heart and mind; results will then be more meaningful. Nor are specific directions and economic programs advanced. The Christian is to act in love and do that which is most appropriate in given situations to meet the physical and spiritual needs of all. The common Christian understanding was to meet human need by direct involvement, in the manner of the good Samaritan. Almsgiving was the most direct and personal way to help the poor.

Chapter 7

Paul, Luke, and the Early Church Fathers

Paul

Though Paul was Jewish, he was the person most responsible for the transition to Greek or gentile Christianity. He put his stamp on Christianity by his mission work and writings, which constitute half of the New Testament.

When we consider Paul's view on theft, poverty, and possessions, we are struck by the paucity of material on this subject. Paul did not address the practical question of long-range economic systems, because he did not expect the world to last. With his expectation of the imminent coming of Jesus, he did not address issues such as slavery, economic rights of the poor, social reform, and others. The inequity of this present age would soon pass away, according to his worldview.

When he does speak of possession it is in hyperbolic or ideal language, such as in his Corinthian correspondence, "If I gave away all I have . . . but have not love, I am nothing" (1 Cor. 13:3). The missionary who traveled the eastern Mediterranean to proclaim a simple gospel did not have time to work out systematic views on property, and in his own personal life he considered concern about possessions unimportant. His emphasis was on grace and faith, not social issues (Dahl, 22–25; Grant, 128).

The communal sharing of property that might have been practiced by contemporary Christians was not advocated by Paul. Christians were to share with one another, and because Paul gave no particular advice, different models appear to have arisen. Often congregations established a common fund for meeting the needs of others. Most members of the Pauline churches were poor, but from his lists of names it seems that some individuals were wealthy. Their generosity would be solicited to help the needs of poorer individuals (Hengel, 36–39; Dahl, 26–31).

In connection with meeting the needs of the poor, Paul did gather a collection for the "saints" in Jerusalem. He alludes to this ongoing collection several times (Gal. 2:10; 1 Cor. 16:1–4; 2 Cor. 8:1–9:15; Rom. 15:23–31); it involved a number of missions. Paul calls it a liturgy (Rom. 15:27) or a service

100

(2 Cor. 8:4; 9:1). The primary purpose may have been the establishment of fellowship between the churches (Rom. 15:26; 2 Cor. 8:4), especially between Greek and Jewish Christians. This would correspond to the motive behind communal sharing in Acts 2 and 4, the establishment of fellowship. Paul did not seek to level economic conditions; he sought a free-will contribution out of a response of love.[156]

There are unanswered questions for us, however. Paul refers to the poor or the saints in Jerusalem. Is the contribution for economically poor individuals, whether Jewish or Jewish Christian, or is he using the word "poor" as a symbol for the pious or righteous? If the former is the case, the collection is a poverty-relief fund; if the latter, the collection is a token display of Christian solidarity between Jews and Gentiles. Paul never clearly equates the poor with Jewish Christians in a way to indicate poverty or piety.

The problem is further compounded by the book of Acts, which may imply that Paul brought the contribution to the temple instead of to Jewish Christians. If so, we are not sure of the meaning of the collection at all. Acts may simply be trying to impress the reader with Paul's piety and continuity with his Jewish roots so as to soften his image as a radical theologian.

The only passage in the Pauline writings that appears to address the issue of theft, in even a loose sense, is in 2 Thessalonians:

> For even when we were with you, we gave you this command: If any one will not work, let him not eat. For we hear that some of you are living in idleness, mere busybodies, not doing any work. Now such persons we command and exhort in the Lord Jesus Christ to do their work in quietness and to earn their own living [3:10–12].

(Some commentators would exclude this from the discussion because they believe it may be a later letter written by a disciple of Paul long after his death.) The passage is often quoted to undergird the principle of private property and the responsibility of every individual to earn a living by gainful employment. But this interpretation is misapplied. The Thessalonians addressed by Paul were living in expectation of Jesus' return. Some of them quit their jobs, sold their possessions, and did little more than wait for Jesus. Even though Paul himself expected the imminent coming of Jesus, he realized that their attitude was not good. So he encouraged them to return to their jobs and live a normal life as they had done, but to anticipate Jesus on a daily basis. This text tried to tone down apocalyptic expectations rather than give social economic directives.

Some commentators also suggest that Paul's advice was addressed to a different problem. Those who do not work might refer to itinerant preachers or teachers (a common phenomenon among Greek philosophical schools) who went around living from the charity of Christian communities. Paul supported himself by his own labor, and this rendered his mission and message more legitimate in the eyes of the people. He may here be condemning preachers who spread their message simply to take advantage of others.[157] Regardless of which interpretation is correct, the passage in 2 Thessalonians does not support modern beliefs concerning the work ethic or the inviolability of private property.

Luke-Acts

The most significant theological contribution to the issue of theft, property, and community is the account of the early church contained in Luke and Acts. Written ca. A.D. 85-100, this two-volume work reflects the theology of the post-Pauline church. After the charismatic missionary endeavors of Paul to implant the church, the generation of Luke-Acts faced the task of organizing, creating institutions, defending itself against heresy, and determining its general mission in the world. With the realization that the second coming of Christ might take longer than initially anticipated, the church realized its mission involved not only the proclamation of the gospel for the spiritual welfare of all peoples, but that fulfilling the gospel included a social ministry to serve human physical needs. With this in mind, the author(s) of Luke-Acts remembered and interpreted the ministry of Jesus and the Apostles to illustrate their spiritual and social ministries. Thus Luke remembered the ministry of Jesus as an outreach to poor and oppressed outsiders.

As we have noted, the Gospel of Luke recalls more of the sayings and deeds of Jesus in regard to possessions and poverty than do the other Gospels. Most notably, the book of Acts records the fleeting memory of the early Jerusalem community as a communalistic economic experience. Luke saw this as an attempt to develop a responsible ethic of wealth and a concern to protect the poor and socially helpless members of society.

Many interpreters have reflected on the two key passages in Acts that describe the community of goods in the primitive church. Any discussion of wealth in Luke-Acts must begin with these passages:

> And all who believed were together and had all things in common; and they sold their possessions and goods and distributed them to all, as any had need. And day by day, attending the temple together and breaking bread in their homes, they partook of food with glad and generous hearts, praising God and having favor with all the people [2:44-47a].
>
> Now the company of those who believed were of one heart and soul, and no one said that any of the things which he possessed was his own, but they have everything in common. And with great power the apostles gave their testimony to the resurrection of the Lord Jesus, and great grace was upon them all. There was not a needy person among them, for as many as were possessors of lands or houses sold them, and brought the proceeds of what was sold and laid it at the apostles' feet; and distribution was made to each as any had need [4:32-35].

José Miranda and others maintain this is nothing other than communism practiced by the early Christians. It failed due to the small number of Christians who were involved, for they were outnumbered in a world of capitalists. But this communistic experience was not recorded simply in memory of an experiment that failed; it is an imperative to all Christians today. We shall succeed, says Miranda, where they failed, because we are stronger and more numerous than they. Furthermore, almsgiving is not just an act of charity; it is a duty, the practice of justice, for almsgiving returns what was once unfairly taken (Miranda, *Marx*, 19; *Communism*, 7-12). Miranda's forceful statement is helpful, even if he does exaggerate, for he confronts a modern society that has become comfortable and has learned to ignore this account in the biblical tradition. But his assessment may not be totally accurate.

Many commentators affirm the historicity of the Jerusalem communal experience. The venture was logical, given their social context. The Christians sought to pattern themselves after the lifestyle of Jesus who owned little property as he moved about the countryside. They expected a quick return of Jesus, so the establishment of such an economic arrangement on a short-term basis seems logical. Other groups in Palestine, such as the Essenes at Qumran and the ascetic Jewish Therapeutae, engaged in such communalistic practices. So the idea of early Christian communism is acceptable to most commentators and even popularizers.

But many observers are quick to point out the differences between this early Christian communism and its modern ideological forms. (1) Sharing was voluntary, not mandatory. (2) It was not complete; private wealth still continued to exist. Mary, the mother of John Mark, still retained her home (Acts 12:12). Later appeals for generous aid indicate continued private ownership. Perhaps they relinquished only what was necessary to relieve temporary needs in their midst. (3) The practice was limited to Jerusalem; Christians in Antioch and elsewhere do not seem to have practiced it. (4) Sharing was done spontaneously and enthusiastically, not in a systematic fashion. Perhaps the program became so disorganized that later the seven deacons had to be entrusted with administrative responsibilities (Acts 6:1-7). (5) The practice was limited in duration. Though it certainly was terminated by the fall of Jerusalem in A.D. 70, the practice may have ended earlier. Perhaps the collection Paul gathered for the saints in Jerusalem—if it was for the poor and not a token of solidarity—implied the failure of the communal experience. (6) The enthusiasm for communal sharing may have been inspired by the expectation of Jesus' imminent return. The practice may have waned as the church perceived the delay of Jesus' return. If so, this communalism was a temporary practice not to be seen as a newly established form for Christian society as a whole.

With the passing of the years Christians realized they could not emulate the practice of Jesus or aspire to his idealistic statements completely. They were an urban church in Jerusalem in contrast with the rural context of Jesus' ministry in Galilee; they had to face deeper poverty in the city and complex problems of management and distribution. Only in a rigorous setting like Qumran out in the wilderness could the experiment be maintained for a significant period of time.

How long the experiment in "modified communism" lasted cannot be ascertained. Lucian's satirical description of Christians from a pagan viewpoint and Tertullian's favorable consideration (provided both authors are not simply referring to the accounts in Acts) do imply that the communalistic experiment in Jerusalem made a noticeable impression on some segments of society.[158]

Closer consideration of these texts has brought some interesting new insights in recent years. There seem to be contradictions among the imperatives or images presented in Luke-Acts. The ideal statements appear to call for the renunciation of wealth (which we have seen is really not the case), the image in Acts 2-4 is one of communal sharing, but the strong imperative to give alms implies that private property is still in force. The Christian cannot aspire to renunciation, communalism, and almsgiving simultaneously. Luke's picture is inconsistent because it is so idealistic. At times there are contradictions —Peter says he has no money for a lame beggar (Acts 3:6) but later he is in charge of community funds (Acts 4:35). Luke may idealistically exaggerate the extent of the communalism in order to emphasize the need for social concern among the more affluent Greek Christians of his day and age (Ehrhardt, 21-22).

In Acts 2:44-47 and 4:32-35 Luke chooses his language very carefully. The expressions "all things in common" (2:44) and "one soul" (4:32) were designed to appeal to Greco-Roman ideals concerning friendship. The phrase "all things in common" can be traced to Plato, Aristotle (*Nichomachean Ethics*), and Cicero (*De officiis*) as the ideal model for sharing among friends in a community. Such a community was envisioned by the Greek philosophers and practiced by the Pythagorean communities described by Diodorus Siculus. In these communities initiates would turn their property over to the group when they became full members. In such communities the goal of the member was to become "one heart" and "one soul" with the other members, and these phrases were taken from Plato.

Luke has chosen this language to appeal to the Hellenistic sense of piety. Philo and Josephus used the same language in their writings to make a similar appeal to their audiences. Luke merges this Hellenistic ideal with the Hebrew ideal, especially as expressed in Deuteronomy. Deuteronomy 15:4-5 promises that if the law is kept, no one among the people would be poor. The community Luke describes is free from need in accord with the Jewish expectations concerning the community of the final messianic age. Thus both Jewish and Greek images are merged in the description of the Jerusalem community.[159]

Acts 2-4 describes a community that rigorously meets the ethic proclaimed by Jesus. Its members have sold their possessions to give to the poor (cf. Luke 12:32 and 18:22, phrases given special emphasis). The Christian community goes beyond the Greek ideal, based on friendship. In Acts the community is motivated by faith not charity, and the authority of the Apostles and the church is strengthened when possessions are laid at the feet of the Apostles (Crowe, 29–30; L. Johnson, *Sharing*, 119).

Why did Luke seek to transcend the Greek ideal in such rigorous fashion, especially when the intent of Luke-Acts is to encourage almsgiving rather than the renunciation of wealth? Because almsgiving was unknown among the Greeks. They would share goods in a community among "noble equals," or they would give loans, but they would not give alms or charity. Their favorite word for love was *eros*, the love between equals; Christians preferred the word *agape*, the love of another regardless of status. Christians would love "inferiors," just as God had loved them as sinners, but Greeks disdained the love of anyone or anything felt to be inferior, or not beautiful, true, and pure.

Luke had to create a new system for his readers based on *agape* love that would encourage them to give alms and engage in charity for the sake of the poor. He portrayed Jesus as the one who loved and forgave sinners, and who brought outcasts (sinners, prostitutes, lepers, gentiles, the thief on the cross) into the kingdom. The Jerusalem community was portrayed as a radical ideal that conformed to the highest Greek and Hebrew expectations. In so doing Luke sought to entreat his audience to strive for this impossible ideal by at least engaging in almsgiving. Elsewhere in Acts it becomes apparent that almsgiving was the basic activity sponsored by the earliest Christians for the welfare of others (Karris, "Poor," 116–17; L. Johnson, *Sharing*, 117–32).

The community of goods envisioned by philosophers and put into practice among Pythagoreans and Jewish Essenes at Qumran appears to be only an ideal. Such tightly constructed communities entailed several characteristics that became self-defeating. They had to retreat from society so as to ensure their harmonious operation. This made them exclusivistic, withdrawn, small, and intolerant of outsiders. The perpetuation of such a community required unity of mind, social control, and authoritarian leadership (L. Johnson, *Sharing*, 117–32).

The church envisioned in Luke-Acts is diametrically opposed to such values. Such a model conflicts with the gospel-oriented ethos that speaks of divine grace, human forgiveness, and individual Christian responsibility. Such a withdrawn attitude would destroy the missionary impetus that the church, and especially the author of Luke-Acts, sought to foster. The tight control of such communities would stifle the effectiveness of both individual Christians and the church as a whole. Hence, Luke's imperative is really oriented to the voluntary giving of alms by individual Christians according to the particular situations in which they find themselves. The Christian acts out of love led by the Spirit to do what is appropriate for each situation.

An excellent assessment of Luke's use of images and language in regard to property and possessions is provided by L. T. Johnson. In Luke-Acts the categories of rich and poor are used to describe the human response to Jesus' message. The poor are the powerless who respond to the message about the kingdom of God and are thus received by Jesus. The rich typify those who reject Jesus; the opponents are called "moneylovers." The poor are symbolized as outcasts, whereas the rich have power and oppress the poor. Poverty refers to the interior response; it does not have an economic implication (L. Johnson, *Sharing*, 1–148; *Function*, 1–222). In Luke's symbols the rich are opponents of the Christian community and the poor are its members (Osiek, 31).

Possessions are used to reflect the interior disposition of the person who responds to Jesus' teachings. Possessions are not evil by themselves but "rather the concentration of energy on one's possessions" (Osiek, 27). Relinquishing possessions signifies conversion, for to follow Jesus means to deny self and possessions. Persons protect the "self" by surrounding it with wealth. Turning possessions over to the community is an affirmation of what is real (Jesus' ethic), and a rejection of the transitory world.

Possessions are also a metaphor for human relationships. When persons come together in community, they share in the outpouring of the Spirit, which results in the sharing of goods. As they share the Spirit, they share possessions. Sharing possessions is the corollary of life together; it is the symbol of perfect unity.

The disciples or leaders of the community have property placed in their administration for the sake of the community they serve. By placing possessions at the feet of the disciples the Christians put themselves totally at the disposal of the disciples. Being at someone's feet is a sign of submission, and laying possessions down gives authority into the hands of the disciples in symbolic fashion. To hold back possessions is to deny the presence of the Spirit in the disciples.

Throughout Acts true authority is administered when control over possessions is demonstrated: (1) the seven deacons (Acts 6:1–7) had delegated authority to administer goods; (2) Ananias and Sapphira tried to "buy" or deceitfully obtain the power of the community, but they failed; and (3) Paul was "in charge" of the collection for Jerusalem. Possessions do not merely refer to wealth; they are a symbol of authority, and their proper administration reflects the true presence of the Spirit (L. Johnson, *Function*, 30, 132–67, 187, 201–20; *Sharing*, 128–29).

Thus in Luke-Acts Christians are not called to a holy poverty that renounces possessions, nor are they called to communalistic distribution of wealth; the goal rather is charity and almsgiving. Such activity must come after a change of heart and attitude on the part of believers. Such activity done with hypocritical intent or wrought in mandatory fashion will fail. The imagery in Luke-Acts is idealized in order to exhort Christians to act. The internal evidence in Luke implies that Jesus did not call for the total renunciation of wealth, and the internal evidence in Acts implies that early Christians did not really engage in a total communalistic experiment. The Greek generation of A.D. 85–100 was called upon to leave apathy behind and take steps to meet the needs of the poor around them with means appropriate to the circumstances—almsgiving. Christians today need to hear this same imperative from Luke-Acts once more (Keck, "Testament," 108–12).

Early Church Fathers

As Christianity spread, the greatest mission expansion occurred in the Greco-Roman culture of the Roman empire. The transition from Jewish Christianity to gentile Christianity initially effected by Paul continued in the following centuries. The next four centuries saw a rich proliferation of Christian thought, literature, and worship forms. The diversity of thought in those first four experimental centuries of rapid growth surpasses even that of our modern pluralistic religious scene.

The response of Christian thinkers on issues such as theft, property, and poverty are diverse, but a broad consensus may be drawn from various authors. The patristic writers did not unanimously condemn the institution of private property. Most of them accepted it as a fixed part of their society, but they critiqued it as being less than the ideal. Human desire for wealth was the target of sermons preached throughout the period. Even among those who attacked the institution of private property, the desire that drove persons to acquire wealth was viewed as a greater evil.

In the articulation of their views, several strands of thought were synthesized: (1) Greek ideals concerning ascetic self-suffering; (2) Old Testament wisdom traditions about hard work, honesty, and frugality; (3) Old Testament prophetic critiques of rich oppressors; and (4) Greek philosophic views about common property and the sharing of goods (Grant, *Christianity*, 113; Hengel, 82).

As the church spread and increased, the majority of Christians were poor, but some were affluent, and a sizeable number might have been freed slaves, small business operators, craftsmen, or what we might call middle-class people. As the Gospel of Luke-Acts called upon these people to be concerned with the less fortunate, so church fathers continued to make the same appeal. The Shepherd of Hermas, for example, dealt with the relationship of "rich" and "poor," and the rich were called upon to repent and be charitable toward the poor. Addressed to the "rich," or more likely, the rising middle class of Rome, this work tried to assess wealth positively. The rich needed the poor, for by sharing their wealth with the poor, they could manifest the love of God (Osiek, 39–57, 78–135).

Certain church fathers, who moved beyond the general statements in the Gospels to a blistering condemnation of the social abuses around them, vehemently denounced the rich. Like Old Testament prophets they were motivated by the expectations willed by a God of love and justice. Their object of criticism was the Roman socio-economic structures that fostered an increasing gap between rich and poor and the gradual destruction of the middle class with the creation of large feudal estates. Roman law perpetuated this by granting absolute sanction to private property—the right of owners over land, goods, and slaves. Laws prevented redistribution of goods and the amelioration of poverty.[160] Thus the church fathers attacked both the depravity of society and its legal institutions.

Poignant statements may be drawn from the writings of the early church fathers. Basil the Great (A.D. 329–379) said:

> When someone steals a man's clothes we call him a thief. Should we not give the same name to one who could clothe the naked and does not? The bread in your cupboard belongs to the hungry man; the coat hanging unused in your closet belongs to the man who needs it; the shoes rotting in your closet belong to the man who has no shoes; the money which you hoard up belongs to the poor [Homily on Luke; quoted in Miranda, *Marx*, 16].

Ambrose's attack on the rich was equally scathing. His most famous work, *De Nabuthe Jezraelita* (ca. A.D. 386–389), was a commentary on 1 Kings 21, Naboth's vineyard; he compared wealthy landowners to Ahab, for they forced the poor from the land as Naboth had been ousted. Elsewhere in this work he wrote:

> You cover walls, but you leave men bare. Naked they cry out before your house, and you heed them not: a naked man cries out, but you are busy considering what sort of marble you will have to cover your floors. A poor man asks for money, and does not get it; a human being begs for bread, and your horse champs a golden bit. You gratify yourself with costly ornaments, while other men go without food. How great a judgment, O rich man, do you draw down upon yourself! The people go hungry, and you close your graneries; the people weep, and you turn your finger-ring about. Unhappy man, who have the power but not the will to save so many souls from death: the cost of the jewel in your ring would have sufficed to save the lives of a whole people [quoted in Lovejoy, 461–62].

John Chrysostom (A.D. 344–407) was so adamant that he was exiled by Empress Eudoxia of Constantinople for his strident accusations of the rich. He believed that wealth in the hands of a few was akin to robbery:

> This is robbery: not to share one's resources. Perhaps what I am saying astonishes you. Yet be not astonished. For I shall offer you the testimony of the Sacred Scriptures, which say that not only to rob other's property, but also not to share your own with others, is robbery and greediness and theft [quoted in C. Avila, 83].

Among church fathers one can find statements to the effect that all persons are equal, because all have come into this world at birth as equals—naked and helpless. This original equality of birth reflects the Creator's plan that all things are intended to be shared by everyone equally. The distribution of property is a human fabrication. Common belief among Greek and Roman philosophers and poets held that there once was a "golden age" with neither private property nor poverty—from which humanity fell into its later inequitable condition. For many church fathers the sinful fall of the man and woman in Genesis 3 corresponded to that belief. The institution of private property came into existence only as an evil result of the fall of humanity from grace.

Land and goods belong to God who distributes them to all. The Roman system had to be overcome in order to return to this original divine plan. Basil articulated a view, adopted by many fathers after him, that there was a difference between *koina*, the common goods that rightfully belong to all, and *idia*, private possessions. His criticism was that the rich appropriated *koina* and thus robbed the poor. Land was such a possession; rightfully it belonged to everyone, just as did wind, air, and sunshine. As a result he and other fathers called for the redistribution of goods (C. Avila, 52-53). Goods should be available to all, and this natural right took priority over the secondary right of private property.

Owners can do with their property only that which God wills them to do, as Clement of Alexandria taught:

> All things therefore are common, and not for the rich to appropriate an undue share. . . . For God has given us . . . the liberty of use, but only so far as necessary; and he has determined that the use should be common [quoted in Hengel, 77].

The rich must give back to the poor what was once theirs. The wealth of a few created the misery and poverty of many; the presence of riches implied a lack of love. Basil reasoned:

> If only each one would take as much as he requires to satisfy his immediate needs, and leave the rest to others who equally needed it, no one would be rich—and no one would be poor [quoted in Hengel, 2].

Injustice existed on a massive scale and redistribution was the solution, and after that the responsibility lay on all persons to take only what they needed. Refusal to engage in almsgiving or the redistribution of wealth on any level was robbery, whether it be by the rich who retained their wealth or the state with its landownership system.

Several church fathers spoke of the ideal of a communal sharing of goods. Ambrose is described as an advocate of primitive communism by some, for his views may have anticipated the modern critique of the competitive system of production and distribution (Lovejoy, 458–68). He grounded the idea of communal ownership in the Stoic concept of the common nature of all human beings. Likewise Chrysostom felt that the gifts of God were intended not for individual ownership but for joint ownership. Augustine declared:

> Those who wish to make room for the Lord must find pleasure not in private, but in common property. . . . Let us therefore abstain from the possession of private property—or from the love of it, if we cannot abstain from possession—and let us make room for the Lord [quoted in C. Avila, 120].

The idealistic affirmation of communal sharing was compromised by the early church as its message penetrated the ranks of the rich. Then church fathers more prudently called upon rich Christians to use their wealth wisely for the benefit of the poor, and almsgiving was encouraged. The fathers accepted private property only as long as wealth was used for the benefit of the church and the poor. Though they attacked the institution of private property in theory, their practical advice called for almsgiving by the rich (Hengel, 3–8, 61–73).

The church strongly encouraged giving help to the poor. Almsgiving was doing justice, not merely charity—though it was that, too. Early second century A.D. literature resonates these ideas:

> Give the unskilled an opportunity to earn their daily bread; give work to those who can do it, take care to look after those who are unable to work [Pseudo-Clementine, 8:6].
>   Do not turn away the needy, but share everything with your brother, and do not say that it is your own [Didache, 4:8].

Clement believed that private property provided the opportunity to create fellowship by sharing. Owners must first realize how little is necessary for self-sufficiency, then sharing may occur abundantly:

> Possessions were made to be possessed. Goods are called goods because they do good, and they have been provided by God for the good of humanity. Indeed, they lie at hand and are put at our disposal as a sort of material and as instruments to be well used [quoted in C. Avila, 43].

Clement rejected renunciation, for giving away wealth limited the opportunity for good. Private property was a just institution when owners were generous in almsgiving (Hengel, 74–78; Grant, 108–9). Ambrose called almsgiving justice or retribution, for therein the rich repaid the poor what was justly theirs. Though he envisioned a better distribution of the goods of this world, the only way this was possible in the Roman empire was via the voluntary sharing of individuals on a grand scale (Lovejoy, 464–68; Miranda, *Marx*, 16). Chrysostom believed the rich had the opportunity to rectify the injustice of the world by freely distributing wealth to the poor. They were accountable to all in their duty to use wealth as a means for correcting social injustice; otherwise their continued greedy possession would constitute new robbery:

> Do you give to the poor? What you give is not yours but your Master's, common to you and your fellow-servants. For which cause you ought especially to be humbled in the calamities of those who are your kindred [quoted in C. Avila, 98–99].

Augustine blamed Roman law for legalizing unfair distribution, which destroyed human solidarity and a sense of community. Good persons used *pecunia*, "money," "goods," wisely when they were indifferent to it and used it in almsgiving. Though he favored the abolition of private property, and he even participated in communal experiments, he was ultimately drawn from the ideal to the more practical admonition for almsgiving (Grant, 119; C. Avila, 108–24).

The social ethos of the church fathers that called for almsgiving and other forms of humanitarian concern may have been a primary element in the rapid spread of Christianity. The eloquent testimony provided by an ardent opponent of Christianity, Emperor Julian the Apostate (ca. A.D. 360), demonstrates this:

> Why do we not observe that it is their benevolence to strangers, their care for the graves of the dead, and the pretended holiness of their lives that they have done the most to increase atheism [Christianity]? . . . It is disgraceful that when no Jew ever has to beg, and the impious Galileans [Christians] support not only their own poor but ours as well, all men see that our people lack aid from us.[161]

Then, as now, the most successful form of evangelism was one that combined social action with gospel proclamation.

The message of the church fathers has a unified ring. Wealth is not evil, but wealthy persons who rob the poor and misuse their money are evil. Robbery consists in private ownerships of goods intended by God to be common property and the refusal to share that wealth. Because of the common origin, nature, and destiny of all human beings, basic goods and property should be shared. Radical almsgiving, or even redistribution, done in voluntary fashion will provide for the self-sufficiency of all individuals and fellowship in the Spirit created by the unity of possessions.

Summary

The ancient church spread quickly, especially due to the mission outreach of Paul and others. Their expectation of Jesus' imminent return prevented them from developing views on society, economics, and the relation of the rich to the poor. With Luke-Acts (A.D. 85) the first serious images are provided. Herein the goal of the Christian is not the renunciation of wealth, but its proper and effective utilization for almsgiving.

The spirit of the New Testament is best summarized by a passage in the Johannine epistles:

> But if any one has the world's goods and sees his brother in need, yet closes his heart against him, how does God's love abide in him? [1 John 3:17].

The strong sermonic rhetoric of the church fathers is a natural development of New Testament thought, especially Luke-Acts. Whereas the New Testament imperative was general, the church fathers were more specific and spoke directly to critical issues. As we listen to their prophetic voices, their message may be interpreted diversely. Are we to radically change social structures or do we engage in almsgiving?

In one sense society has radically changed in the past two centuries. We know something that the church fathers could not have comprehended—that religious inspiration can join forces with the urge for social reform in order to effect significant change. Nor are we as otherworldly as were they. Now that Christianity has been in this world for two thousand years, many theologians have come to realize that the actualization of Jesus' imperatives is partially to be realized in this world.

We need not compromise the highest of our dreams. The question that remains is, What direction should we take to further actualize the prophetic vision of social, political, and economic quality for all? What is the most practical and functional model for society to emulate in order to achieve such a vision?

Chapter 8

Beyond the Biblical Tradition

The same fate will overtake those who turn the free public market into a carrion-pit and a robber's den. Daily the poor are defrauded. New burdens and high prices are imposed. Everyone misuses the market in his own willful, conceited, arrogant way, as if it were his right and privilege to sell his goods as dearly as he pleases without a word of criticism. We shall stand by and let such persons fleece, grab, and hoard. But we shall trust God, who takes matters into his own hands. . . . If when you meet a poor man who must live from hand to mouth, you act as if everyone must live by your favor, you skin and scrape him right down to the bone, and you arrogantly turn him away whom you ought to give aid, he will cry to heaven. Beware of this, I repeat, as of the devil himself. Such a man's sighs and cries will be no joking matter. They will have an effect too heavy for you and all the world to bear, for they will reach God, who watches over poor, sorrowful hearts, and he will not leave them unavenged. But if you despise and defy this, see whom you have brought upon yourself [Martin Luther on the Seventh Commandment, from "Ten Commandments," *Large Catechism*, 397–98].

Throughout two millennia Christian theologians and preachers have decried the unjust oppression of the poor by the rich. Yet somehow this has been forgotten by many Christians in contemporary society. Popular religious interpretation has used the commandment against theft to justify the accumulation of wealth and the refusal to help the poor. Too often the official theologies of the churches permit social concerns to take a subordinate role to other concerns, and this allows such popular religious misunderstandings.

During the Middle Ages and into the modern era, the institutional church had concerns that distracted theologians and church administrators from social issues. The demise of the Roman empire and the barbarian incursions left church leaders the only educated persons in society capable of exercising any effective leadership. Simply surviving the Dark Ages and bringing society back to civilized behavior was the burning concern of church leaders. In order to do this the church developed as an institution in the same structural form as the Roman empire, and it inherited many of the same unfortunate characteristics. The chief concern of the church was the maintenance of its position in society, the care of souls, and the propagation of the Christian message.

The social ethos and the imperative to share possessions was remembered by certain noble individuals within the institutional structures, but more frequently the mandates of the New Testament and early church fathers were implemented by noninstitutional movements.

Religious and Social Movements Concerned with Communal Sharing

The bold rhetoric of the early church fathers regarding the communal sharing of property never materialized for their society as a whole. However, dedicated individuals sought to actualize this lifestyle in the monastic movement of the early Middle Ages, and this grand experiment in Christian communal life continues today.

The roots of monasticism may be traced to pre-Christian origins, for there have always been solitary individuals who retreated to the wilderness for meditation. The early centuries of Christianity saw such hermits, or eremitic monks, withdraw from a society that they viewed as corrupt and transitory. Their quest for God led them to the wilderness to live an austere lifestyle. One such early example was St. Anthony (A.D. 251?-356) who withdrew far into the wilderness, but ironically his fame attracted emulators to him. Pachomius of Egypt (A.D. 286-346) is credited with the founding of the first organized order of monks who lived in community. Jewish Essene communities (e.g., Qumran), several centuries before, may have provided inspiration for Christian initiatives.

Orders of monks flourished in Egypt and Palestine during the fourth century A.D. Perhaps the triumphant conquest of the Roman empire by Christianity caused even more Christians to withdraw from society and from a church that had begun to compromise with the values of that society. Monasticism was brought in organized form to Europe by St. Benedict of Nursia (A.D. 480-547), who formulated the Rule of the Benedictine Order and founded the monastery at Monte Cassino. This undertaking, in the early Middle Ages, was the beginning of monasticism in the West, and it would contribute mightily to the civilization of Europe.

Monasticism gave the West a vision of communal sharing of possessions and community living. With the structures provided by the Rule of Benedict and later developments, monasticism has proven that communal living need not be an idealistic, transitory experiment. Although other experiments in communal living have so often failed, especially in America, the monastic tradition has endured faithfully for fifteen hundred years.[162]

Nor can it be said that monasticism is escapist and otherworldly. In many ways it has been very "worldly," for in the monasteries of Western Europe the sparks of civilization were kindled and preserved. Monasteries were bastions where literacy was maintained, literature was preserved, and agricultural activity was fostered. Culture was kept alive in the medieval monasteries until society was ready to receive its riches once more. Monasteries provided religious service to the church: religious reform movements originated there, as was the case with the monastery at Cluny, and monasteries were the chief missionary arm of the church in the conversion of all Europe. The monastic movement was not only a successful attempt to fulfill the mandate of sharing possessions; it was the cultural repository and tutor of Western civilization (Decarreaux, 271–368; Knowles, 25–244).

In contrast to the more orthodox and well-ordered monastic movement, there were radical and spontaneous attempts to create communal sharing of property. Throughout the Middle Ages and into the modern period, society has witnessed apocalyptic movements that often teetered on the edge of revolution. Monasticism was the peaceful end of the spectrum; millenarianism was often the violent end.

Millennial movements attracted persons who expected the imminent coming of Jesus Christ and the final judgment. They were inspired by literature from the early Middle Ages and later writers such as Joachim de Fiore and Savonarola (McGinn, *Spirituality*, 17–275; *Visions*, 1–283). Persons dispossessed by social and economic change were often drawn to these movements, which offered an outlet for their frustrations with society and the established church.

These revolutionary and mystical millenarians were anarchists who sought to prepare for the second coming or the "golden age" by radical spiritual and social transformation. Some movements burned out quickly in a rapid and futile uprising. Others attempted to create a communal sharing experience. This was particularly true of north European movements of the late Middle Ages, such as John Zizka's Taborite movement, Hans Böhm's activity at Niklashausen, Thomas Müntzer's Thuringian revolution, the Anabaptist communities of Melchior Hoffmann (Strasbourg), and the combined efforts of Jan Bockelson and Jan Matthys (Münster). Communal sharing could include not only property but sometimes even wives and families. In some instances, however, a community became the chattel of a totalitarian leader (Jan Bockelson). Invariably such movements ended with defeat and the slaughter of their adherents (Cohn, 19–286).

The millenarian movements with their violence were not as successful as the more peaceful monastic movements, which lay within the spectrum of orthodoxy. However, millenarian movements did contribute to the fabric of Western civilization. Their radical ideas were inherited and developed by liberal socio-political thinkers in the Enlightenment and eventually provided input for the development of democratic and socialist thought. The millenarian affirmation of universal racial equality became the cornerstone for modern social thought. Their attempt to redistribute goods was an inspiration to socialist thinkers such as Jacques Rousseau, Friedrich Engels, and Marx. Finally, the millenarian movements left descendants to the modern era in a more pacific form. Mennonites (Germany), Amish (Poland), and Hutterites (Russia) are those heirs of Anabaptist thought who survived the sixteenth-century revolutions and withdrew to form nonviolent communities in central and eastern Europe. (The origins of the modern Baptist denominations may also be found in the same Anabaptist movements.)

Theological Heritage of the Institutional Church

It was not until the modern era that the institutional churches directed official attention to issues such as property, the redistribution of wealth, and the deeper meaning of theft. However, throughout the Middle Ages and early modern period concern was expressed by leading theologians, and awakened social consciousness may be found among many Christian thinkers. There were also isolated reform movements of dedicated and caring individuals. Eighteenth-century Pietism in Germany and Methodism in England brought the creation of home missions, hospitals, orphanages, and other charitable institutions. These movements contributed to socio-religious reform in America in the nineteenth and twentieth centuries.

The insights of the early church fathers were not lost during the Middle Ages. Thomas Aquinas affirmed their critical views on property and possessions, but somehow his views on these issues were later forgotten. It has been hypothesized that the crucial misinterpretation of Aquinas was made by Cardinal Cajetan in the sixteenth century when he interpreted references to "common purpose" to mean "private property," and thus the institution of private property was legitimated. Though other interpreters have criticized this misinterpretation, it remained part of the theological tradition of the Catholic Church until the modern era. By that time it had become a natural reaction of church authorities to defend pure capitalism against socialist theories or even social reform.

The modern Catholic Church has rediscovered the roots of social reform inherent in the Christian tradition. Modern encyclicals have inspired social reform movements in the church at large.

Among Protestants similar popular misinterpretations have led well-intentioned believers to affirm a divine right for the institution of private property and to deny economic reform for the sake of the poor and oppressed. Luther and Calvin authored a multitude of works from which later generations could establish a diverse range of opinions by selecting appropriate passages, some of which could be contradictory to others. The writings of Luther prior to the 1524 Peasants' Revolt appear revolutionary as he encouraged peasants to seek their rights and chides the nobility. However, he may be portrayed as an advocate of the old order of authoritarianism by quoting his statements made during the Peasants' Revolt when he called upon nobles to crush revolutionaries. Calvin may also be portrayed in dual fashion on economic matters. Attributed to him is the so-called Calvinistic work ethic, which undergirds principles of modern capitalism, but at the same time he sought a society that would help the poor, and for this reason he opposed interest rates (Rushdoony, 474).

Max Weber postulated that the theology of Calvin and Protestantism in general had produced the work ethic that undergirded the development of modern capitalism. Weber's observations are true; capitalism did develop and thrive in northern Europe because of Reformed theology (Weber, *Ethic*, 13–183). However, Calvin and the Reformed theologians did not set forth to create a competitive capitalistic ethos; rather, it was an unforeseen side effect of their teachings. Reformed theology and Protestant theology in general had a strong humanitarian ethos and could critique unscrupulous merchants, as the quote by Luther at the beginning of this chapter demonstrates. Christians were called upon to assist their neighbor in need; almsgiving was an imperative, just as it had been in the ancient church.

Modern industrialists who aggrandize wealth in the name of the work ethic and quote the Seventh Commandment to protect their wealth overlook an important aspect of the commandment's interpretation. Christian tradition does not support a ruthless capitalism that creates or widens a gap between rich and poor, nor does the Seventh Commandment justify the accumulation of wealth in the hands of a few while others are in need. Theft means the taking from a person things that are necessary for that individual's development as a complete and contributing member of society. Theft includes even the "legal" acquisition of goods from persons, if the loss of those goods reduces them physically, psychologically, educationally, or emotionally.

Review of the Biblical Tradition

An initial consideration of the commandment not to steal might seem to justify accumulation, but closer consideration reveals that biblical tradition has interpreted this command by laws and sermonic rhetoric designed to protect the poor against excessive accumulation of wealth in the hands of a few. The Israelite preacher would declare: "You shall take care of the poor, the widow, the orphan, the stranger in your land; for once you were slaves in Egypt, and I the Lord your God brought you out with an outstretched arm and a mighty hand!"

Biblical law was geared to tribal solidarity, the concern for the greater society or "family at large." Laws rejected massive accumulation of wealth by encouraging redistribution. Unlike later classical Greco-Roman laws, which sought only to maintain the status quo, biblical law sought to reform society and ensure justice for weaker members (Miranda, *Marx*, 30). Although the laws defended the freedom of all, they sought to maintain the welfare of the weak in particular. Biblical laws serve as a model for our society, for we face the same tensions. As George Wright has written of Israelite society:

> There was no separation of freedom and welfare, so that the one was in opposition to the other. Freedom in any institution was precisely to fulfill a function, and the chief function was community welfare ["Deuteronomy," 427].

Though our society is more advanced and complex than theirs, we may still learn from them.

As we have studied Israelite laws, we have perceived insights different from many of ours. Situations wherein property had come into another person's possession legally could also be instances of theft. The recipient of property could not retain it if the well-being of another was threatened thereby.

Laws in the Covenant code (Exod. 21–23), Deuteronomic code (Deut. 12–26), and other legal corpora are replete with examples, many of which we have considered. If the coat of a poor person has been taken as a pledge, it had to be returned before the night brought freezing weather (Exod. 22:26–27; Deut. 24:12–13). Loans had to be provided interest-free for the poor (Lev. 25:35–38). In the seventh year the poor had a right to whatever grew in uncultivated fields (Exod. 23:10–11). The poor also had a right to garner grain left in the field after harvesting (Lev. 19:9–10). Land reform was envisioned by the jubilee year: it was to be returned to its original owners every fifty years (Lev. 25:8–17). Slaves had to be released after seven years of service (Exod. 21:1–6; Deut. 15:12–18), or else Israel would forfeit the freedom from slavery won for it by Yahweh in the historic exodus.

Such legislation reflects the attempt of Israel to restore and maintain the equality of the early pastoral period. Some legislation may be an idealistic projection that never was observed. Nevertheless, the religious ethos sought to restore the essential equality of Israelites before God in all human endeavors. Their mere attempt to do this so many eons ago should inspire us today.

Israel idealized the past over against the Canaanite or sedentary ethos. The history of Israel was a struggle between these two philosophies until the exile of the sixth century B.C. The record of that struggle and the proclamations of the prophets have become part of our heritage and have entered into the development of our own liberal democratic ethos.

The Ten Commandments are rooted in this ethos, and the prohibition of theft reflects it. The commandment spoke against those who would appropriate goods for their own use to the detriment of others. Such hoarding would result in the lowering of the quality of life or even lead to death in that precarious environment. There was no notion of the inviolability of private property. That notion is our invention.

In a pastoralist milieu, flocks and land were owned by the community as a whole, and even after the settlement process land was considered to be the property of an extended family. The commandment did not protect private property, for the truly important property was owned by the community or family. Some have called this a primitive democracy or a primitive socialism, though both are naive generalizations. We could speak of a theocratic egalitarianism, for God was viewed as the true owner who gave the land to the people at large. Families, tribes, and communities had a right of access to those things upon which their lives depended. This right was vital for their continued marginal existence; impoverishment or death of members in the community adversely affected everyone, even those who hoarded.

The history of Israel shows that the settlement process caused Israel to move from early pastoral models for society based on tribal and kinship structures to models in the monarchical period that were based on mercantilistic economics and state-oriented politics. The prophets saw the abuses in their society created by this process and called for a return to the Mosaic covenant, which idealized earlier social, political, and economic norms.

The idealistic theologians of Israel did not demand the communalization of all goods. The commandment not to steal did not legislate against the possession of personal items or heirlooms that gave persons a sense of meaning and value. Such items reinforce personal identity in any age, and to destroy them is to undermine individual existence and selfhood, and so to eat away at the identity of a people. The commandment not to steal protected such individual possessions as well as the communal property of the people.

The commandment applied to both private and public property. But we have misinterpreted it by considering certain things to be private property that then were viewed as public. What must be shared are those significant things in society that sustain the quality of life for everyone, such as access to productive resources, to food, and to the necessities for a healthy and fruitful life within society.

The postexilic experience of the Jews saw a new spiritual dimension added. Poverty became idealized as a virtue when it came to be equated with humility vis-à-vis God. It also signaled the frustration of faithful Jews who found themselves socially, religiously, and economically oppressed. They longed for the future when God would act in a new decisive manner for them.

The New Age was something that Christians appropriated to themselves, for they were sure that God had acted in the new and decisive way that had been so long awaited. Whether they called themselves "the poor" is questionable, but they imbibed deeply of the traditions from which they sprang. Most importantly they took on the spiritual insight of the postexilic era that viewed poverty as an interior attitude. They perceived that the interior attitude of poverty or indifference to wealth was necessary before any social action was possible. Once this interior attitude was attained by the grace of God, the Christian would be able to reach out in love to those in need.

The social ethic of the nascent church was practical. Beginning with Jesus and continuing through the patristic era, the imperative was not upon renunciation of wealth or coerced redistribution but upon voluntary almsgiving. This appeared to them to be the best way to manifest the love of God to others.

Implications for the Modern Age

The biblical tradition offers us a plethora of insights. Close study is necessary to correct misunderstandings. The Bible does not endorse pure capitalism and the concentration of wealth in the hands of a few. Nor does it endorse forcible redistribution of goods. Readers are called upon to be moderate and practical in meeting human needs effectively.

We notice a range of options in the biblical tradition. From the fiery revolutionary invective of the prophets to the calm didactic response of the wisdom literature, we detect different approaches to the problem of property and community. The common denominator is a concern for human welfare, but rhetoric and policy differ from generation to generation.

There is a message there for the modern Christian. The Christian must be flexible, able to meet different situations with different responses. Times change and so do economic systems. Christian social responses must be ready to change. The patristic church, for example, advocated almsgiving as a practical way to meet social needs. That does not have to be the modern response. The church fathers could not envision the radical social transformation of their world, certainly not of the Roman empire. However, we can envision such radical social change, for in the past two centuries we have embarked upon reform in our society with a frequency and effectiveness that would have astounded the church fathers. Perhaps Christians in our world need to think on a grander scale. Certainly our potential, skills, ability, and power to transform society are greater than that of our ancestors in the ancient church.

Christians today may need to be involved in programs of social change effected by government legislation and reform. Above all we must remain open to different models of response in our modern world. Modern Christians may work the will of God for the welfare of the poor in radically diverse economic and social structures. Each of us must make our own decision and commitment in this matter. Some may be committed to capitalistic systems, and others to socialist forms. Both, in their own place and time, may be appropriate for particular social settings.

Writers and theologians have drawn upon the biblical tradition to derive insights valid for our modern world. Some have seen the similarity with feudal latifundia condemned by the prophets of Israel and the economic policies of the ruling elite in Latin America. Their observations are piercing and often valid. One author compares the treatment of Naboth by Ahab with the American treatment of Third World countries (Napier, "Inheritance," 3–11). Others have deduced that only a socialistic or communistic system is the viable Christian alternative. If such a form of government were wedded to Christianity, the result would be a significant step forward in the history of human institutions. A true Christian must be committed to communism, says Miranda, for that system alone can alleviate injustice, close the gap between rich and poor, and thus bring to fruition the vision of Jesus and the prophets.

The institution of private property is nothing more than "legalized, institutionalized, civilized, canonized robbery" (Miranda, *Marx*, 11). Such an extreme position is naive, though the rhetoric may be necessary in situations of extreme oppression in Latin America. (The old story of hitting a mule with a club to get his attention before you speak comes to mind.) Nonetheless, to maintain that socialism or communism is the *only* option for Christians fails to take into consideration the broader traditions of the Bible. They cannot be brought to light by a literalistic reading of biblical texts. A more critical and historically conditioned reading is necessary.

A sensitive consideration of the biblical imperatives and attitudes vis-à-vis property, theft, and community tells us that we should meet the physical needs of the poor in whatever fashion is most beneficial for them. We are to prevent injustice, dishonesty, and oppression of the weaker members of society. We are to create a society in which all members have authentic equality of opportunity in economic matters. Finally, we are to provide the possibility for all individuals to develop their own full potentials in social and economic, as well as educational and personal, categories. These are gargantuan imperatives for any society! Nevertheless, they are the ideals toward which we must strive if we are to remain faithful to the biblical tradition. There remains the very practical question of which socio-economic system is most suited for meeting such high ideals. The biblical tradition is not concerned with economic systems or ideologies, but with human needs. The commandment against theft is designed not to protect property but rather the life of members in the community and the quality of life they experience. In different periods of history different economic systems may be the answer. The Christian ought to address human need by whatever economic system is most appropriate for a given situation. The Christian is committed to persons, not systems.

The biblical and patristic traditions of the church give us no program for reforming society. Throughout the development of the tradition we note changing values as the historical process moved forward. The constant appeal was to serve human need. Christians are to be "detached" in their relationship to wealth, which is the moderate norm between covetous hoarding and indiscriminate renunciation. With this spirit of detachment, Christians will be better able to see the needs of others and determine what is necessary for their historical, social, and economic situation.

Such a response may take the form of Israelite tribal, pastoral egalitarianism with its ideal of periodic redistribution, or the voluntary communism of some New Testament communities, or the patristic demand for radical almsgiving. The response of responsible Christians today will probably include a totally new option. But it must avoid dogmatic adherence to any doctrinaire ideology. The Christian ethic may lead some to a more radical, others to a more conservative, ethic for a given situation; it does not single out any one system (Hengel, 84–88; Barr, 97, 133).

The Bible does not mandate either capitalism or socialism. The extreme position of Miranda is matched by the equally extreme position of Michael

Novak. Just as Miranda calls communism the solution (salvation!), so Novak naively sings the praises of ''democratic capitalism'' as the panacea for human woes (Novak, *Vision*, 1–60; *Spirit*, 13–360). Both authors are dogmatically committed to their respective ideologies, as are many others in their two respective ''camps.'' Both of them lack the ability to be self-critical, and they have overlooked the potential of their systems to oppress human beings. The Christian is committed to persons, not ideologies and systems.

The best statement in this regard is provided by L. T. Johnson after his evaluation of possessions in the ancient church:

> The Scriptures do not present for our consideration or implementation any grand scheme for the proper disposition of possessions. There is no Christian economic structure or educational system. The Bible does not tell us how to organize our lives together, and still less which things we should call private and even which public. Nor does it propose a clear program of social change. It does not even present one way of sharing possessions as uniquely appropriate. A Christian social ethic must be forged (repeatedly, as in theology) within the tension established by two realities; the demands of faith in the one God who creates, sustains, and saves us and the concrete, changing structures of the world we encounter in every age. . . . This lack of a utopian vision or specific ethic may be regarded by some as a loss, but it is not. It is a blessing. If the scriptural witness on possession could be reduced to an ideology, it would not be God's word to the world, but humankind's [*Sharing,* 115].

His final insight is worth emphasis. The lack of a particular economic theory in the Bible is a blessing. For this frees Christians to implement whatever programs or policies are most beneficial and appropriate to specific situations.

The biblical tradition does not advocate any particular economic system, because it does not blame economic systems for human suffering, injustice, and oppression. Unlike modern theorists who see the problem in terms of economic policies and systems, the biblical tradition lays the blame squarely on inordinate human desire. The problem is selfishness, and no political system can completely remedy that problem.

An economic system is no better or worse than the persons who live under it. Jesus and the theologians of the ancient church saw human renewal as the regulative purpose of almsgiving and communal sharing. Any wholesale redistribution of goods is impractical without a change in human nature. Because inordinate human desire is the problem, a radically authoritarian structure could safeguard economic redistribution. However, such a system, stifling individual creativity and the potential for human development, would be as oppressive as the structure it is replacing (L. Johnson, *Sharing,* 124–39; Hengel, 86). The idealist adamantly committed to an ideology easily overlooks the simple human flaw of selfishness, which is the bane and downfall of perfection-seeking in any system. The biblical tradition welcomes any system that truly meets the needs of a given society.

The biblical commandment prohibiting theft is a two-edged sword. The commandment condemns the individual who uses a capitalistic ethos to justify selfish individualism and a rapacious desire for wealth that deprives others of their livelihood. But the commandment also condemns doctrinaire ideologies of the left that would seek to redistribute wealth on a large scale regardless of the cost in human life and misery. How often have would-be liberators become oppressors of the poor!

Political movements of right and left are capable of subordinating the great human needs of the masses to the ideals of a few. Whereas rightists may oppress in the name of individual property rights, leftists may oppress for the ideology of a "new order." Wrenching goods from the hands of the needy in the name of justice, fair play, competition, national security, or any ideology violates this commandment. Laws in the Old Testament called for reform and redistribution, but they did so in the name of human need, not ideology.

The prohibition can function in any economic system, because it addresses not so much the issue of property as the issue of human need. Designed to protect the quality of life, the command insists that both capitalistic and socialistic systems do justice to the higher goal of human need. Capitalism is permitted the free and competitive exchange of goods and services, provided the weaker members of society are not victimized. The socialistic system is permitted the regulation of public property for the best interests of all, provided the initiative, zeal, and personal goals of individuals are not crushed in the process. The commandment prohibits the destruction, limitation, or erosion of the selfhood of individuals and communities.

The commandment rebukes those who maintain that the successful and rich have been blessed for their hard work, whereas the poor are receiving their just rewards for laziness. This popular notion is really a misunderstanding of the old Calvinistic ethos, which also had a place for almsgiving and help for the less fortunate. The modern ethos too often forgets the merciful side of the old ethos.

The biblical tradition indeed praises hard work, diligence, patience, and related virtues, but it also teaches that the fruits of labor produced by those virtues are meant to be shared by society as a whole. Selfish individualism is condemned.

Individuals must view themselves as part of a greater organic whole, a community, a family that works together and shares the common abundance. A society that ignores the poor for the sake of productivity may soon lose that productivity, for it has stolen from the poor the right to livelihood that the poor have by virtue of their humanity.

We are to view individual persons as part of a community, an organic whole, in which the needs of all are to be met. The biblical ethos calls for a society where everyone has a right to access to the food, clothing, housing, education, and basic services that not only sustain life but improve the quality of life, so that individuals can develop their full potential in society. Martin Hengel says it well:

> The goal would be to grant each individual the chance of personal development in accordance with his capabilities and wishes, for the well-being of and in responsibility for the whole society [87].

Christians are to strive for this goal in whatever economic system they may live. In different historical periods and in differing social conditions the economic system may change. We must realize in our modern world that different economic systems may be necessary for different cultures and societies. The goal of the Christian is to promote the system that most effectively meets human needs.

Finally, the biblical tradition tells us that one's interior attitude is the most important dynamic. The modern Christian may not be able to reshape the hearts and minds of everyone in society. But it is the responsibility of each of us to actualize the biblical message in our lives, practice it, and then proclaim it to the world.

We must perceive that our goods and possessions are a gift from God. As such we are called upon to share them with those in need. A precondition for giving is owning, so we are not called to an out-and-out renunciation of wealth or material possessions. According as our economic system has permitted the distribution of goods, we are to use that which is in our possession to serve others. We must never become a slave to our own possessions, for this blinds us to the needs of others. Nor can we ever let possessions function as the measure of human value, for true human worth includes the spiritual and intellectual possessions bequeathed to us by God (L. Johnson, *Sharing*, 115, 124–39). Before God, we are all equals. Touched by the grace of God we are to reach out to those around us, the others with whom we are to have total community—and bear each other's burdens and share each other's joys.

Abbreviations

AB	Anchor Bible
ASORDS	American Schools of Oriental Research Dissertation Series
BA	*Biblical Archaeologist*
BAR	*Biblical Archaeologist Reader*, 3 vols.
BASOR	*Bulletin of the American Schools of Oriental Research*
Bib	*Biblica*
BZ	*Biblische Zeitschrift*
BZAW	Beihefte zur Zeitschrift für die alttestamentliche Wissenschaft
CB	Century Bible
CBC	Cambridge Bible Commentary
CBQ	*Catholic Biblical Quarterly*
CBQMS	Catholic Biblical Quarterly Monograph Series
HAT	Handbuch zum Alten Testament
Herm	Hermeneia: A Critical and Historical Commentary on the Bible
HUCA	*Hebrew Union College Annual*
IB	*Interpreter's Bible*, 12 vols.
ICC	International Critical Commentary
IDB	*Interpreter's Dictionary of the Bible*, 4 vols.
IDBS	*Interpreter's Dictionary of the Bible, Supplement*
Int	*Interpretation*
JBL	*Journal of Biblical Literature*
JHI	*Journal of the History of Ideas*
JNES	*Journal of Near Eastern Studies*
JQR	*Jewish Quarterly Review*
JSS	*Journal of Semitic Studies*
JTS	*Journal of Theological Studies*
KD	*Kerygma und Dogma*
NCB	New Century Bible
NICNT	New International Commentary on the New Testament
NICOT	New International Commentary on the Old Testament
NTM	New Testament Message: A Biblical Theological Commentary
OBT	Overtures to Biblical Theology

OTL	Old Testament Library
RB	*Revue biblique*
SBLDS	Society of Biblical Literature Dissertation Series
SBLMS	Society of Biblical Literature Monograph Series
SBT	Studies in Biblical Theology
TLZ	*Theologische Literaturzeitung*
VT	*Vetus Testamentum*
VTS	Supplements to Vetus Testamentum
WHJP	*World History of the Jewish People*
WMANT	Wissenschaftliche Monographien zum Alten und Neuen Testament
WO	*Die Welt des Orients*
ZAW	*Zeitschrift für die alttestamentliche Wissenschaft*
ZNW	*Zeitschrift für die neutestamentliche Wissenschaft*

Notes

1. See Harrelson, *Commandments,* 137–39; Park, I, 987; Greenberg, I, 741.

2. Hamel, 22–23; Wittenberg, 3–17. However, some scholars believe they are later, for the reference to "house" and "testimony" reflect the postsettlement condition, and the fear of human desire (coveting) and a fear of taking the divine name in vain reflect the postexilic morality (Weber, *Judaism,* 235–39). In response to Weber, other scholars argue that these particular nuances or vocabulary are really later developments in the Decalogue (e.g., Nielsen, 94–131). The basic core of the Decalogue is early and reflects pastoralist concerns. Whether its origin is in the wilderness or the early settlement period cannot be definitely ascertained.

3. Stamm and Andrew, 13–22; Phillips, *Law,* 37–152; Nielsen, 78–86; Harrelson, *Commandments,* 40–48.

4. Phillips (*Law,* 3–189) shows how the commandments might be reworded so as to function as a criminal law code in the wilderness under Moses. Nielsen (132–38) believes it was the law of the royal court in northern Israel. However, Harrelson (*Commandments,* 22, 139, and passim) shows how the commandments are too dissimilar from other law codes to have functioned as a civil law code.

5. Stamm and Andrew, 22–75; Nielsen, 94–118, 132–43; Schmidt, 201–2.

6. Alt, "Origins," 103–71; Stamm and Andrew, 30–35; Nielsen, 56–71.

7. Gervitz, 137–58; Gerstenberger, 130–38 and passim (Gerstenberger also believes that the wisdom tradition in Israel contains such apodictic forms, and the Ten Commandments may come from the wisdom tradition); Kilian, 185–202; Phillips, *Law,* 13; Weinfeld, 63–75.

8. Gese, 147–50; Kilian, 185–202; Fohrer, "Rechte," 49–74; Nielsen, 71–78; Phillips, *Law,* 13; Boecker, 191–207.

9. Alt, "Verbot," I, 33–340; Noth, *Exodus,* 165–66; idem, *Leviticus,* 121; Stamm and Andrew, 101–7; Nielsen, 91; Hamel, 84–86; Phillips, *Law,* 130, 141; idem, *Deuteronomy,* 161; Craigie, 161, 307; Mayes, 324.

10. Alt, "Inschriften," 274–79; Stamm and Andrew, 101–4; Nielsen, 92, 110. Phillips (*Law,* 151–52) believes a different word was used originally, and it implied that the offender deprived a person of his or her status in the community by seizing his or her "house." As such, this crime would entail the deprival of status and freedom in the democratic society of early Israel and it would lead to improper administration of justice after repeated offenses, and therefore it was a capital crime. With Jehoshaphat's reform in the early ninth century B.C., the verb *ḥmd* was inserted, and the command was spiritualized.

11. Stoebe, 11, 126; Hyatt, *Exodus,* 215–16; Harrelson, *Commandments,* 138.

12. Driver and Miles, 8–10; North, *Jubilee,* 5–11; Boecker, 53–73.

13. Weber, *Judaism,* 61–63; Harrelson, "Law," 83; Childs, 456–57; Boecker, 142.

14. Phillips, *Law,* 91; Childs, 459; Boecker, 137, 143.

15. Finkelstein, *Edict,* 91-104; Paul, 75-77; Childs, 472.

16. Rylaarsdam, 1009-10; Harrelson, "Law," 83; Brueggemann, *Land,* 65-66.

17. Von Rad, *Studies,* 15; Loewenstamm, "Law," 246-47; Mayes, 72.

18. Greenberg, 734, 741; Hamel, 83; Boecker, 84, 166. Barr (109) compares this to modern England where theft, until the nineteenth century, was punished by hanging.

19. Pedersen, II, 403; Greenberg, 741; Hempel, 126 (because theft was the crime of the hungry poor, the Old Testament was biased in their favor); Hamel, 83; Loewenstamm, "Law," 265; Mendenhall, *Generation,* 207; Boecker, 84, 166-67.

20. Some scholars believe the first verse refers to burning rather than grazing, because the Israelites respected the rights of pastoralists to graze (Childs, 449, 475). Childs also cites Hittite laws that place burning and grazing damage together, which tends to mitigate the other opinion.

21. Rylaarsdam, 1004-5; Noth, *Exodus,* 185; Hyatt, *Exodus,* 239; Childs, 476; Boecker, 168-71.

22. Driver and Miles, 183-84; Scott, "Weights," 22-40; Craigie, 316-17; Mayes, 331.

23. Rylaarsdam, 1002; Noth, *Exodus,* 183; Hyatt, *Exodus,* 237; Childs, 474. But Beer (*Exodus,* 113), as quoted by Rylaarsdam (1002), believes the expression "sun rising" refers to his subsequent capture away from the house, and thus killing the thief would not be unlawful.

24. S. Driver, *Deuteronomy,* 250; Rylaarsdam, 1010; Wright, "Deuteronomy," 464; Noth, *Exodus,* 189; von Rad, *Deuteronomy,* 140; Phillips, *Deuteronomy,* 145; Childs, 480-81 (he finds a parallel in Hittite laws); Hyatt, *Exodus,* 246; Craigie, 287; Mayes, 306-7.

25. Mendelsohn, *Slavery,* 26; Weber, *Judaism,* 63-64; Gamoran, 127; Maloney, 1-20.

26. S. Driver, *Deuteronomy,* 267; Taeusch, 317-18; Wright, "Deuteronomy," 472; North, "Yad," 196-99; Neufeld, 359-62, 395-410; von Rad, *Deuteronomy,* 148; Gamoran, 128; Wenham, 322.

27. S. Driver (*Deuteronomy,* 266), North (*Jubilee,* 177), Neufeld (357), de Vaux (*Israel,* 172), and Gamoran (131-32) view *neshek* and *tarbith* as amounts either withheld initially or added upon payment. Loewenstamm ("Neshek," 79-80) views them as forms of interest on money and produce, respectively. Stein (163) and Snaith (*Leviticus,* 166) view the former as regularly paid interest and the latter as a lump sum.

28. Wright, "Deuteronomy," 472; Neufeld, 359-62, 375-410; Phillips, *Deuteronomy,* 25; Craigie, 302.

29. Neufeld, 363-74; Hyatt, *Exodus,* 243; Porter, 205. Because of the use of the word "anything" in Deuteronomy, its concern for aliens, and its expansion of *neshek* to include food as well as money, Gamoran (129-33) believes it to be the last legislation to be created. Exodus mentions only money, and Leviticus mentions only food.

30. Stein, 164-67; Gamoran, 131. Historical texts refer to persons reduced to slavery because of unpaid interest: 1 Sam. 22:2; 2 Kings 4:1.

31. S. Driver, *Deuteronomy,* 180; Cohen, 191; North, *Jubilee,* 179.

32. S. Driver, *Deuteronomy,* 274; Rylaarsdam, 1008; Wright, "Deuteronomy," 474-75; Noth, *Exodus,* 187; de Vaux, *Israel,* 172; von Rad, *Deuteronomy,* 151; Hyatt, *Exodus,* 244; Loewenstamm, "Law," 246; Childs, 479; Craigie (308) refers to the example of a farm worker who appealed against the decision of a minor govern-

ment official who had taken his garment (quoted from J.L.C. Gibson, *Textbook of Syrian Semitic Inscriptions,* I, 27, on the Yavneh-Yam ostracon); Mayes, 324; Boecker, 183.

33. Von Rad, *Deuteronomy,* 106; Daube, 429; Phillips, *Deuteronomy,* 105.

34. Mendelsohn, *Slavery,* 123; Weber, *Judaism,* 64; Noth, *Leviticus,* 43; Croatto, *Exodus,* 36.

35. De Vaux, *Israel,* 88; Noth, *Exodus,* 177; von Rad, *Deuteronomy,* 107; Mendelsohn, "Slavery, ANE," 139; Hyatt (*Exodus,* 228) points out that many think this refers to Israelites, not classless *habiru;* Childs, 447, 468.

36. Mendelsohn, *Slavery,* 49; Rylaarsdam, 994; Falk, 86–88; Fensham, "Eshnunna," 160–61; Loretz, 167–75; Noth, *Exodus,* 178; Hyatt (*Exodus,* 229) quotes a parallel law in the code of Eshnunna, ##36–37.

37. Rylaarsdam, "Exodus," 994; Noth, *Exodus,* 177; Westbrook, 209; Boecker, 158–59.

38. Wright, "Deuteronomy," 430; von Rad, *Deuteronomy,* 107; Hyatt, *Exodus,* 229; Phillips, *Deuteronomy,* 106; Craigie, 238; Boecker, 182.

39. North (*Jubilee,* 33), Morgenstern ("Sabbatical," 142), Phillips (*Deuteronomy,* 250), and Wacholder ("Year," 762–63) believe the release to be part of a fixed cycle, but Craigie (238) thinks it is an individual release for each slave after six years of service.

40. Wright, "Deuteronomy," 430; de Vaux, *Israel,* 83; Mendelsohn, *Slavery,* 138; Mayes, 250.

41. Mitchell, 263; Micklem, 125; North, *Jubilee,* 135, 153; Porter, 205.

42. North ("Flesh," 206) translates: "he shall not curtail her physical satisfaction, her honorable standing in the harem, or her right of parenthood."

43. Edwards, 44; Mendelsohn, *Slavery,* 13; idem, "Slavery, ANE," 128–29.

44. Rylaarsdam, 999; Noth, *Exodus,* 181; Hyatt, *Exodus,* 234; Loewenstamm, "Law," 261–62; Childs, 473; Boecker, 162.

45. Mendelsohn, *Slavery,* 18–19; idem, "Slavery, OT," 388; idem, "Slavery, ANE," 138.

46. S. Driver, *Deuteronomy,* 264; von Rad, *Deuteronomy,* 147; Mendelsohn, "Slavery, ANE," 136; Phillips, *Deuteronomy,* 156; Mayes, 319; Boecker, 86.

47. Edwards, 72; Mendelsohn, *Slavery,* 63–64; idem, "Slavery, OT," 389.

48. Noth (*Leviticus,* 172) sees Lev. 23:22 as a repetition of Lev. 19:9–10, but Wenham (305) thinks it is separate and necessary in this context because of the reference to the spring festival of weeks earlier in the chapter.

49. Wright, "Deuteronomy," 477; von Rad, *Deuteronomy,* 152; Noth, *Leviticus,* 141; Porter, 153; Craigie, 311; Mayes, 327; Boecker, 91.

50. S. Driver, *Deuteronomy,* 269; Weber, *Judaism,* 67; Mayes, 322.

51. Von Rad (*Deuteronomy,* 159–60), Phillips (*Deuteronomy,* 102), and Mayes (335) take the custom to be a later creation, but Loewenstamm ("Law," 247) believes it was in practice earlier.

52. Wright, *Deuteronomy,* 486; von Rad, *Deuteronomy,* 103; Phillips, *Deuteronomy,* 102, 174–75; Mayes, 246.

53. Rylaarsdam, 1011–12; Noth, *Exodus,* 189; Childs, 482; Wacholder, "Year," 762; Porter, 198; Boecker, 91–92.

54. Cazelles (91–92), North (*Jubilee,* 114–19), Micklem (121), Childs (482), and Porter (198) suggest that the land was available for the poor to use; Alt ("Origins," 165–66) thinks that the poor rented it; Hoenig (229) thinks the land was not used: it lay fallow for only two months.

55. Micklem, 120; Elliger, 350; Snaith, *Leviticus,* 161-62; Mendelsohn, "Society," 196-98.

56. Von Rad (*Deuteronomy,* 105) and Mayes (246) think that slave release was now attached to debt release. North (*Jubilee,* 33), de Vaux (*Israel,* 173), Morgenstern ("Sabbatical," 142), and Phillips (*Law,* 104) think that their presence together in this chapter is just a coincidence.

57. S. Driver (*Deuteronomy,* 174, 178-79), von Rad (*Deuteronomy,* 106), Wacholder ("Year," 762), and Mayes (246) believe the debts were canceled, but North (*Jubilee,* 186-87) and Craigie (236-38) suggest they were only suspended.

58. Weber (*Judaism,* 68) and North (*Jubilee,* 156) suggest that the reforms were never systematically put into effect. However, Wacholder ("Year," 762) attributes them to the early period. Wright ("Deuteronomy," 428) and Morgenstern ("Sabbatical," 142) attribute them to the divided monarchy.

59. Gordon, "Parallèles," 39; North, *Jubilee,* 65; Wiseman, 163; Wenham, 318. However, Loewenstamm ("Law," 335) thinks this is a coincidence.

60. Morgenstern, "Sabbatical," 142-44; Snaith, *Leviticus,* 161-62; Wacholder, "Calendar," 154; idem, "Year," 762-63.

61. North, *Jubilee,* 82; de Vaux, *Israel,* 174; Wacholder, "Calendar," 158-84; idem, "Year," 762-63.

62. North, *Jubilee,* 90; de Vaux, *Israel,* 174; Morgenstern, 142-43.

63. Wacholder, "Chronomessianism," 201-18; "Year," 763.

64. Pedersen, I, 88-90; North, *Jubilee,* 35; Westbrook, 211; Noth, *Leviticus,* 44; Pixley, 35; Wenham, 320-23; Boecker, 91; Sloan, 7.

65. Eichrodt, I, 96-97; de Vaux, *Israel,* 173; Van Selms, 498; Wenham, 323; Sloan, 4-8.

66. North, *Jubilee,* 109-10, 129-33; Elliger, 351-52; Van Selms, 496.

67. De Vaux, *Israel,* 175; Porter, 199-202; R. Avila, 22.

68. Elliger, 356; Westbrook, 223; Porter, 202; Van Selms, 497; Boecker, 92. However, Snaith (*Leviticus,* 165) and Wenham (321) maintain that urbanization and rapid development in the cities made it difficult to redeem houses in them; thus the "exceptions" in Lev. 25:29-31 are really newer additions to the law rather than exceptions created by the old Canaanite law.

69. Snaith, *Leviticus,* 176; Noth, *Leviticus,* 206; Porter, 223; Wenham, 340.

70. Pedersen, I, 89; Weber, *Judaism,* 71; Micklem, 122; Morgenstern, "Jubilee," 1002; Elliger, 351; Snaith, *Leviticus,* 163; Westbrook, 221-22; Wacholder, "Calendar," 154; Porter, 196-98; Wenham, 317.

71. Gordon, "Parallèles," 39; North, *Jubilee,* 62-65; Van Selms, 497.

72. Lewy, 21, 27 (cited in Westbrook, 216).

73. Fenton, *Life,* 70-74; Ginzberg, 364-91; van den Ploeg, 169-71; Alt, "Origins," 165; Loewenstamm, "Law," 245; Van Selms, 497. Van den Ploeg (171) cites a number of earlier scholars who held this view: Bernardus Eerdmans, *Alttestamentliche Studien* 4 (1912) 121ff.; Nicolaj Nicolsky, *ZAW* 44 (1932) 216; and Anton Jirku, "Das israelitische Jobeljahr," *Von Jerusalem nach Ugarit: Reinhold Seeberg Festschrift,* Leipzig, Scholl, 1929, II, 169-79.

74. Lewy, 21, 27 (cited in Westbook, 220).

75. Van Selms (497) also believes the words "release," *deror* (which also occurs in the presumably old text of Num. 36:4), and "jubilee," *yobel,* are archaic words, which point to the early settlement period.

76. Fenton (*Life*, 71–74) theorizes that the Sabbath year called for land redistribution every seven years, but jubilee replaced this custom even at an early period. Land was redistributed only every seventh Sabbath year or jubilee until the rise of the monarchy terminated the custom. North (*Jubilee*, 3, 199–212) thinks jubilee was designed to occur only once—the fiftieth year after the entry into the land under Joshua. This gave Israelites inexperienced at agriculture a second chance to farm their land if they had lost it through mismanagement. The actual restoration never took place; instead later generations tried to incorporate aspects of the legislation into existing social and economic practices. The whole tenor of the institution is too optimistic to reflect exilic or postexilic reforms, which were pessimistic attempts at immediate change. Neufeld ("Yobel," 53) believes common lands were redistributed every seven years (fallow year). Jubilee was performed only once during the reform of Jehu, king of Israel, after the overthrow of the Omride dynasty in 840 B.C.

77. Klostermann, 723–42; Mahler, 109; Zeitlin, "Notes," 354 (all cited in North, *Jubilee*, 125); Zeitlin, "Stages," 6ff.; idem, *State*, I, 216; Hoenig, 222, 229–36; Morgenstern, "Jubilee," 1001–2; Wenham, 318.

78. Leviticus says that the jubilee is introduced by a horn blast in the seventh month. This might be a reference to the civil calendar. The Israelite religious calendar began in the fall, but the civil calendar after the exile began in the spring. The reference to the seventh month would be a civil calendar reference to a fall month, the time when this theory posits the occurrence of the intercalary year. A civil calendar reference is used because the religious calendar is the one dislocated by the forty-nine days. Hoenig (229–36) believes the Book of Jubilees tried to restore the old calendar.

79. Weber, "Agrarverhältnisse," 87; Menes, 81; Weil, 171 (all cited and discussed in North, *Jubilee*, 173–88).

80. Von Rad, *Deuteronomy*, 151; Snaith, *Leviticus*, 130; Phillips, *Deuteronomy*, 163; Rushdoony, 505; Boecker, 184.

81. S. Driver, *Deuteronomy*, 199; von Rad, *Deuteronomy*, 114; Phillips, *Deuteronomy*, 115–16. However, Wright ("Deuteronomy," 436) believes it refers to local elders in villages.

82. Rylaarsdam, 1007; Kramer, 84; Hyatt, *Exodus*, 243; Phillips, *Deuteronomy*, 165–66.

83. Weber, *Judaism*, 32–36; Rylaarsdam, 1007; North, *Jubilee*, 74–75; de Vaux, *Israel*, 75; Loewenstamm, "Law," 249–50; Boecker, 203.

84. Habel (13–118) outlines the nature of this religious conflict very effectively. See also Heaton, 44–55.

85. Gaster, 124–29; Kapelrud, 45–46. Gordon (*Ugaritic*, 3–5) and M.D. Coogan (84–85) believe it refers to a period of years. G. Driver (*Myths*, 20–21) believes the cycle merely recounts how Baal replaced El as the chief deity in the pantheon.

86. Hyatt, *Religion*, 61–62; Mendenhall, "Conquest," 100–120; idem, *Generation*, 23; Mendelsohn, "Society," 42–43; Pixley, 32–33; Brueggemann, *Land*, 65; Frick, 57–59, 91–94; Dietrich, 16–20; Gottwald, *Tribes*, 388–409.

87. Brueggemann, *Land*, 65; Frick, 57–59, 91–94; Matthews, 179–81 and passim.

88. Rowton, "Autonomy," 201–15; idem, " 'Apirû," 13–20; idem, "Parasocial," 181–98; Matthews, 17–29, 179–81.

89. Hyatt, *Religion*, 61–62; Weber, *Judaism*, xvii, 5–10, 206; Heaton, 48–51; Scott, *Prophets*, 18–33; Dietrich, 14–20.

90. Hyatt, *Religion,* 61-62; Weber, *Judaism,* 254; Noth, *History,* 142; Frick, 205-7; Dietrich, 21-31; Ahlström, "Israelites," 133-38.

91. Alt, "Settlement," 173-221; idem, "Erwägungen," I, 126-74; Noth, *History,* 53-84; Weippert, 5-46, 102-26; Herrmann, 86-111; Aharoni, "Nothing," 55-76.

92. Albright, "Archaeology," 10-18; idem, "Light," 22-26; idem, "Conquest," 11-23; idem, *Period,* 24-34; Wright, "Joshua," 105-11; idem, *Archaeology,* 69-85; Bright, *History,* 110-27; Aharoni, *Land,* 200-229 (which represents his earlier position, before archeological work in the Negev [see n. 91, above]). Weippert (46-55, 126-44) summarizes and responds to this position.

93. Noth, "Beitrag," 262-82; Pritchard, 313-24; de Vaux, "Archaeology," 64-80; Weippert, 46-55; Gottwald, *Tribes,* 192-203. The Albright reconstruction of Israelite history has been criticized in other areas as well; its views on the patriarchal era have come under increasing criticism: see T. Thompson, 1-330; Van Seters, 1-312.

94. Rowton, " 'Apirû," 13-20; idem, "Parasocial," 182, 193-98; Frick, 199.

95. Astour, 6-17; Mendenhall, "Conquest," 66-86 (100-120); idem, *Generation,* 1-226; idem, "Organization," 132-51; idem, "Migration," 135-43; Luke, 35-38, 272-75; McKenzie, 76-120; Glock, 558-605; Gottwald, "Nomads," 223-55; idem, "Domain," 89-100; idem, *Tribes,* 210-19, 389-587; Dus, 26-41; de Geus, 120-92; Frick, 186-200; Ahlström, "Moses," 65-69; Bright, *History,* 3rd ed., 129-43 (where he modifies his earlier position taken in the 1st edition [1959] in which he advanced an Albright viewpoint). Weippert (55-102) summarizes and responds to this position.

96. Weber, *Judaism,* 338-39; Frick, 186-200. Milgrom (169-76) incorrectly concludes that there was no early conversion of Canaanites, because he assumes that the xenophobia of later exilic texts is a reflection of attitudes at an early period.

97. Matthews, 83, 158; Marfoe, 33; Ahlström, "Israelites," 133-34.

98. Pedersen, I, 81-83; Weber, *Judaism,* 71; North, *Jubilee,* 158-63; R. Avila, 22.

99. Ring, 50, 71 (quoted in North, *Jubilee,* 49); Hyatt, *Religion,* 61-62; de Vaux, *Israel,* 164; Loewenstamm, "Law," 235, 239; Kaiser, 65-66; Boecker, 89.

100. Elliger, 356; Frick, 86-91; Pixley, 32-33; Boecker, 92.

101. Kübel, 28; Fenton, "Tenure," 498; Verinder, 16; Mitchell, 266; Schaeffer, *passim*; Lurje, 5; Kirschner, 506; Kennett, 76 (quoted by North, *Jubilee,* 161-65, 170-71, who gives an excellent discussion of this issue); Scott, *Prophets,* 20-29; Kippenberg, 30-31.

102. Fenton, *Life,* 64-80; S. Driver, *Deuteronomy,* 177; North, *Jubilee,* 200; Mayes, 246; Kaiser, 65-66.

103. Fenton, *Life,* 22-26; Damaschke, 8 (quoted by North, *Jubilee,* 172) (Damaschke believes the Tenth Commandment, on coveting, was designed to undergird this special system of land tenure); Weber, *Judaism,* 70-74; Fohrer, *Elia,* 79; Porter, 201; Scott, *Prophets,* 23, 31; Pixley, 33-35; R. Avila, 22.

104. Buhl, *Verhältnisse,* 56-62; idem, "Institutions," 738 (quoted in North, *Jubilee,* 212, as affirming the coexistence of communal and private property). Pedersen (I, 85) and North (*Jubilee,* 212) point out that familial ownership cannot be communistic by definition: modern communism is really state ownership, and early Israel disavowed that system. Hyatt (*Exodus,* 247) believes private ownership was the rule, but

there may have been communal cultivation of particular portions of the land.

105. Pedersen, I, 85-88; Hyatt, *Religion,* 63; Weber, *Judaism,* xvii-xviii; Noth, *History,* 217; de Vaux, *Israel,* 73; Gelin, 16-17; Heaton, 21-29; Mendenhall, *Generation,* 208-9; idem, "Monarchy," 157; Scott, *Prophets,* 30-33; Brueggemann, *Land,* 100; idem, *Imagination,* 28-43; Boecker, 93; Davisson and Harper, 79-85.

106. Mendenhall, "Monarchy," 162-69; Dietrich, 32-117; Ahlström, "Israelites," 135-36.

107. De Vaux, *Israel,* 140-42; Heaton, 30-31; Mendelsohn, "Society," 41; Pixley, 44-45.

108. Alt, "Gaue," 76-89; de Vaux, *Israel,* 140-42; Halpern, 529; Brueggemann, *Land,* 85-88; Gottwald, *Tribes,* 368-71; Aharoni, *Land,* 309-17.

109. Fenton, *Life,* 70; de Vaux, *Israel,* 124-25; Andersen, 47-48; Heaton, 21-29, 32, 34-42; Croatto, 42.

110. Weber, *Judaism,* 101; Mendenhall, "Monarchy," 162; Dietrich, 40-51; Ahlström, "Israelites," 134-36.

111. Gray, *History,* 91-96; idem, "Vestibule," 365-78; idem, "Temple," 872-74; Frank, *Bible,* 144-46.

112. Weber, *Judaism,* 202; Heaton, 51-55; Mendelsohn, "Slavery," 140; Brueggemann, *Land,* 28-43; Gottwald, *Tribes,* 371; R. Avila, 50-51.

113. Dietrich (52-117) attempts the most detailed analysis of this fluctuating policy among the royal houses. Though his work is conjectural at many points, his analysis of each king in Israel and Judah is interesting and illuminating. His theory is as follows: Jeroboam (922-901 B.C.) and Baasha (900-877 B.C.) of Israel were Yahwists, but the Canaanite party was strong and created instability. The civil war between Zimri (Canaanite) and Tibni (Israelite) saw the ultimate rise of Omri (876-869 B.C.), who initially was neutral, but his successors—Ahab (869-850 B.C.), Ahaziah (850-849 B.C.), and Jehoram (849-842 B.C.)—moved to a Canaanite position. In Judah at this time Jehoshaphat (873-849 B.C.) was pro-Canaanite because his successors—Joram (849-842 B.C.) and Ahaziah (842 B.C.)—were allied with the Omrides. The Canaanite queens Jezebel in Israel and Athaliah in Judah (842-837 B.C.) were ousted by pro-Yahweh kings, Jehu in Israel (842-815 B.C.) and Jehoash (837-800 B.C.) in Judah. The Jehu dynasty in Israel gradually compromised with Canaanite culture until Jeroboam II (786-746 B.C.), who was thoroughly Canaanite. In Judah Jehoash was assassinated and replaced by pro-Canaanite Amaziah (800-783 B.C.) and Azariah (783-742 B.C.). In the declining days of Israel there was fluctuation between Canaanite advocates such as Shallum (745 B.C.) and Pekah (737-732 B.C.) on the one hand, and Yahwists such as Zechariah (746-745 B.C.), Menahem (745-738 B.C.), and Pekahiah (738-737 B.C.) on the other. Though prophets tried to remain neutral in the political struggle between Yahwistic "elders" and Canaanite "officers," they favored the former, and they even favored foreign powers who could overthrow their own "Canaanitized" kings (Hos. 8). In Judah the Yahwist Hezekiah (715-687 B.C.) sought to reverse the policy of pro-Canaanite kings before him, Jotham (742-735 B.C.) and Ahaz (735-715 B.C.). His revolt failed and he was replaced by pro-Canaanite Manasseh (687-642 B.C.) and Amon (642-640 B.C.), who allowed Judah to be vassal to Assyria. "People of the land" assassinated Amon and put the pro-Yahwist reformer Josiah (640-609 B.C.) on the throne. His death at Megiddo devastated the Yahwist reform movement, and the final kings of Judah—Jehoiakim (609-598 B.C.) and Zedekiah (597-587 B.C.)—were pro-Canaanite as the opposition of Jeremiah indicates.

(Throughout it should be noted that Israel had dynastic changes with many of these fluctuations, whereas the same Davidic family stayed on the throne in Judah; the various members of the family were simply swayed by one of the two parties in the court.)

114. Noth, "Krongut," 211-13, 230-31; Alt, "Fragen," 309; de Vaux, *Israel,* 137; Mazar, 134; Gray, *Kings,* 331-32.

115. Loud, 1-2, 10, and passim; Crowfoot et al., I, 5-20; II, 49-53; III, 94-96; Kenyon, 74.

116. Alt, "Samaria," 258-302; idem, "Monarchy," 321-24; Fohrer, *Elia,* 74-77; Herrmann, 206-9.

117. Frost, 510-14; Andersen, 50 (he notes that Jezebel was like a Canaanite queen in that she owned land and had followers in the court who paid her tribute—2 Kings 10:11); Mendenhall, "Monarchy," 164-65.

118. Parrot (29) relates that many potsherds from Samaria indicate that Yahweh was a common name among the people, which points up the failure of the Omride movement to take complete control of the popular mind. See also MacLean, 601; Dietrich, 66.

119. Montgomery, 332; Napier, "Omrides," 366-78; Fohrer, *Elia,* 63; Gray, *Kings,* 435-38; Robinson, 237, 240; Seebass, 474-88.

120. Andersen (49) states that even among Canaanites the sale of land was more difficult than in Mesopotamia. At Mari and Ugarit the purchase of land could occur only under a fictitious adoption of the buyer by the seller, or as a gift exchange. Tribalism among West-Semitic peoples caused this reticence. Thus Ahab had to offer Naboth the "gift" of another vineyard or good value in silver.

121. Hyatt, *Religion,* 61-62; Snaith, "Kings," 173; idem, *Leviticus,* 163-64; Fohrer, *Elia,* 79; Heaton, 34-42; Gray, *Kings,* 439; Kaiser, 65-66; Robinson, 236; Scott, *Prophets,* 29; Brueggemann, *Land,* 93-94.

122. Napier, "Omrides," 366-78; Mauchline, "Kings," 347; Baltzer, 73-88; Fohrer, *Elia,* 79-80; Gray, *Kings,* 435; Robinson, 235; Welten, 18-32; Herrmann, 212; Brueggemann, *Land,* 93-94; Frick, 109. Hammershaimb (95-96) goes against the prevailing consensus maintained by other scholars, for he thinks Naboth held to his land due to a Canaanite tradition and that is why Ahab respected him; thus Naboth's reticence only represents the typical West-Semitic attitude mentioned previously.

123. Montgomery, 331; Frost, 508; Fohrer, *Elia,* 26-27; Gray, *Kings,* 440-41.

124. Gray (*Kings,* 440-41) and Seebass (474-88) think Naboth's reply was misconstrued as a curse; Andersen (52-55) thinks that falsified documents led to Naboth's being found guilty; Beek (27-28) proposes the hypothesis of a vicarious sacrifice.

125. Hammershaimb (96) and Seebass (474-88) believe that property belonging to someone found guilty of a capital offense went to the crown; de Vaux (*Israel,* 55) calls it simple confiscation; Fohrer (*Elia,* 25), Dietrich (65-66), and Wifall (91-92) believe this to be an example of Canaanite business practices applied by brute force; Andersen (46-57) thinks the property went to Ahab because of forged documents.

126. Hyatt, *Religion,* 62; Weber, *Judaism,* xviii-xix; Wolfe, 910-11; de Vaux, *Israel,* 167; Heaton, 41; Mays, *Amos,* 94; idem, *Micah,* 64; McKeating, 165; Dietrich, 87-91; Wenham, 317. A totally different assessment is given by the recent work of Morris Silver (1-251), who believes that Israelite peasants willingly sold their land because land consolidation created a better economy and benefits for everyone. He

postulates that Israelite economic life was improving up to 750 B.C. because of a free market economy. This healthy economy was destroyed by idealistic intellectuals, the prophets, who were advisors to kings and spokesmen in the cult. The powerful and elite prophets caused social reform movements by their exaggerated cry for social justice. The result was three disastrous social reforms under kings Jeroboam II of Israel (751 B.C.), Hezekiah of Judah (716–715 B.C.), and Josiah of Judah (621 B.C.), which destroyed the economy and led to the downfall of both the states of Israel and Judah. His theory is bizarre, and it has serious flaws: (1) He offers little concrete evidence for his theory, especially for the supposed reform of Jeroboam II, who was the target of prophetic criticism. (2) He naively ignores the dynamics of the interplay between merchants and peasants, especially the prophetic references to dishonest weights and manipulative grain-selling tactics, which explain how a few rich people could impoverish many peasants. (3) Economic historians in general would not call Israel's economy a free market economy. But Silver brazenly dismisses their views as the opinions of "marxist idealists." In turn his evidence for a free market economy is very superficial, and he often interprets ambiguous and sometimes outdated archeological evidence in a very subjective fashion. (4) His assessment of the prophets is based on outdated and idiosyncratic scholarship, especially when he views prophets as cultic priests. To call them powerful and elite members of society is absurd in view of the traditions about their rejection and persecution (consider Jeremiah). (5) His declaration that Deuteronomy was not reflective of traditional Yahwism, but that the syncretism attacked by the prophets was the authentic Yahwist faith is a bold statement. However, he does not defend this argument; he merely states it, and then uses it to undergird his general thesis. Such a procedure is weak scholarship. Unfortunately Silver's work will be used by those who seek to blunt the message of social reformers today by declaring that the prophets were intellectual losers who caused the downfall of society by their own power politics. In reality, prophets pointed the finger at those who destroyed society, but too few people listened.

127. Hyatt, *Religion,* 61–68; Weber, *Judaism,* xxi–xxii, 277–79; Heaton, 37–42, 55–59; Scott, *Prophets,* 171–92; Anderson, 40–45. Humbert (97–118) and Causse (53ff.) believe the prophets were anti-Canaanite and opposed to the culture of settled civilization.

128. Hammershaimb (79–94) believes the prophets inherited their ideals from other parts of the ancient Near East. Fensham ("Widow," 129–34) points out that kings such as Urukagina, Ur-Nammu, and Hammurabi in Babylon boast of protecting the weak.

129. Weber, *Judaism,* 370; Fensham, "Widow," 138; Noth, *Leviticus,* 46; Greengus, 536; Pixley, 48.

130. Harper, 49; Fosbroke, 786–87; Mays, *Amos,* 45; McKeating, 22–23; Wolff, 165.

131. Fosbroke, 840; Mays, *Amos,* 142–44; Wolff, 327.

132. Mauchline, 698–99; Mays, *Hosea,* 165–76; McKeating, 144.

133. Wolfe, 910–11, 914; Alt, "Micah," 373–81; Heaton, 41; McKeating, 164–65; Mays, *Micah,* 64, 71.

134. Scott, "Isaiah," 199; Kaiser, 20, 65–66; Clements, 35, 62.

135. Harper, 186; Bright, *Jeremiah,* 141–42; J. Thompson, 478; Gunneweg and Schmithals, 83–86.

136. S. Driver, *Deuteronomy,* 234; Wright, "Deuteronomy," 453; Craigie, 268; Mayes, 288.

137. Mowinckel, I, 227–29; II, 1–8; Westermann, *Psalms,* 64–67; idem, *Praise,* 188–94.

138. S. Driver, "Poor," IV, 19–20; Gelin, 34–44; Hengel, 19.

139. Gelin, 57–59; Snaith, *Ecclesiasticus,* 169 (he calls these examples of common injustices); L. Johnson, *Sharing,* 99.

140. Fenton, *Matthew,* 80; Gelin, 66–74; Keck, "Poor," 66; Hengel, 19; L. Johnson, *Sharing,* 127.

141. Loeb, 1–42, 161–206, esp. 179; S. Driver, "Poor," 19–20; Danker, 81; Gelin, 26–55, 108–14 (he offers the best description of this development in terms of spiritual categories); Hengel, 19; Dibelius, 42, 87, 137–39; Osiek, 16–17. Only a few writers maintain that the literal meaning of these terms refers to the economic categories of rich and poor (e.g., Miranda, *Communism,* 22–48), but such interpretation ignores the entire postexilic development (which moves in a religious-spiritual direction) as well as the actual context from which many of the passages are taken.

142. Fenton, *Matthew,* 80; Gelin, 27–34; Danker, 81; Dibelius, 39.

143. Dupont, *Béatitudes,* 291–95; Nineham, 271; Danker, 81; Dibelius, 40.

144. Gelin, 105; R. Williams, 131–32; Hengel, 26–27; Dibelius, 41–42.

145. Miranda (*Communism,* 18–56) would call Jesus a communist and a revolutionary against the socio-economic structures of his day, but the more balanced view is advocated by the majority of scholars, including Hyatt (*Religion,* 67–68), Gelin (102–4), and Hengel (27–30).

146. Gilmour, 118; Caird, 102; Schweizer, *Matthew,* 80–85.

147. Luccock, 804; Gilmour, 314–15; Taylor, 429; Nineham, 271; Schweizer, *Mark,* 212–15; idem, *Matthew,* 388; Lane, 367. But Miranda (*Communism,* 18) takes this literally for all Christians and understands it as an imperative to be a communist.

148. S. Johnson, 486; Gilmour, 315; Taylor, 431; Fenton, *Matthew,* 316; Schweizer, *Mark,* 213–14; Danker, 188; Grant, 97.

149. Luccock, 807; Taylor, 431; Fenton, *Matthew,* 316; Lane, 369.

150. S. Johnson, 486; Taylor, 430; Nineham, 271.

151. Gilmour, 230–31; Danker, 152–53; Karris, "Poor," 120–21.

152. Dupont, *Béatitudes,* 107–13; Caird, 188; Karris, "Poor," 196; L. Johnson, *Sharing,* 17–18.

153. R. Williams, 131–32; Adamson, 29–31, 182–90; Dibelius, 235–40; Kügelman, 54–57; Laws, 7–10, 194–208.

154. Keck ("Poor," 116–17) and Hengel (47–48) believe he is attacking the Palestinian latifundia system; but Dibelius (39, 44) thinks he merely inherited old prophetic elements that he dispassionately included.

155. Dibelius (87, 137–39) believes the categories of rich/evil and good/poor apply to non-Jews as well as Jews; but Miranda (*Communism,* 55) sees this passage as an attack on all wealthy persons and any profit-making transaction.

156. Keck, "Testament," 100–129; Dahl, 31–32; L. Johnson, *Sharing,* 112–13.

157. Bailey, 336–37; Hengel, 35; Reese, 106–7.

158. MacGregor, 73; C. Williams, 71–72; Haenchen, 233–35; Rushdoony, 451; Hengel, 31–34; Dibelius, 43; Grant, 100–101; White, 128; L. Johnson, *Sharing,* 21–22; Krodel, 25.

159. Haenchen, 233; Hengel, 8–9; Grant, 100; Mealand, 96–99; L. Johnson, *Func-*

tion, 5; idem, *Sharing,* 119–30 (he offers the best discussion of this issue); Karris, *Acts,* 64–65; idem, "Poor," 116–17; Crowe, 29–30; Dupont, *Salvation,* 85–102.

160. C. Avila (14–32) provides the best description of this system and its origin.

161. Julian, "Epistle," 84a, Loeb Classical Library, quoted in John Gager, *Kingdom and Community: The Social World of Early Christianity,* Prentice-Hall Studies in Religion Series, Englewood Cliffs, N.J., Prentice-Hall, 1975, 130–31.

162. Decarreaux, 39–116, 214–368; Lacarriere, 21–221; Chitty, 1–181; Knowles, 9–244.

Works Cited

Adamson, James, *The Epistles of James,* NICNT, Grand Rapids, Eerdmans, 1976.

Aharoni, Yohanan, *The Land of the Bible: A Historical Geography,* Philadelphia, Westminster, rev. ed., 1979.

——, "Nothing Early and Nothing Late: Re-Writing Israel's Conquest," BA 39 (1976).

Ahlström, Goesta, "Another Moses Tradition," JNES 39 (1980).

——, "Where Did the Israelites Live?," JNES 41 (1982).

Albright, William F., *The Archaeology of Palestine,* Baltimore, Penguin, 1949.

——, "Archaeology and the Date of the Hebrew Conquest of Palestine," BASOR 58 (1935).

——, *The Biblical Period from Abraham to Ezra,* New York, Harper & Row, 1963.

——, "Further Light on the History of Israel from Lachish and Megiddo," BASOR 68 (1937).

——, "The Israelite Conquest of Canaan in the Light of Archaeology," BASOR 74 (1939).

Alt, Albrecht, "Archäologische Fragen zur Baugeschichte von Jerusalem und Samaria in der israelitischen Königszeit," *Kleine Schriften,* III.

——, "Erwägungen über die Landnahme der Israeliten in Palästina," *Kleine Schriften,* I.

——, *Essays on Old Testament History and Religion,* Garden City, N.Y., Doubleday, 1966.

——, "Israels Gaue unter Salomo," *Kleine Schriften,* II.

——, *Kleine Schriften zur Geschichte des Volkes Israel,* Munich, Beck, 3 vols., 1953.

——, "Micah 2, 1-5," *Kleine Schriften.* III.

——, "The Monarchy in the Kingdoms of Israel and Judah," in *Essays.*

——, "The Origins of Israelite Law," in *Essays.*

——, "Die Phönikischen Inschriften von Karatepe," WO 1 (1947-1952).

——, "The Settlement of the Israelites in Palestine," in *Essays.*

——, "Der Stadtstaat Samaria," *Kleine Schriften,* III.

——, "Das Verbot des Diebstahls im Dekalog," *Klein Schriften,* I.

Andersen, Francis, "The Socio-Juridical Background of the Naboth Incident," JBL 85 (1966).

Anderson, Bernhard, *The Eighth Century Prophets: Amos, Hosea, Isaiah, Micah,* Proclamation Commentaries, Philadelphia, Fortress, 1978.

Astour, Michael, "The Amarna Age Forerunners of Biblical Anti-Royalism," in *For Max Weinrich on His Seventieth Birthday: Studies in Jewish Languages, Literature, and Society,* ed. L. S. Davidowicz, et al., Mouton, 1964.

Avila, Charles, *Ownership: Early Christian Teaching,* Maryknoll, N.Y., Orbis, 1983.

Avila, Rafael, *Worship and Politics,* Maryknoll, N.Y., Orbis, 1981.

Bailey, John, "II Thessalonians," IB, vol. 9.

Baltzer, Klaus, "Naboths Weinberg (I Kön. 21). Der Konflikt zwischen israelitischen und kanaanäischen Bodensrecht," *Wort und Dienst,* Jahrbuch der Theologischen Schule Bethel (new ser.) 8 (1965).

Barr, James, *The Scope and Authority of the Bible,* Philadelphia, Westminster, 1980.

Beek, Martinus. "Der Ersatzkönig in der altisraelitischen Literatur," *Congress Volume (Geneva, 1965);* VTS, vol. 15, Leiden, Brill, 1966.

Boecker, Hans Jochen, *Law and Administration of Justice in the Old Testament and Ancient East,* Minneapolis, Augsburg, 1980.

Bright, John, *The History of Israel,* Philadelphia, Westminster, 3rd ed., 1981.

———, *Jeremiah,* AB, vol. 21, Garden City, N.Y., Doubleday, 1965.

Brueggemann, Walter, *The Land,* OBT, vol. 1, Philadelphia, Fortress, 1977.

———, *The Prophetic Imagination,* Philadelphia, Fortress, 1978.

Buhl, Frantz, "Social Institutions of the Israelites," *American Journal of Theology,* 1 (1897).

———, *Die sozialen Verhältnisse der Israeliten,* Berlin, 1899.

Buttrick, George A., ed., *Interpreter's Bible,* Nashville, Abingdon, 12 vols., 1951-1957.

———, ed., *Interpreter's Dictionary of the Bible,* Nashville, Abingdon, 4 vols., 1962.

Caird, George, *The Gospel of St. Luke,* Pelican Commentaries, Baltimore, Pelican, 1963.

Carney, T. F., *The Economics of Antiquity: Controls, Gifts and Trade,* Lawrence, Kan., Coronado, 1973

Campbell, Edward, and Freedman, David, *Biblical Archaeologist Review,* Garden City, N.Y., Doubleday, 3 vols., 1961-1970.

Causse, Antonin, *Les pauvres d'Israël,* Paris, 1922.

Cazelles, Henri, *Etudes sur le Code de l'Alliance,* Paris, Gabalda, 1946.

Childs, Brevard, *The Book of Exodus,* OTL, Philadelphia, Westminster, 1974.

Chitty, Derwas, *The Desert a City,* Crestwood, N.Y., St. Vladimirs, 1966.

Clements, Ronald, *Isaiah 1-39,* NCB, Grand Rapids, Eerdmans, 1980.

Cohen, Boaz, "Antichresis in Jewish and Roman Law," in *Alexander Marx Jubilee Volume,* ed. Saul Liberman, New York, KTAV 1950.

Cohn, Norman, *The Pursuit of the Millennium,* New York, Oxford University Press, rev. ed., 1970.

Coogan, Michael D., *Stories from Ancient Canaan,* Philadelphia, Westminster, 1978.

Coogan, Morton, *Imperialism and Religion: Assyria, Judah, and Israel in the Eighth and Seventh Centuries B.C.E.,* SBLMS, vol. 19, Missoula, Mont., Scholars Press, 1974.

Craigie, Peter, *The Book of Deuteronomy,* NICOT, Grand Rapids, Eerdmans, 1976.

Crim, Keith, ed., *Interpreter's Dictionary of the Bible, Supplement,* Nashville, Abingdon, 1976.

Croatto, Severino, *Exodus: A Hermeneutic of Freedom,* Maryknoll, N.Y., Orbis, 1981.

Crowe, Jerome, *The Acts,* NTM, vol. 18, Wilmington, Glazier, 1979.

Crowfoot, John W., et al., *Sebaste: Reports of the Work of the Joint Expedition in 1931-1933 and of the British Expedition in 1935,* London, Palestine Exploration Fund, vol. 1, 1938; vol. 2, 1942; vol. 3, 1957.

Dahl, Nils Alstrup, "Paul and Possessions," in *Studies in Paul: Theology for the Early Christian Mission,* Minneapolis, Augsburg, 1977.

Damaschke, Adolph, *Geschichte der Nationalökonomie,* Jena, 1929.

Danker, Frederick, *Jesus and the New Age according to St. Luke,* St. Louis, Clayton, 1972.

Daube, David, *Studies in Biblical Law,* New York, KTAV, 1969.

Davisson, William, and Harper, James, *European Economic History,* vol. 1: *The Ancient World,* New York, Appleton-Century-Crofts, 1972.

Decarreaux, Jean, *Monks and Civilization: From the Barbarian Invasions to the Reign of Charlemagne,* Garden City, N.Y., Doubleday, 1964.

de Geus, C.H.J., *The Tribes of Israel,* Studia Semitica Neederlandica, vol. 18, Amsterdam, Van Gorcum, 1976.

Dibelius, Martin, *James,* Herm, Philadelphia, Fortress, 1976.

Dietrich, Walter, *Israel und Kanaan: Vom Ringen zweier Gesellschaftssysteme,* Stuttgarter Bibelstudien, vol. 94, Stuttgart, Katholisches Bibelwerk, 1979.

Driver, Godfrey R., *Canaanite Myths and Legends,* Old Testament Studies, vol. 3, Edinburgh, Clark, 1956.

———, and Miles, John, eds., *The Babylonian Laws,* vol. 1: *Legal Commentary,* Oxford University Press, 1952.

Driver, Samuel R., *Deuteronomy,* ICC, Edinburgh, Clark, 3rd ed., 1902.

———, "Poor," in *A Dictionary of the Bible,* James Hastings, ed., New York, Scribner's, 1903.

Dupont, Jacques, *Les Béatitudes,* Louvain, Nauvelaerts, 1958.

———, "Community of Goods in the Early Church," in *The Salvation of the Gentiles: Studies in the Acts of the Apostles,* New York, Paulist, 1979.

Dus, Jan, "Moses or Joshua? On the Problem of the Founder of the Israelite Religion," *Radical Religion* 2 (1975).

Edwards, Chilperic, *The Hammurabi Code and the Sinaitic Legislation,* Port Washington, N.Y., Kennikat, 1904.

Ehrhardt, Arnold, *The Acts of the Apostles,* Manchester University Press, 1969.

Eichrodt, Walter, *Theology of the Old Testament,* Philadelphia, Westminster, 2 vols., 1961.

Elliger, Karl, *Leviticus,* HAT, vol. 4, Tübingen, Mohr, 1966.

Falk, Zeev, "Exodus xxi 6," VT 9 (1959).

Fensham, Charles, "New Light on Exodus 21:6 and 22:7 from the Laws of Eshnunna," JBL 78 (1959).

———, "Widow, Orphan, and the Poor in Ancient Near Eastern Legal Literature," JNES 21 (1962) (= *Studies in Ancient Israelite Wisdom,* James L. Crenshaw, ed., New York, KTAV, 1976).

Fenton, John, *Early Hebrew Life: A Study in Sociology,* London, Trubner, 1880.

———, *Gospel of St. Matthew,* Pelican Commentaries, Baltimore, Pelican, 1963.

———, "The Primitive Land Tenure," *Theological Review* 14 (1877).

Finkelstein, Jacob J., "Ammi-saduqa's Edict and the Babylonian 'Law Codes,' " *Journal of Cuneiform Studies* 15 (1961).

———, "Some New Mishnarum Material and Its Implications," in *Studies in Honor of Benno Landsberger on his Seventy-fifth Birthday, April 21, 1965,* Oriental Institute of the University of Chicago Assyriological Studies, vol. 16, Chicago University Press, 1965.

Fohrer, Georg, *Elia,* Abhandlungen zur Theologie des Alten und Neuen Testaments, vol. 53, Zurich, Zwingli, 1968.

————, "Das sogenannte apodiktisch formulierte Recht und der Dekalog," KD 11 (1965).

Fosbroke, Hughell, "Amos," IB, vol. 6.

Frank, Henry, *Bible, Archaeology, and Faith,* Nashville, Abingdon, 1971.

Frick, Frank, *The City in Ancient Israel,* SBLDS, vol. 36, Missoula, Mont., Scholars Press, 1977.

Frost, Stanley, "Judgment on Jezebel, or a Woman Wronged," *Theology Today* 20 (1963-64).

Gamoran, Hillel, "The Biblical Law against Loans on Interest," JNES 30 (1971).

Gaster, Theodor, *Thespis: Ritual, Myth, and Drama in the Ancient Near East,* Garden City, N.Y., Doubleday, 2nd rev. ed., 1961.

Gelin, Albert, *The Poor of Yahweh,* Collegeville, Minn., Liturgical Press, 1964.

Gerstenberger, Erhard, *Wesen und Herkunft des "Apodiktischen Rechts,"* WMANT, vol. 20, Neukirchen, Neukirchener Verlag, 1965.

Gervitz, Stanley, "West-Semitic Curses and the Problem of the Origins of Hebrew Law," VT 11 (1961).

Gese, Hartmut, "Beobachtungen zum stil alttestamentlicher Rechtssätze, TLZ 85 (1960).

Gilmour, MacLean, "Luke," IB, vol. 8.

Ginzberg, Eli, "Studies in the Economics of the Bible," JQR 22 (1932).

Glock, Albert, "Early Israel as the Kingdom of Yahweh: The Influence of Archaeological Evidence on the Reconstruction of Religion in Early Israel," *Concordia Theological Monthly* 41 (1970).

Gordon, Cyrus, "Cultural and Religious Life," WHJP, vol. 3.

————, "Parallèles nouziens aux lois et coutumes de l'Ancien Testament," RB 44 (1935).

————, *Ugaritic Literature,* Rome, Pontifical Biblical Institute, 1949.

Gottwald, Norman, "Domain Assumptions and Societal Models in the Study of Pre-Monarchic Israel," *Congress Volume (Edinburgh, 1974)*; VTS, vol. 28, Leiden, Brill, 1975.

————, *The Tribes of Yahweh: A Sociology of the Religion of Liberated Israel, 1250-1050 B.C.E.,* Maryknoll, N.Y., Orbis, 1979.

————, "Were the Israelites Pastoral Nomads?," in Jackson and Kessler, *Rhetorical Criticism.*

Grant, Robert, *Early Christianity and Society,* San Francisco, Harper & Row, 1977.

Gray, John, *I and II Kings,* OTL, Philadelphia, Westminster, 2nd rev. ed., 1970.

————, *A History of Jerusalem,* New York, Praeger, 1969.

————, *The KRT Text in the Literature of Ras Shamra: A Social Myth of Ancient Canaan,* Documenta et Monumenta Orientis Antiqui, vol. 5, Leiden, Brill, 1964.

————, "The Temple of Solomon," IDBS.

————, "Le vestibule du temple de Salomon était-il un bît halâni?," RB 78 (1969).

Greenberg, Moshe, "Crimes and Punishment," IDB, vol. 1.

Greengus, Samuel, "Law in the Old Testament," IDBS.

Gunneweg, Antonius, and Schmithals, Walter, *Authority,* Biblical Encounters Series, Nashville, Abingdon, 1982.

Habel, Norman, *Yahweh versus Baal: A Conflict of Religious Cultures,* New York, Bookman, 1964.

Haenchen, Ernst, *The Acts of the Apostles,* Philadelphia, Westminster, 1971.

Halpern, Baruch, "Sectionalism and Schism," JBL 93 (1974).

Hamel, Edouard, *Les dix paroles: Perspectives bibliques,* Essais pour notre temps, vol. 7, Montreal, Bellarmin, 1969.

Hammershaimb, E., "On the Ethics of the Old Testament Prophets," *Congress Volume (Oxford, 1959);* VTS, vol. 7, Leiden, Brill, 1960.

Harper, William R., *Amos and Hosea,* ICC, Edinburgh, Clark, 1905.

Harrelson, Walter, "Law in the Old Testament," IDB, vol. 3.

————, *The Ten Commandments and Human Rights,* OBT, vol. 8, Philadelphia, Fortress, 1980.

Heaton, Eric W., *The Hebrew Kingdoms,* New Clarendon Bible, vol. 3, Oxford University Press, 1968.

Hempel, Johannes, *Das Ethos des Alten Testaments,* Berlin, Gruyter, 2nd ed., 1964.

Hengel, Martin, *Property and Riches in the Early Church: Aspects of a Social History of Early Christianity,* Philadelphia, Fortress, 1974.

Herrmann, Siegfried, *A History of Old Testament Times,* Philadelphia, Fortress, 1975.

Hoenig, Sidney, "Sabbatical Years and the Year of Jubilee," JQR 59 (1969).

Humbert, Paul, "Osée, le prophète bedouin, *Revue d'histoire et philosophie religieuses* 1 (1921).

Hyatt, James P., *Exodus,* NCB, London, Oliphants, 1971.

————, *Prophetic Religion,* Nashville, Abingdon, 1947.

Jackson, J., and Kessler, Martin, eds., *Rhetorical Criticism: Essays in Honor of James Muilenburg,* Pittsburgh, Pickwick, 1974.

Johnson, Luke T., *The Literary Function of Possessions in Luke-Acts,* SBLDS, vol. 39, Missoula, Mont., Scholars Press, 1977.

————, *Sharing Possessions: Mandate and Symbol of Faith,* OBT, vol. 9, Philadelphia, Fortress, 1981.

Johnson, Sherman, "Matthew," IB, vol. 7.

Kaiser, Otto, *Isaiah 1–12,* OTL, Philadelphia, Westminster, 1972.

Kapelrud, Arvin, *The Ras Shamra Discoveries and the Old Testament,* University of Oklahoma Press, 1963.

Karris, Robert, *Invitation to Acts,* Garden City, N.Y., Doubleday, 1978.

————, "Poor and Rich: The Lukan Sitz im Leben," in Charles Talbert, ed., *Perspectives on Luke-Acts,* Perspectives in Religious Studies, vol. 5, Danville, Va., Association of Baptist Professors of Religion, 1978.

Kautsky, John. *The Politics of Aristocratic Empires,* Chapel Hill, N.C., University of North Carolina, 1982.

Keck, Leander, "The Poor among the Saints in Jewish Christianity and Qumran," ZNW 57 (1966).

————, "The Poor among the Saints in the New Testament," ZNW 56 (1965).

Kennett, Robert, *Ancient Hebrew Social Life and Custom,* London, 1933.

Kenyon, Kathleen, *Royal Cities of the Old Testament,* New York, Schocken, 1971.

Kilian, Rudolf, "Apodiktisches und kasuistisches Recht im Licht ägyptischer Parallelen," BZ (new ser.) 7 (1963).

Kippenberg, Hans, *Religion und Klassenbildung im Antiken Judäa,* Studien zur Umwelt des Neuen Testaments, vol. 14, Göttingen, Vandenhoeck und Ruprecht, 1978.

Kirschner, Bruno, "Soziale Gesetzgebung der Juden in der Bibel," *Jüdisches Lexicon,* Berlin, 1930.

Klostermann, August, "Kalendarische Bedeutung des Jobeljahres," *Theologische Studien and Kritiken* 53 (1880).

Knowles, David, *Christian Monasticism,* New York, McGraw-Hill, 1969.

Kramer, Samuel N., *The Sumerians,* University of Chicago Press, 1963.

Krodel, Gerhard, *Acts,* Proclamation Commentaries, Philadelphia, Fortress, 1981.

Kübel, Franz, *Soziale und wirtschaftliche Gesetzgebung des Alten Testaments,* Wiesbaden, 1970.

Kügelman, James, *James and Jude,* NTM, vol. 19, Wilmington, Glazier, 1980.

Lacarriere, Jacques, *Men Possessed by God: The Story of the Desert Monks of Ancient Christianity,* Garden City, Doubleday, 1964.

Lane, William, *The Gospel according to Mark,* NICNT, Grand Rapids, Eerdmans, 1974.

Laws, Sophie, *The Epistle of James,* Harper's New Testament Commentaries, New York, Harper & Row, 1980.

Lewy, Hildegard, "The Biblical Institution of Deror in the Light of Akkadian Documents," *Eretz-Israel* 5 (1958).

Loeb, Isidore, "La littérature des pauvres dans la Bible," *Revue des études juives* 20 (1890).

Loewenstamm, Samuel, "Law," in WHJP, vol 3.

———, "Neshek and m/tarbith," JBL 88 (1969).

Loretz, Otto, "Ex 21, 6; 22, 8 und angebliche Nuzi-Parallelen," Bib 41 (1960).

Loud, Gordon, *The Megiddo Ivories,* University of Chicago Oriental Institute Publications, vol. 8, University of Chicago Press, 1939.

Lovejoy, Arthur, "The Communism of Saint Ambrose," JHI 3 (1942).

Luccock, Halford, "Mark: Exposition," IB, vol. 7.

Luke, J.T., "Pastoralism and Politics in the Mari Period: A Re-examination of the Character and Political Significance of the Major West Semitic Tribal Groups on the Middle Euphrates, ca. 1828–1758 B.C.," diss., University of Michigan, 1965.

Lurje, M., "Studien zur Geschichte der wirtschaftlichen und Sozialen Verhältnisse im israelitischen-jüdischen Reiche," BZAW, vol. 45 (1927).

Luther, Martin, "The Large Catechism," in Theodore Tappert, ed., *Book of Concord,* Philadelphia, Fortress, 1959.

MacGregor, G.H.C., "Acts," IB, vol. 9.

MacLean, Hugh, "Omri, King," IDB, vol. 3.

Mahler, Eduard, *Handbuch der jüdischen Chronologie,* Leipzig, 1916.

Maine, Henry S., *Village Communities in the East and West,* Classics in Legal History, vol. 15, London, Murray, 1872 (reprint ed., 1978).

Maloney, Robert, "Usury and Restrictions on Interest-Taking in the Ancient Near East," CBQ 36 (1974).

Marfoe, Leon, "The Integrative Transformation: Patterns of Socio-Economic Organization in Southern Syria," BASOR 234 (1980).

Matthews, Victor H., *Pastoral Nomadism in the Mari Kingdom (ca. 1830–1760 B.C.),* ASORDS, vol. 3, Cambridge, Mass., ASOR, 1978.

Mauchline, John, "Hosea," IB, vol. 6.

———, "I and II Kings," in Matthew Black and Harold H. Rowley, eds., *Peake's Commentary on the Bible,* New York, Nelson, 1962.

Mayes, A.D.H., *Deuteronomy,* NCB, London, Oliphants, 1979.

Mays, James L., *Amos,* OTL, Philadelphia, Westminster, 1969.

———, *Hosea,* OTL, Philadelphia, Westminster, 1969.

———, *Micah,* OTL, Philadelphia, Westminster, 1976.

Mazar, Benjamin, "The Aramean Empire and Its Relations with Israel," BAR, vol. 2.

———, ed., *The World History of the Jewish People,* 21 vols., Rutgers University Press, 1961–.

McGinn, Bernard, ed., *Apocalyptic Spirituality,* Classics of Western Spirituality, New York, Paulist, 1979.

———, *Visions of the End: Apocalyptic Traditions in the Middle Ages,* Columbia University Press, 1979.

McKay, John, *Religion in Judah under the Assyrians 732–609 B.C.,* SBT (2nd ser.), vol. 26, London, SCM, 1973.

McKeating, Henry, *The Books of Amos, Hosea, and Micah,* CBC, Cambridge University Press, 1871.

McKenzie, John, *The World of the Judges,* Englewood Cliffs, N.J., Prentice-Hall, 1966.

Mealand, David, "Community of Goods and Utopian Allusions in Acts II-IV," JTS 28 (1977).

Meek, Theophile J., *Hebrew Origins,* New York, Harper and Brothers, rev. ed., 1950.

Mendelsohn, Isaac, *Slavery in the Ancient Near East,* New York, Oxford University Press, 1949.

———, "Slavery in the Ancient Near East," BAR, vol. 3.

———, "Slavery in the Old Testament," IDB, vol. 4.

———, "Society and Economic Conditions," WHJP, vol. 3.

Mendenhall, George, "The Hebrew Conquest of Palestine," BA 25 (1962) (= BAR, vol. 3).

———, "Migration Theories vs. Cultural Change as an Explanation for Early Israel," *SBL Seminar Papers,* Missoula, Mont., Scholars Press, 1976.

———, "Social Organization in Early Israel," in Frank Cross et al., eds., *Magnalia Dei: The Mighty Acts of God,* New York, Harper & Row, 1976.

———, *The Tenth Generation: The Origins of the Biblical Tradition,* Johns Hopkins University Press, 1973.

———, "The Monarchy," Int 29 (1975).

Menes, Abraham, "Die vorexilischen Gesetze Israels," BZAW, vol. 50 (1928).

Micklem, Nathaniel, "Leviticus," IB, vol. 2.

Milgrom, Jacob, "Religious Conversion and the Revolt Model for the Formation of Israel," JBL 101 (1982).

Miranda, José Porfirio, *Communism in the Bible,* Maryknoll, N.Y., Orbis, 1981.

———, *Marx and the Bible: A Critique of the Philosophy of Oppression,* Maryknoll, N.Y., Orbis, 1974.

Mitchell, Hinckley, *Ethics of the Old Testament,* Chicago, 1912.

Montgomery, James, *Book of Kings,* ICC, New York, Scribner's, 1951.

Morgenstern, Julian, "Jubilee, Year of," IDB, vol. 2.

———, "Sabbatical Year," IDB, vol. 4.

Mowinckel, Sigmund, *The Psalms in Israel's Worship,* Nashville, Abingdon, 2 vols., 1962.

Napier, Davie, "The Inheritance and the Problem of Adjacency," Int 39 (1976).

———, "The Omrides of Jezreel," VT 9 (1959).

Neufeld, Edward, "The Prohibitions against Loans at Interest in Ancient Hebrew Laws," HUCA 26 (1955).

———, "The Socio-Economic Background to Yobel and Semitta," *Revista degli Studi Orientali* 33 (1958).

Nielsen, Eduard, *The Ten Commandments in New Perspective,* SBT (2nd ser.), vol. 7, Naperville, Ill., Allenson, 1968.

Nineham, Dennis, *The Gospel of St. Mark,* Pelican Commentaries, Baltimore, Pelican, 1962.

North, Robert, "Flesh, Covering, and Response, Ex. xxi 10," VT 5 (1955).

———, *Sociology of the Biblical Jubilee,* Rome, Pontificial Biblical Institute, 1954.

———, "Yad in the Shemitta-Law," VT 4 (1954).

Noth, Martin, "Der Beitrag der Archäologie zur Geschichte Israels," *Congress Volume (Oxford, 1959);* VTS, vol. 7, Leiden, Brill, 1960.

———, *Exodus,* OTL, Philadelphia, Westminster, 1962.

———, *The History of Israel,* New York, Harper & Row, 2nd ed., 1960.

———, "Das Krongut der israelitischen Könige und seine Verwaltung," *Zeitschrift des Deutschen Palästina-Vereins* 50 (1927).

———, *Leviticus,* OTL, Philadelphia, Westminster, 1974.

Novak, Michael, *The American Vision: An Essay on the Future of Democratic Capitalism,* Washington, American Enterprise Institute for Public Policy Research, 1978.

———, *The Spirit of Democratic Capitalism,* New York, Simon and Schuster, 1982.

Oppenheim, A. Leo, "A Bird's-Eye View of Mesopotamian Economic History," *Trade and Market in the Early Empires,* Glencoe, Ill., Free Press, 1957.

Osiek, Carolyn, *Rich and Poor in the Shepherd of Hermas: An Exegetical-Social Investigation,* CBQMS, vol. 15, Washington, D.C., Catholic Biblical Association, 1983.

Park, Edgar, "Exodus," IB, vol. 1.

Parrot, Andre, *Samaria: The Capital of the Kingdom of Israel,* Studies in Biblical Archaeology, vol. 8, New York, Philosophical Library, 1958.

Paul, Shalom, *Studies in the Book of the Covenant in the Cuneiform and Biblical Law,* Leiden, Brill, 1970.

Pedersen, Johannes, *Israel: Its Life and Culture,* London, Cumberlege, 4 vols., 1926.

Phillips, Anthony, *Ancient Israel's Criminal Law: A New Approach to the Decalogue,* Oxford, Blackwell, 1970.

———, *Deuteronomy,* CBC, Cambridge University Press, 1973.

Pixley, George, *God's Kingdom: A Guide for Biblical Study,* Maryknoll, N.Y., Orbis, 1977.

Poggioli, Renato, "Naboth's Vineyard or the Pastoral View of the Social Order," JHI 24 (1963).

Polanyi, Karl, "Marketless Trading in Hammurabi's Time," *Trade and Market in the Early Empires,* Glencoe, Ill., Free Press, 1957.

Porter, J.R., *Leviticus,* CBC, Cambridge University Press, 1976.

Pritchard, James, "Culture and History," in James Hyatt, ed., *The Bible and Modern Scholarship,* Nashville, Abingdon, 1965.

Reese, James, *1 and 2 Thessalonians,* NTM, vol. 16, Wilmington, Glazier, 1979.

Ring, Emanuel, *Israels Rechtsleben,* Stockholm, 1926.

Robinson, J., *The First Book of Kings,* CBC, Cambridge University Press, 1972.

Rowton, Michael, "Dimorphic Structure and the Parasocial Element," JNES 36 (1977).

———, "Dimorphic Structure and the Problem of the 'Apirû-'Ibrîm," JNES 35 (1976).

———, "Urban Autonomy in a Nomadic Environment," JNES 32 (1973).

Rushdoony, Rousas J., *The Institutes of Biblical Law,* Nutley, N.J., Craig Press, 1973.

Rylaarsdam, Coert, "Exodus," IB, vol. 1.

Schaeffer, Henry, *Hebrew Tribal Economy and the Jubilee as Illustrated in Semitic and Indo-European Village Communities,* Leipzig, 1923.

Schmidt, Werner, "Überlieferungsgeschichtliche Erwägungen zur Komposition des Dekalogs," *Congress Volume (Uppsala 1971);* VTS, vol. 22, Leiden, Brill, 1972.

Schweizer, Eduard, *The Good News according to Mark,* Atlanta, John Knox, 1970.

———, *The Good News according to Matthew,* Atlanta, John Knox, 1975.

Scott, Robert B.Y., "Isaiah," IB, vol. 5.

———, *The Relevance of the Prophets,* New York, Macmillan, rev. ed., 1976.

———, "Weights and Measures of the Bible," BA 22 (1951).

Seebass, Horst, "Der Fall Naboth in 1 Reg. XXI," VT 24 (1974).

Silver, Morris, *Prophets and Markets: The Political Economy of Ancient Israel,* Boston, Kluwer-Nijhoff, 1983.

Sloan, Robert Bryan, *The Favorable Year of the Lord,* Austin, Schola, 1977.

Snaith, Norman, *Ecclesiasticus,* CBC, Cambridge University Press, 1974.

———, "First and Second Books of Kings," IB, vol. 3.

———, *Leviticus and Numbers,* CB, New York, Nelson, 1967.

Stamm, Johann Jakob, and Andrew, Maurice, E., *The Ten Commandments in Recent Research,* SBT (2nd ser.), vol. 2, Naperville, Ill., Allenson, 1967.

Stein, S., "The Laws on Interest in the OT," JTS (new ser.) 4 (1953).

Stoebe, Hans Joachim, "Das achte Gebot (Exod. 20, vers 16)," *Wort und Dienst* (new ser.) 3 (1952).

Taeusch, Carl, "The Concept of 'Usury': The History of an Idea," JHI 3 (1942).

Taylor, Vincent, *The Gospel according to St. Mark,* London, Macmillan, 1955.

Thompson, John, *The Book of Jeremiah,* NICOT, Grand Rapids, Eerdmans, 1980.

Thompson, Thomas L., *The Historicity of the Patriarchal Narratives: The Quest for the Historical Abraham,* BZAW, vol. 133, Berlin, Gruyter, 1974.

van den Ploeg, Jean, "Studies in Hebrew Law," CBQ 13 (1951).

Van Selms, Adrianus, "Jubilee, Year of," IDBS.

Van Seters, John, *Abraham in History and Tradition,* Yale University Press, 1975.

de Vaux, Roland, *Ancient Israel: Its Life and Institution*, trans. John McHugh, New York, McGraw Hill, 1961.

———, "On Right and Wrong Uses of Archeology," in *Near Eastern Archaeology in* the Twentieth Century, ed. James Sander, Garden City, New York, Doubleday, 1970.

Verinder, Frederick, *My Neighbor's Landmark: Short Studies in Bible Land Laws,* London, 1911.

von Rad, Gerhard, *Deuteronomy,* OTL, Philadelphia, Westminster, 1966.

———, *Studies in Deuteronomy,* SBT, vol. 9, London, SCM, 1953.

Wacholder, Ben Zion, "The Calendar of Sabbatical Cycles during the Second Temple and Early Rabbinic Period," HUCA 44 (1973).

———, "Chronomessianism: The Timing of Messianic Movements and the Calendar of Sabbatical Cycles," HUCA 46 (1975).

———, "Sabbatical Year," IBDS.

Weber, Max, "Agrarverhältnisse im Altertum," *Gesammelte Aufsätze zur Sozial- und Wirtschaftsgeschichte,* Tübingen, 1924.

———, *Ancient Judaism,* Glencoe, Ill., Free Press, 1952.

———, *The Protestant Ethic and the Spirit of Capitalism,* New York, Scribner's, 1958.

Weil, Hermann, "Gage et cautionment dans la Bible," *Archives d'Histoire de Droit Oriental* 2 (1938).

Weinfeld, Moshe, "The Origin of the Apodictic Law," VT 23 (1973).

Weippert, Manfred, *The Settlement of the Israelite Tribes in Palestine,* SBT (2nd ser.) vol. 21, Naperville, Ill., Allenson, 1971.

Welten, P., "Naboth's Weinberg (I Kön. 21)," *Evangelische Theologie* 33 (1973).

Wenham, Gordon, *The Book of Leviticus,* NICOT, Grand Rapids, Eerdmans, 1979.

Westbrook, Raymond, "Jubilee Laws," *Israel Law Review* 6 (1971).

Westermann, Claus, *Praise and Lament in the Psalms,* Atlanta, John Knox, 1981.

———, *The Psalms: Structure, Content, and Message,* Minneapolis, Augsburg, 1980.

White, Reginald, *Biblical Ethics,* Atlanta, John Knox, 1979.

Wifall, Walter, *The Court History of Israel: A Commentary on First and Second Kings,* St. Louis, Clayton, 1975.

Williams, C.S.C., *A Commentary on the Acts of the Apostles,* New York, Harper and Brothers, 1957.

Williams, R.R., *The Letters of John and James,* CBC, Cambridge University Press, ,1965.

Wiseman, Donald, "The Laws of Hammurabi Again," JSS 7 (1962).

Wittenberg, Gunther, "The Tenth Commandment in the Old Testament," *Journal of Theology for Southern Africa* 21 (1978).

Wittfogel, Karl, *Oriental Despotism: A Comparative Study of Total Power,* New Haven, Yale, 1957.

Wolfe, Rolland, "Micah," IB, vol. 6.

Wolff, Hans Walter, *Joel and Amos,* Herm, Philadelphia, Fortress, 1977.

Wright, George E., *Biblical Archaeology,* Philadelphia, Westminster, 2nd ed., 1962.

———, "Deuteronomy," IB, vol. 2.

———, "The Literary and Historical Problem of Joshua 10 and Judges 1," JNES 5 (1946).

Zeitlin, Solomon, "Notes relatives au calendrier juif," *Revue des Etudes Juives* 89 (1930).

———, "Some Stages of the Jewish Calendar," *SAJ Review* 8 (May 31, 1929) 6ff.

Index of Scriptural References

NEW TESTAMENT

General Index

Abel, 3, 58
Abiathar, 70
Abiesuh, 41
Absalom, 67, 69
Achan, 7
Adamson, James, 97, 136, 139
Aegean islands, 56
agape, 105. *See also* love
aged, 89
agrarian economy: Canaanite, 55 ff.; festivals in, 54, 129; laws and, 13, 16; vs. pastoralism, 56-58. *See also* pastoralism; poor
Agrippa I, 35
Ahab, 72, 73, 74, 75, 108, 120, 133, 134
Aharoni, Yohanan, 132, 133, 139
Ahaz, 133
Ahaziah, 133
Ahlström, Goesta, 132, 133, 139
Ai, 59
Alalakh, 55
Albright, William Foxwell, 59, 61, 132, 139
Alexander the Great, 35, 87
almsgiving, 89, 94-96, 99, 103-07, 109-12, 117, 119, 120, 121
Alt, Albrecht, 5, 8-9, 58, 60, 69, 127, 129, 130, 132, 133, 134, 135, 139
Amaziah, 133
Ambrose, 108, 109, 110
Ammiditana, 41
Ammisaduqa, 41
Amon, 133
Amorites, 11, 41
Anabaptists, 115-16
Ananias, 106
Anat, 54
Andersen, Francis, 61, 133, 134, 139
Anderson, Bernhard, 135, 139

Andrew, Maurice E., 127, 147
Anthony, 114
Antioch, 103
apocalyptic movement, 89-90. *See also* Kingdom of God
apodictic law, 4-5, 127. *See also* commandment against theft, Ten Commandments
Apostles, 105
Aqhat epic, 54
Aquinas, 116
Arabs, 61
Aramaic, 92
Arameans, 64
archeology, 59, 61, 73, 132
aristocratic empires, 56
Aristotle, 104
Ark of the Covenant, 4, 68
Asa, 69
Asherah, 54
Assyrians, 19, 22, 72, 77, 81, 82, 84, 133
Astarte, 70, 73
Astour, Michael, 132, 139
Athaliah, 133
Augustine, 110, 111
Avila, Charles, 108-11, 137, 140
Avila, Rafael, 130, 132, 133, 140
Azariah, 133
Boal, 54, 70, 75
Boal Melqart, 73-74
Baasha, 133
Babylon, 135; calendar of, 43; class structure in, 46; conquest of Judah by, 72, 81, 84; Israel's exile in, 11, 13, 14, 41, 44, 53, 77, 83, 84, 86, 98, 118; punishment for theft in, 7, 15; restitution in, 15; slavery in, 22, 25-28. *See also* Hammurabi
Bailey, John 136, 140

Other Orbis Titles . . .

OWNERSHIP: EARLY CHRISTIAN TEACHING
by Charles Avila
"A rich anthology of a stream of Christianity which offers a striking vision of what the Redemption ought to imply normatively for a Christian-inspired organization of economic and social life. Prophetic reminders of basic truths about wealth and poverty are never out of date." *Denis Goulet*

"An important recovery of the patristic teachings on wealth and poverty."
Rosemary Radford Ruether

"This book will do a great amount of good for people who are searching into this question of property all across the world. It should be read in every sociology as well as every economics class."
Msgr. John J. Egan, Archdiocese of Chicago

Item no. 384   *240pp. Paper $9.95*

BIBLE OF THE OPPRESSED
by Elsa Tamez
"Elsa Tamez leads us through a systematic study of the words for oppression in the Bible. The theme of oppression and liberation is seen as the substance within history through which divine revelation unfolds. This is a careful and critical study in biblical theology. Tamez has written a biblical study that is both scholarly and usable for lay Bible study groups." *Sojourners*

"For those of us eager to hear the voices of Latin American women, this book is doubly welcome! Writing from a perspective of those oppressed by poverty and sexism, Elsa Tamez has brought us a wealth of analysis of the biblical understanding of oppression." *Letty M. Russell, Yale University*

Item no. 035   *80pp. Paper $5.95*

THE WEALTH OF CHRISTIANS
by Redmond Mullin
Lamenting the lack of a Christian alternative to either capitalist or Marxist systems, an English businessman takes a substantial look at how Christians have dealt with the pursuit of wealth throughout history. The author argues for a greater connection between economic behavior and faith, while simultaneously offering an interesting antidote to the ethic of total renunciation within Christianity.

Item no. 709   *256pp. Paper $9.95*

COMMUNISM IN THE BIBLE
by José Porfirio Miranda

"Miranda presents, with detailed proof based on the original texts of Scripture, three topics. First, he shows that the original Christians were communists and that communism is the Christian ideal. Secondly, he demonstrates that Jesus condemned 'differentiating' or relative wealth and explains what this statement means. Thirdly, he shows that Jesus engaged in politics and approved violence."   *Theology Digest*

"A scholarly study in biblical teaching—brief, direct, powerful—which puts the burden of proof on those who would deny that original and authentic Christianity is communistic (*not,* to say, Marxist). This is vintage Miranda—erudite, passionate, persuasive, and above all, disturbing."

Robert T. Osborn, Duke University

Item no. 014   *96pp. Paper $6.95*

THE BIBLE AND LIBERATION
Political and Social Hermeneutics
edited by Norman K. Gottwald

"Norman K. Gottwald, professor of biblical studies at New York Theological Seminary, has brought together over 25 previously published book reviews, articles and portions of books that deal with the Bible from a political and social perspective.

"The book is divided into five main parts. Part One deals with the social-scientific methods of studying the Bible. The articles in the second part of the book explore how social class is a determining factor in our interpretation of the Bible. The subsequent two major sections of the book present a variety of sociological readings of the Old and New Testaments. The final portion of the book treats of the Bible in political theology and Marxist thought.

"The editor has made a major scholarly contribution in bringing together such a wide variety of articles inaccessible to the ordinary reader. He has also tapped the thought of a diversity of authors including some scholars widely revered in their fields."   *America*

Contributors include noted scholars Walter Brueggemann, Bruce Malina, Elizabeth Schüssler Fiorenza, Carlos Mesters, Luise Schottroff, Gerd Thiessen, and others who answer the need for a basic text or reader in the field of biblical studies.

Item no. 044   *624pp. Paper $18.95*

THE TRIBES OF YAHWEH
A Sociology of the Religion of Liberated Israel, 1250-1050 B.C.E.
by Norman K. Gottwald

"In this massive work on the sociology of religion in premonarchic ancient Israel, Gottwald meticulously examines the biblical theories of such scholars as Noth, von Rad, Alt, and Mendenhall and sociological and historical-cultural views of Durkheim, Marx, and Weber to define such concepts as tribalism, social structure, and the cultic-ideological and tradition history in the various books of the Bible. He discusses the social systems and economic modes of the other peoples of the Near East and compares the ancient Israelite social structure to the Greek city states. The comprehensiveness of this work in using primary as well as secondary sources makes it a valuable scholarly contribution to the study of this period." *Library Journal*

Item no. 499 *944pp. Paper $19.95*

GOD'S KINGDOM
A Guide for Biblical Study
by George V. Pixley
Foreword by Harvey Cox

"This is a book that analyzes the vital connections between political economy and religious faith in all the major periods of biblical history. Compactly and clearly written, with abundant biblical references, Pixley's work will be a tremendous asset for study groups that want to grasp the Bible as a resource for social change." *The College Store Journal*

Item no. 156 *128pp. Paper $5.95*

MATERIALIST APPROACHES TO THE BIBLE
by Michel Clévenot

The publication in English of Fernando Belo's *A Materialist Reading of the Gospel of Mark* (Orbis, 1981) was hailed as a major event in the world of scripture scholarship. Those who have recognized the importance of this pioneering, but difficult, work will welcome Michel Clévenot's accessible, extended introduction to Belo's ideas and the materialist "school" of biblical interpretation. Reconstructing the social conditions in which the scriptures were produced is central to materialist readings of the Bible.

Michel Clévenot has served as national chaplain of the Christian Students' Movement in France and is one of the editors of the Paris-based journal *La Lettre*.

Item no. 343 *160pp. Paper $8.95*

GOD OF THE LOWLY
Socio-Historical Interpretations of the Bible
edited by Willy Schottroff and Wolfgang Stegemann
trans. by Matthew J. O'Connell

A German theological best-seller now available in translation from Orbis. Stegemann, Sölle, Luise and Willy Schottroff, and other members of the rising "materialist school" of biblical interpretation in Europe elaborate their method and expose the Bible's partiality for the weak, the underprivileged, and the poor.

"These essays combine the expected German thoroughness in critical exegesis with an acute analysis of social context to build 'a bridge of love' between our world and the biblical world. This is an important contribution to a liberating knowledge of scripture." *Norman K. Gottwald*

Item no. 153   *176pp. Paper $9.95*

POLITICAL ISSUES IN LUKE-ACTS
edited by Richard Cassidy & Philip Scharper

A collection of essays by outstanding Lucan scholars: Danker, Derrett, Ford, O'Toole, Quesnell, Schmidt, Swartley, Talbert, and Via.

"The excellent essays in this volume sharpen our perception of Luke's theo-political vision. They also confront us with the enduring claim and challenge of the distinctive dominion of Jesus."
David Tiede, Luther Northwestern Theological Seminary

"The editors of this symposium deserve our thanks for bringing together this series of useful essays which no student of the social teaching in the New Testament and of Luke's writings in particular ought to miss."
I. Howard Marshall, University of Aberdeen

"I am happy to commend this new volume of studies to the serious attention of students and teachers of the New Testament and early Christian history."
F. F. Bruce, University of Manchester

Item no. 390   *192pp. Cloth $16.95*
Item no. 385   *Paper $9.95*

MY ENEMY IS MY GUEST
Jesus and Violence in Luke
by J. Massyngbaerde Ford

For this noted scholar, Luke differs dramatically from his predecessors in portraying Jesus as an advocate of nonviolence. Into the "seething cauldron" of first-century Palestine comes Luke's Jesus, whose approach to pacifism confounds even his peace-making contemporaries: he forgives and loves enemies. A signal contribution to Lukan redactional studies. Must reading for biblical scholars and all Christians opposing the arms race.

". . . an excellent, lively, and timely book."
David Daube, University of California, Berkeley

Item no. 348   *192pp. Paper $9.95*